Space, Culture and Power

Space, Culture and Power:
New identities in globalizing cities

edited by

AYŞE ÖNCÜ AND
PETRA WEYLAND

Zed Books
LONDON AND
NEW JERSEY

Space, Culture and Power: New identities in globalizing cities was first published by Zed Books Ltd, 7 Cynthia Street, London N1 9JF, UK, and 165 First Avenue, Atlantic Highlands, New Jersey 07716, USA, in 1997.

Cover designed by Andrew Corbett.
Set in Monotype Ehrhardt by Ewan Smith.
Printed and bound in the United Kingdom by Biddles Ltd, Guildford and King's Lynn.

A catalogue record for this book is available from the British Library.

Library of Congress Cataloging-in-Publication Data

Space, culture, and power : new identities in globalizing cities / edited by Ayşe Öncü and Petra Weyland.
p. cm.
Papers from a workshop held at Boğaziçi University, Istanbul, in 1994.
Includes bibliographical references and index.
ISBN 1-85649-503-5. – ISBN 1-85649-504-3 (pbk.)
1. Metropolitan areas–Congresses. 2. Sociology, Urban–Congresses. 3. Social groups–Congresses. 4. Social networks–Congresses. 5. International economic relations–Congresses. I. Öncü, Ayşe. II. Weyland, Petra, 1954– .
HT330.S63 1997
307.76–dc21 96-39525
CIP

ISBN 1 85649 503 5 cased
ISBN 1 85649 504 3 limp

Contents

Acknowledgements

The present volume has grown out of a workshop held at Boğaziçi University, Istanbul, in the spring of 1994. We are grateful to the Thyssen Foundation of Cologne, Germany, and the German Orient Institute of Istanbul/Beirut for their generous support, and to Boğaziçi University for hosting the workshop. We would also like to thank our colleagues from different metropolises across the world for their contributions, personal friendship and encouragement in making this undertaking possible.

Contributors

Erhard Berner is a research fellow and assistant lecturer at the Sociology of Development Research Centre, University of Bielefeld, Germany.

Beng-Huat Chua is professor of sociology at the National University of Singapore.

Farha Ghannam is a PhD candidate in the Department of Anthropology at the University of Texas at Austin.

Suzanne Kassab is assistant professor of philosophy at the American University of Beirut, Lebanon.

Ulrich Mai is professor of geography at the University of Bielefeld, Germany.

Ayşe Öncü is professor of sociology at Boğaziçi University in Istanbul, Turkey.

Jan Nederveen Pieterse is professor of sociology at the Institute of Social Studies in The Hague, the Netherlands.

Ayşe Saktanber is assistant professor of sociology at the Middle East Technical University in Ankara, Turkey.

Günter Seufert is a research fellow at the Department of History and Science of Religion, University of Lausanne, Switzerland.

Petra Weyland is a lecturer in sociology at the Federal Armed Forces Command and General Staff College in Hamburg, Germany.

I

Introduction: struggles over *lebensraum* and social identity in globalizing cities

Ayşe Öncü and Petra Weyland

Large metropolises are everywhere caught in the contradictory logics of globalization and localization. Symbolizing the accelerated momentum of globalization are the glossy façades of megacapital which have changed the skyline of major cities around the world. Office towers housing multinational corporations, transnational banks, world trade centres and five-star hotels, once the exclusive hallmark of a small number of 'world cities', now signify the integration of almost every major metropolis into global capitalism. The extension of information technologies and travel possibilities have created a new network of 'global spaces' within the interstices of metropolitan life across continents, inhabited by a growing coterie of transnational professionals and specialists. From the optics of this high-rise corporate economy and corporate culture, the city down below appears to be inhabited by a swirling mass of immigrant populations, competing for low-wage jobs in an increasingly informalized urban economy as the state retreats from its welfare functions. The combined economic and political imperatives of globalization seem to sweep away particularities of time and place to generate common outcomes everywhere: growing ethnic, racial and cultural heterogeneity, coupled with social and spatial polarization.

The present volume adopts the optics of the local, to provide a view of the changing skylines from below. Rather than treat globalization as a unitary and homogenizing process, to be described in terms of its putatively generic outcomes, we attempt to understand how it articulates with distinctive ensembles of class and culture, power constellations and patterns of state/society relations specific to each locality. Hence our focus is upon processes of localization, not as an imagined repository of resistance and opposition, but as actually playing a central role in shaping the power-laden processes and outcomes of globalization.

The cities we are immediately concerned with, such as Beirut, Cairo, Istanbul, or Manila and Singapore, share an important commonality. In the abundant accounts of globalization as a phenomenon which penetrates spatially to shape the life-worlds in distant corners of the planet, these are 'other' cities in 'other' places which illustrate the impasses and paradoxes of globalization. This is presumably why they have so far remained on the edges of scholarly interest. Our aim in turning to these cities is neither to rehearse the contradictions of globalism, nor to re-iterate the plight of individual cities which are absorbed into its fold. Taking these for granted, we aim to move beyond them by raising a series of questions.

Every metropolis has a unique history of cohabitation among groups fragmented along racial, ethnic, sectarian as well as gender lines. The social and cultural boundaries between these groupings are constituted within a multitude of networks which serve as the locus of identification and belonging, as well as the source of power and legitimation. How are these boundaries renegotiated as new social networks and circuits of global trade and finance selectively create new opportunity spaces? What are the political agendas and strategies of groups who mobilize to seize upon these new opportunity spaces? Metropolitan culture is everywhere the locus of hybrid forms, a product of exchanges and borrowings over time and space. How are symbolic elements from contemporary global discourses of consumerism, of Islam, of human rights, selectively appropriated by various groupings in the metropolitan arena to voice new cultural alternatives? How are prevailing social distinctions of inclusion and exclusion redrawn as pivotal urban actors pursue their political visions by inscribing them on to the physical space of the metropolis?

Our aim in posing these questions is not so much to report on individual cities, as to juxtapose evidence from different research sites to delineate how the 'global' is translated by different groups of urban actors into practices which transform the physical as well as social and cultural spaces of the city.

An initial positioning

Globalization and localization are not singular and homogeneous processes to be characterized neatly by their opposing essences. Rather than being mutually exclusive, they are 'in' one another in ways that make their interpenetration as important as their differentiation. Any attempt to make practical and political sense of contemporary metropolitan experience must therefore begin by recognizing that processes of globalization and localization interconnect and intertwine to produce place-based political struggles. Acknowledging their interconnectedness does not mean that we cannot generalize about globalization and localization as separable concepts. But to treat localization as a separate focus of generalization, without reducing it to the workings of the global capitalist economy, requires some elaboration of the differentiated forms and meanings of globalization.

At the most general level, it is possible to think of globalization in terms of movement and circulation, complexity of criss-crossing flows, some of it capital and trade, some of it people, and some of it signs, symbols, meanings and myths. A common thread which runs through the existing body of literature is the idea that such flows and mobility across space have accelerated, speeded up, or have gained a new momentum in the contemporary era, captured in such key phrases as 'time–space compression' (Harvey 1989); 'time–space distantiation' (Giddens 1990); 'intersecting scapes' (Appadurai 1990). Hence the concept of globalization does not imply a shift from one period to another, or a historical rupture, as do other encompassing terms most frequently used to describe contemporary metropolitan experience, namely post-Fordism (Amin 1994) and postmodernity (Soja 1989; Watson and Gibson 1995). Rather, it denotes intensification and stretching out of movements and flows, as captured for instance in Giddens's definition of globalization as 'the intensification of world-wide social relations which link distant localities in such a way that local happenings are shaped by events occurring many miles away and vice versa' (Giddens 1990: 64).

Globalization then, has to do with movement and circulation. It also has to do with power, i.e. the differing relationship of distinct social groups to these flows and movement. This is what Massey (1993: 61) refers to as the 'power-geometry' of globalization. Some social groups initiate flows and movement, others do not; some are more on the receiving end of it than others; some are effectively imprisoned by it. There is thus a dimension of movement and circulation; there is also a dimension of control and initiation. The ways in which different social groups are inserted into, placed within and seize upon these flows, which are themselves differentiated, can both reflect and reinforce existing power relations; it can also undermine them.

What does *not* follow from the considerations above, and yet continues to inform much of the literature on global flows, is the social imaginary of a 'borderless' world. Inherent to the concept of global flows, differentiated and differentiating, is the capacity to transgress taken-for-granted boundaries between nation-states, between racial, ethnic and gender groups, between public and private spheres. This does mean, however, an increasingly 'borderless' world, one in which boundaries have lost their meaning, as implied by the almost obligatory use of such phrases as 'spatially fluid', 'territorially unbounded', 'profoundly disconnected', and so forth, in the existing literature. On the contrary, 'borders' have become the locus of struggles among a variety of social actors, mobilized to reassert or redefine their boundaries *vis-à-vis* other relevant actors, and translate them on to the space of the metropolis.

We will below first turn to various types of global flows which have become objects of study, to trace how the social imaginary of a progressively borderless world underpins an otherwise highly diverse literature. This will pave the ground for a subsequent discussion on processes of 'localization', as we understand the term, in terms of place-based struggles between contending social actors, variously located within networks of global flows.

On global flows

To try to weld together a grand synthesis out of the variety of disciplinary perspectives, ranging from geography to anthropology, where the concept of globalization has gained increasing currency and become interlaced with the long-standing divergence between the concerns of political economy and cultural studies, would not be a meaningful enterprise. A less presumptuous and more workable strategy of finding our way in this conceptual maze is to trace the different types of flows and circuits which have become objects of study.

Flows of capital Circuits of capital and trade flows associated with the workings of the world economy have a lengthy tradition in studies of colonialism and capitalism. But it is only in the past ten years that attention has shifted to large cities as nodal points in this process. Underpinning much of this recent scholarly interest in the role of cities in the global economy, is the idea that centralized states are progressively losing their capacity to monitor their economic borders. On the one hand, the fixity of investment has lost much of its meaning with the newly available technologies of communication and transportation. On the other, the wave of structural adjustments, liberalizations and privatization in one national economy after another have weakened political restrictions on movements of globalized capital flows. Accordingly, cities have assumed increasing significance in the articulation of global circuits of capital, becoming networks of trade and finance on their own, that is, without the intermediation of the political centre. While admittedly oversimplified, this line of reasoning has constituted the underpinning of a new interest in cities in the global economy, and a growing body of detailed studies.

Much of this recent literature was stimulated by Friedmann's article 'The World City Hypothesis' (1986). Cautioning that he was providing 'neither a theory nor a universal generalization about cities' but rather a 'loosely joined ... framework for research', Friedmann argued that a city's internal structure and economic prospects would depend upon how it was integrated into circuits of global capital. Certain 'world cities' had become 'key basing points' for transnational corporate headquarters and the other institutions that organize and control the economy. For Friedmann, the paradox is that world cities will prosper as important nodes in the global economy, but the structure of their prosperity generates new forms of spatial and class polarization which they can neither redress nor manage.

Subsequent research on the relatively small number of cities which have surged ahead in the global context has by and large supported Friedmann's arguments. In one of the most ambitious attempts to follow up Friedmann's perspective, Saskia Sassen (1991) suggested that 'global cities' function more as centres of complex international transactions than as command posts for multinational organizational hierarchies. Her emphasis was on the role of producer services, especially finance, which play a pivotal role in global cities. Similarly, Matthew Drennan in his work on 'gateway cities' (1992) argued that it is the flexible networks of advanced corporate-services firms which constitute the most dynamic element of most large US cities, rather than headquarters of multinational industrial firms. Castells's earlier treatise on the 'informational city' (1989) emphasized that the increasingly dense pattern of communications within and between organizations creates a 'space of flows', so that location is driven by 'the need for the organization to be connected simultaneously with the financial markets, the pool of professional labor, the strategic alliances in the world economy and the ability to install and update the necessary technology'.

Not all recent analyses emphasize the primary importance of advanced corporate services in capital flows. Fujita and Hill (1993), for instance, have argued that manufacturing remains integral to Tokyo's economy. They find that Japanese manufacturing firms, in contrast to US firms, do not make strong spatial distinctions between headquarters, research and development and production, pointing out that Tokyo has retained all these functions. But while cities which retain a strong manufacturing base in their metropolitan region may grow most rapidly, this does not appear to be a necessary condition for surging ahead in the global context. Both Budd and Whimster (1992) and Fainstein et al. (1992), in their comparative analysis of New York and London, show that these de-industrialized metropolises in what might be argued to be economically declining regions, prospered during the 1980s.

Questions of how capital flows and networks are shaped by local and national political alignments, to produce distinctive social geographies in 'world cities', remain a Pandora's box, in the studies cited above. Or, perhaps more accurately, these studies uniformly emphasize a drift towards economic polarization and ethnic cleavages, simultaneously with the decreased capacity of local and national politics to control either one. Sassen (1991), for example, discerns the same trajectory towards income polarization and ethnic fragmentation in New York, Tokyo and London, notwithstanding each city's distinct history, socio-economic make-up and politics. She sees each as having produced a new upper class of (male) professionals, a low-paid class of (female) clerical workers, and a new immigrant working class that caters to the professionals, often through an informal economy and 'downgraded' manufacturing. Castells (1989) depicts the 'informational city' as a place where not even elites can control the trajectory of economic development or the allocations of its benefits. Fainstein et al. (1992) find that, both in London and New York, conservative national policies and local pro-business coalitions have weakened the basis of opposition and succeeded in disorganizing large-scale political opposition.

What conclusions, then, can we draw from the metropolitan experiences described in these works? Taken together, they provide a grand systemic framework which initially appears to invite debate and to inspire further studies of specific regions and individual cities. Yet, they collectively create an image of the world that is empty beyond global cities, a borderless space which can be reordered, integrated, neglected or put to use according to the demands of globally articulated capital flows. Hence they simultaneously close off new lines of inquiry, by theoretically relegating all but global cities to irrelevance.

Flows of people Flows of people across borders is once again not a new topic of study. Conventional migration analysis has long been concerned with the movement of populations, within or across national borders, focusing upon alternative paths of integration and/or strategies of survival of populations often categorized as internal and external migrants. Archetypal accounts of the third world city have been more or less coterminous with the study of migrants in informal labour and housing markets. This genre of research, far from losing its vitality, has acquired a new lease of life in studies of informalization and immigrant labour in 'global cities' (e.g. Glick Schiller et al. 1992).

In addition, new lines of inquiry on mobile populations have begun to explore crossings over time and cultural space, thus opening up novel terrains of study and interdisciplinary arenas. What used to be conceptualized and studied as discrete movements of people – as workers, as pilgrims, as tourists – is progressively becoming a part of a much richer body of work on mobile populations across complex social and cultural time–spaces. This redrawing of boundaries of topical areas has been stimulated by critical rethinking on concepts of time and space, for which the work of cultural geographers and sociologists has been a reinforcing inspiration (e.g. Bird et al. 1993; Boyarin 1994; Friedland and Boden 1994). There is thus a growing body of literature which traces movements of people in and through different cultural sites and time-zones, problematizing the very notion of borders which underpins traditional genres of migration research. For example, Rouse (1991) follows his Mexican subjects across borders in the conventional mode of migration studies, but his object of study is that of a diasporic world independent of the mere movement of subjects from one place to another. Behar (1994) crosses the Mexican border through a relationship forged between two women. Fischer and Abedi (1990) use the life-story as a strategy to juxtapose alternative visions of Islam as collective reality across time and cultural space. Naficy (1993) focuses on exile narratives in Iranian television in Los Angeles, to explore transcultural and postcolonial experience. Phillips (1995) explores histories of interaction between natives and non-natives by contrasting ethnologists' collection of museum objects and tourists' accumulation of souvenirs. Eickelman and Piscatori (1990) have focused upon Muslim travellers, bringing together studies of ritual pilgrimage with research on immigrant workers in large European cities.

A major point of intersection between these studies is the common strategy of following people in and through different cultural sites. Marcus (1995) names this genre of research 'multi-sited ethnography', suggesting that it entails 'juxtapositions of phenomena that conventionally have appeared to be (or conceptually have been kept) "worlds apart"' (Marcus 1995: 102) Hence it would be misleading to view this genre of study as merely adding new topics, peripherally, to the usual migration research, for example adding perspectives on diasporas or exiles, or placing a new emphasis on migrant cultures. Rather, it constitutes an intellectually self-conscious attempt to map out new objects of study and interdisciplinary terrains of research. By framing the life-worlds of subjects across and within diffuse time-zones, this mode of inquiry destabilizes the local/global distinction and merges, in its theoretical concerns, with questions of identity and belonging in cultural contexts where an assortment of images, symbols and expressions from the larger world circulate.

Flows of images, signs and symbols That the veritable traffic in people, consumer products, brand names and media images across the world is not equivalent to the homogenization of cultures, is perhaps the most important single common point of emphasis in the various strands of current thinking on cultural flows across the world. The long-standing assumptions of the cultural imperialism perspective, with its two-fold tendency to emphasize the hegemonic power of Western forms, and the authenticity of cultures it threatens to massify, standardize, or uniformize, now appear frozen in the realities of the 1970s. Theoretical emphasis has shifted to questions of cultural bricolage, hybridization and creolization.

One major source of inspiration for this line of thinking has come from media research. Arguments about the polysemy of media texts (e.g. Fiske 1987) and the diversity of interpretive frameworks audiences bring to bear upon them (e.g. Liebes and Katz 1990) have served to challenge the long-standing assumptions of the media imperialism perspective by emphasizing the ways in which 'Western' media products are selectively appropriated and negotiated by audiences. Moreover, the possibilities of 'domestic' production offered by new media technologies have led to a proliferation of hybrid cultural forms, ranging from popular Indian cinema – a creative mixture wryly described as 'curry eastern' (Jain 1990) – to a variety of blended musical genres circulating through burgeoning cassette markets in one country after another (Stokes 1992; Manuel 1993).

The idea that elements from metropolitan cultures can be selectively appropriated to 'construct' hybrid forms to articulate historically and socially specific experiences elsewhere in the world has brought into question older notions of culture(s) as being located in place(s). A variety of terms has been suggested to capture the ways in which contemporary cultures are actively produced through a fusion of disparate elements. Thus, for instance, Ulf Hannerz has suggested that, as with creole languages, the blending of disjunct and distinct cultural forms creates something qualitatively new. Rather than one global, homogeneous, mass culture, what we observe is a process of creolization and that 'we are all being creolized' (Hannerz 1987; 1991). Appadurai (1990) has used the term 'global cultural economy' in his well-read article to describe a complex multi-sited process of production, driven by the growing momentum with which images, sounds and idioms lose their original moorings in time and space, to acquire new meanings as they circulate around the globe. In Featherstone's work, the trans- and cross-cultural flows which shape 'global culture' and 'global consumer culture' are conceptualized in contrast to the homogeneous and integrated culture of the nation-state (Featherstone 1990; 1991).

This major shift in theory and research, away from what Straberny-Mohammedi (1991) has described as the 'top-down hypodermic-injection needle' assumptions of cultural imperialism perspective, towards a 'bottom-up resistance through indigenization' and assumptions of cultural bricolage and hybridization, coincided with the high-water mark of postmodernist thinking about identities. In very broad strokes, the postmodernist scenario on questions of identity is a two-part tale: the fracturing of national identities and the emergence of neo-tribes.

First, the emphasis is on the erosion of cultural boundaries organized round nation-states, as well as the implosion of time and distance which transforms the experience of cultural difference. The fracturing of national identities ostensibly opens up new cultural spaces for tolerance of the stranger, and fosters new bases of identity and bonding rooted in cultural distinctiveness. In contrast with written cultures that are directly linked to languages and therefore to a territory, the new identities of audio-visual culture have no roots in territorial memory, but offer a choice of life-styles with shorter time-spans and more flexible, easily reshaped identities. Thus in the second part, 'neo-tribes' are formed 'as concepts rather than as integrated social bodies by the multitude of individual acts of self-identification' (Bauman 1991: 249). Feminist, gay, environmentalist, anti-nuclear, pro-natalist, and so on, movements have been among the most frequently cited examples of such flexi-identities and neo-tribes.

Predictably, the second part of this scenario – notions of 'flexi-identities' which seem open to choice as though individuals were consumers in the shopping mall of culture – has come under criticism. But the first part of the scenario, that is the fracturing of national identities, the legacy of nineteenth-century political evolution, and the concomitant quest for alternative bases of identity and bonding, both old and new (Hall 1991), continues to inform contemporary discussions of identity politics. It also constitutes a major point of intersection between current conceptualizations of global cultural flows, consumer cultures and the presumed fluidity of cultural identities.

Needless to point out, perhaps, that the growing body of literature concerned with questions of global cultural flows and cultural identities, both old and new, can be quite varied in political mood. The spectrum ranges from those who portend a 'happy bricolage' of multi-culturalism across the globe, all the way to the melancholy prognoses of resurgent ethnic nationalisms and fundamentalist movements, with, somewhere in between, cautious optimists who foresee the possibilities for revitalization of local identities as tools of mobilization *vis-à-vis* both national and global forces.

The variety of political affinities notwithstanding, however, there are a number of common underlying premises which run through this body of literature. One common emphasis is that contemporary cultures are everywhere increasingly the products of hybridization, a complex bricolage of cultural icons and images from different locations and time periods which circulate across the globe. There is also agreement that this blending of disjunct and different cultural forms which yields new diversities offers no simple reading in such binary oppositions as traditional/modern, indigenous/foreign or local/global. Indeed, the increasingly slippery terrains of the global and local are consistently reiterated. But the most important commonality, one that is of immediate relevance here, is the evacuation of the 'national' from the analysis. Thus, in the ongoing cultural re-mapping of the globe, wherein all cultural identities are presumed to be in flux, the locus of political struggles over cultural identities – that is, the national arena – has become all but invisible.

Contemporary metropolitan experience: the struggle for *lebensraum* and cultural identity

To shift from the analysis of global flows to the dynamics of contemporary metropolitan experience requires various kinds of 'translation': from space to place, from movement and circulation to social agents positioned within specific power constellations, from the social imaginary of a borderless world to practices of boundary maintenance. This is not simply moving from one level of abstraction to another, but entails coming to grips with a different order of complexity, with its own logic and coherence. The multiple political–cultural struggles played out at the level of the metropolis are not intelligible without contextualizing them in the power constellations of a different order, one whose logic is not reducible to the 'power geometry' of global flows.

Power-laden as global flows may be, social groups with differing relations to these flows are mobilized to reassert or redefine their political and cultural boundaries *vis-à-vis* other relevant social actors in the metropolitan arena. Place-based struggles entail contending social actors whose frames of reference, projects and practices have their logic and coherence within distinctive ensembles of the class and culture of the metropolis.

It is only by taking into account the cultural frames and life strategies of social actors who are positioned within the power constellations of a different social order, with its own logic, that it becomes possible to make practical and political sense of metropolitan experience in the globalizing world.

It is self-evident that a variety of commodities, images and words from the larger world circulate in and through metropolitan life everywhere. But it does not follow that metropolitan experience in various regions of the world has now become a motley blend of cultures, mixed together with ketchup, McDonalds and Rambo films. As Ekholm-Friedmann and Friedmann (1995: 135) have pointed out, the concepts of creolization and hybridization imply a blending, combination and mixture of images, words and commodities whose sources can be identified as disparate, but only from the bird's-eye view of the cosmopolitan cultural expert. For the people involved in the daily struggle for life-space, *lebensraum*, 'the genealogies of the objects, people, ideas which circulate are only of secondary museocological importance' (Ekholm-Friedmann and Friedmann 1995: 165).

This is not to deny that metropolitan experience in various regions of the world is intricately involved in the global circulation of images and commodities. But these are assimilated into fields of experience and life strategies of social groups which have the capacity to maintain coherence in their daily existence. The ways in which a variety of icons and tropes are appropriated from the global field and combined in the life projects of a population can be understood only within the cultural frames of relevant social actors; that is, social groups which are positioned differentially within the power constellations of a different system. Inhabitants of metropolises across the world engage in active struggles to maintain their conditions of social existence and cultural distinctiveness *vis-à-vis* other relevant actors, including the state elite. The fact that people now drink Coca-Cola or watch Rambo films does not change this. Struggles over cultural identity are not about 'preserving a culture' in the conventional anthropological meaning of the phrase, but about *lebensraum*, an obvious point which is frequently overlooked when 'other' cities, in 'other' places are in question.

It is also self-evident that national borders have become increasingly permeable in the contemporary world. But it does not follow that national identities have now become a chimera, or that the state elite have lost the capacity to develop and pursue strategies which are contiguous with, albeit transformed versions of, older nationalisms. On the contrary, the rapid integration of national economies into global markets sets limits upon the viability of projects the state elite may initiate, but not upon their capacity to develop or implement them on the ground, remoulding the physical map of the metropolis in line with their visions. Hence, contrary to the social imaginary of a borderless world wherein national states have become invisible, the chapters in the present volume underscore the capacity of the state elite ruthlessly to inscribe their visions upon the metropolis through bulldozers.

The state elite and the renegotiation of collective identities The significance of the state elite as key actors in reshaping metropolitan space is emphasized in many of the papers in this volume, albeit from different perspectives. Some authors focus directly upon the visions and discursive strategies of the state elite in their attempts to reassert collective identities *vis-à-vis* the encompassing global social order, and the ways in which these are moulded by the cultural matrix of forces in national space. In the context of Singapore, for instance, Beng-Huat Chua argues that the search for a 'Singaporean' culture which encompasses the Chinese, Indian and Malay populations of the city represents a significant political turn in the ideological frame of 'multi-culturalism' which had been the basis of nation-building over the past thirty years. His sophisticated interpretation of this political turn emphasizes the ethno-religious differences which have been reproduced and solidified during Singapore's 'miracle' of growth and prosperity. Having successfully integrated the population into the global capitalist structure, suggests Chua, the state elite are now seeking to homogenize discursively the differences among the population and unify them as a 'people' in the collective imaginary. Thus, Singaporean culture is inscribed as essentially one of 'Asian communitarianism', against the arch-alternative of the unitary 'West' which symbolizes individual self-interest.

The reinvention of Singapore's new 'Asian' identity, built upon the self-confidence of capitalist success, stands in stark contrast to Cairo and Istanbul, two ancient cities which came to symbolize the promise of miracle growth and future prosperity in the national imaginary. In both Egypt and Turkey the state elite have embraced the rhetoric of opening up to the global, the outside, to the rest of the universe, conceived as the new path to economic growth through private and foreign investment and tourism. In the case of Cairo, Farha Ghannam points out that the political discourse of *infitah* (opening up to the outside) to construct a 'modern national identity' was bound with the vision of a 'modern Cairo', fit to be gazed upon by upper-class Egyptians and foreign visitors, and inscribed upon the city. In the case of Istanbul, Ayşe Öncü describes how visions of a new Istanbul as the showcase of Turkey's new era of opening to global markets inspired, in the political juncture of the 1980s, a series of massive urban renewal projects 'to re-create Istanbul's past glory in the present'. As in the case of Cairo, the projects to preserve the glory of Istanbul's historical monuments and sites blotted out from memory what were once thriving areas of the city, re-creating them through the tourist gaze.

Perhaps the most dramatic example is that provided by Suzanne Kassab on the ongoing physical reconstruction of Beirut. In a city ravaged by two decades of civil war, where the struggle for daily existence under severe inflationary conditions has become paramount, popular hopes have become attached to the Hariri government's economic agenda, which addressed political questions very timidly, if at all. Kassab underlines that an official discourse venerating conviviality, openness and tolerance, emphasizing civil liberties and democracy, did not provide a very convincing ground for making real peace, in the absence of a political agenda addressing the issue of tribalism. But after two decades of civil war, Lebanese society has been too exhausted to dream itself, to dream its identity and its future, too preoccupied with sheer survival to salvage the vital forces of imagination and critique, argues Kassab. It was in this prevailing mood of exhaustion, shortly after the end of fighting, that a plan of reconstruction was announced by the government and laws were quickly passed for its implementation. The government reconstruction plan, with colourful sketches of a modern, clean and grandiose centre to be built upon the ruins of the old one, applied what Kassab terms 'a *tabula rasa* approach'. The idea was to replace the old Beirut with a modern and global one, inspired by models of Manhattan, Hong Kong and Arab oil cities; more than two-thirds of the remaining buildings were to be destroyed to make room for sparkling towers, imposing boulevards, entertainment centres, ornamented with touches of traditional folkloric cosmetic. Kassab's discussion of the controversy surrounding the implementation of the plan, and her graphic description of the actual costs it imposed upon the population of the city, are revealing. But the analytical centrepiece of Kassab's argument emphasizes how images of a new Beirut are intertwined with the state elite's vision of the 'Second Republic', and the disjuncture between the physical reconstruction of the city and the political reconstruction of the country. She suggests that the ongoing feverish construction activity is based on the dubious political assumption that Beirut will regain its pre-war regional position and functions.

The chapters we have all too briefly touched upon above underline the variety of discursive strategies the state elite adopt to renegotiate collective identities *vis-à-vis* the encompassing global order. They also indicate that regardless of the viability of such strategies, or the extent to which they find resonance in the public imagination, the state elite actively pursue them on the ground, inscribing their visions upon the physical as well as the cultural map of the city. These visions and discursive strategies are shaped by, and in turn shape, the political struggles for physical space and *lebensraum* in the metropolitan arena.

The symbolism of space and the struggle for **lebensraum** That space is never 'empty' but always culturally inscribed with meanings, is perhaps most forcefully demonstrated when the state elite pursue their grand visions through bulldozers. Less immediately obvious, perhaps, is that geographical space is a social and cultural category for all relevant actors in the urban arena, including newcomers whose 'history' in the metropolis is of recent origin.

Erhard Berner's discussion of the urban poor in Metro Manila, for instance, underlines how 'locality', as a socially defined and 'created' spatial entity, becomes the basis of social cohesion and community-based efforts in the struggle for survival. He argues that in the endemic conflicts and confrontations over precious land, locality supersedes ethnic and religious networks as the basis of solidarity and of resistance for the immigrant populations of the city. He thus criticizes current strands of theorizing which conceive economies and cultures of the emergent global order as increasingly '*placeless*'. Not only is 'the global' anchored in space in the contemporary metropolis, he points out (as evinced by foreign investments in real estate, particularly Japanese and Taiwanese, which have fuelled land speculation and contributed to skyrocketing prices in Metro Manila), but also locally-based groups are composed of a multitude of territorial communities.

Petra Weyland in her contribution also problematizes the notion of 'placelessness'. Taking up the issue of female global migrants, she stresses the crucial significance of gender in the globalization of metropolitan space. Based upon an empirical case study of Filipina maids and their employers, wives of corporate executives employed by multinational firms in Istanbul, she argues that global space is 'gendered' space. Global space in the metropolis is internally divided into female 'privatized' space – which is basically identical to the corporate executives' domestic space – and into male space which is equated with 'public' multinational business space. This construction of a female 'privatized' global space has an ideological as well as a practical dimension, Weyland points out, in securing the reproduction of the global managerial labour force by the female occupants of the household. She thus questions the male-biased assumption that the constructions of maps in the globalizing metropolis is a sexually neutral undertaking; a point that is also underscored by Farha Ghannam's and Ayşe Saktanber's contributions in the present volume.

The symbolism of space as a significant component of collective identities is also emphasized by Ulrich Mai, Ayşe Öncü and Farha Ghannam, but from the perspective of divergent social groups in very different cities. Mai offers an nuanced account of how inhabitants of East German cities have become strangers in their own cities, as the most conventional, routine, taken-for-granted aspects of daily existence were dramatically transformed: street signs, the odour of disinfectants used in public spaces, names of avenues and plazas, as well as the looks, shapes and tastes of daily consumer items. Their experience of homelessness, Mai suggests, takes a more symbolic than existential form, a profound sense of loss as helpless victims of a superior strange power. In the context of Istanbul, Öncü is similarly concerned with the symbolism of space and social identities, but with specific reference to the upwardly mobile segments of the middle strata. She suggests that the domestic ideal of the private home, the symbolic construct from which the experiences and consumption practices of a middle-class way of life and identity derive their meaning, has travelled across cultural borders to adorn the dreams and desires of Istanbul's middle strata. They have invested their savings in housing developments on the periphery of the city to distance themselves, symbolically and spatially, from what they have come to perceive and define as the urban chaos and 'social pollution' of metropolitan Istanbul. Öncü notes that the majority of Istanbul's newly constructed residential estates, composed of uniform high-rise apartment blocks, fall dramatically short of what an outside observer might perceive as the domestic ideal of a private home. But in the lives and experiences of their residents, she argues, it is the very homogeneity and uniformity of such neighbourhoods, with their antiseptic social and cultural spaces, which have become the symbolic markers of a distinctively middle-class life-style in contemporary Istanbul.

In the context of Cairo, Ghannam's analysis once again underlines the significance of place in the constitution of collective identities. Her research focuses on the former residents of Bulaq, an inner-city neighbourhood which was literally razed to the ground, as unfit to be gazed upon by upper-class Egyptians and foreign visitors; its inhabitants were relocated in public housing units described as 'modern'. The process of relocation not only destroyed the group's informal economy and access to many cheap goods and services but also their social relationships, and it reordered their lives. Fifteen years after the move, the relocated people still refer to themselves as 'people of Bulaq' and are known as 'those from Bulaq' by other groups in the community, a negative construction perpetuated by the physical segregation of uniformly-built public housing. Ghannam describes how Bulaq has become an anchor for the group's sense of belonging in the face of stigmatization and hostility, and has assumed significance as the shared geographical place of origin and common history in the collective imaginary of the group, thus taking precedence over other identifications. But what facilitates the group's interaction with other groups which live in the area, Ghannam argues, is the space of the mosque, through its promise of an equal and unified community. Below, we turn to the question of how religious discourses are actively negotiated as a variety of commodities, images and words from the larger world circulate in and through the everyday life of the metropolis.

Rediscovering Islam through the prism of the global The ways in which Islam is articulated in everyday practices and forms of sociability in the cosmos of the contemporary metropolis, bringing people together as connected selves, is the focal point of analysis in a series of chapters in the present volume. Their concern is not with 'fundamentalism', 'extremism' or 'militant Islam', that is often construed as 'response' or 'resistance' to the global; rather, they focus upon the everyday lives of people at the neighbourhood level, in an attempt to understand how global discourses and consumer goods are appropriated and negotiated in the struggle of Muslims to live in the present. In this connection, Ghannam emphasizes the centrality of the mosque as a distinctive space in the Cairo neighbourhood she has studied. The naturalized relationship of the mosque with religion is currently being reinforced, she suggests, particularly among women who actively associate the unity of prayers with feelings of communal bonding, and being part of a collectivity. The opening of the mosque to women, not only for regular prayers but also as mothers, sisters and wives responsible for the morals of the community, capable of actively shaping their own practices as well as those of family members, has facilitated their participation in a variety of mosque-related activities.

The centrality of women in the politically conscious effort to render Islam a living social practice is the focal point of Saktanber's research as well. Her analytical emphasis is on the significance of a middle-class ethos in the creation of an Islamic order, capable of replacing 'national civil religion' in the Turkish context. To the extent that Islamic revitalization is a response of civil society to the failures of the state, and takes the form of a reaction to state practices, it is primarily shaped within the context of the nation-state, she argues. The significance of globalization resides, according to Saktanber, in increasing the possibility of infiltrating different opportunity spaces hitherto monopolized by the state elite. Viewed from this perspective, Islamic circles in Turkey need to create not only their own intelligentsia, capable of replacing the existing ones, but also their own middle classes who can play a leading role in the production, dissemination and consolidation of new models of sociabilities, she emphasizes. This is why women, who were once perceived as an adjunct to the more important issues of polity and social order, have now become crucial agents in the daily articulation and reproduction of Islamic ideologies. Based upon her field research in a Muslim urban complex in Ankara, the capital of the secular Turkish republic, Saktanber analyses how the inhabitants have rallied together to 'live Islam' as conscious Muslims, organizing their daily lives in accordance with Islamic codes. She focuses upon the efforts of women to carry out daily life in accordance with Islamic precepts, in a secular modern system. In the consolidation of an alternative Islamic life-style, she suggests that their aim is not to reject the comforts and opportunities of modern life, but to question the price a Muslim should pay for their attainment. Following Saktanber's line of thinking, it becomes apparent that the process termed 'revitalizing Islam' by 'outsiders' corresponds, in the experience of so-called Islamist people, to a politically informed effort to render Islam a living practice.

Following Günter Seufert's line of thinking, it becomes evident that the process termed 'resurgence of ethnic nationalisms' is once again a response of civil society to the failures of the cultural hegemony of the nation-state, one that has received an uplift from the global discourse of human rights, but cannot be reduced to it. Seufert offers a richly detailed analysis of the competing claims of religious sectarianism and ethnic nationalism in the identity politics of an Alevi Kurdish tribe in the urban cosmos of metropolitan Istanbul. He describes how a symbiosis of tribal Kurdish and Alevi Muslim identity served as the basis of a binding moral economy and network of reciprocity through which the immigrant group acquired a foothold in the urban economy and managed to construct a distinctive socio-cultural space. In the national political arena, the Alevi Kurdish identity of tribe was defined *vis-à-vis* the historical hegemony of the Sunni Turkish centre and the repressive practices of the state elite. Excluded and stigmatized both as Alevis and as Kurds, the group engaged in oppositional politics under the ideological banner of the 'secular left'. The declining appeal of leftist ideologies and parties, however, coupled with the ascendence of Sunni Islam as the major oppositional discourse in Turkish national politics, has currently left few options for the younger generation of Kurdish Alevis other than defining their cultural distinctiveness and political identity through Kurdish nationalism. In contrast to Sunni youth, Seufert suggests, for whom political Islam has begun to gain credibility as an internationally 'valid' identity, Alevism fails to provide a serious political alternative to secular ideologies. Thus, for the politicized, literate young members of Koçkìrì tribe, nationalist Kurdishness becomes the only way of marking an internationally valid identity in global times.

With Jan Nederveen Pieterse's chapter, we turn to the question of how Islam changes in the process of migration to European metropolises. He uses 'travelling Islam' as the central metaphor to discuss how the Muslim diasporas of Europe bear the imprint of cultural cohabitation. His contrast between multi-culturalism in Britain and pillarization in the Netherlands, as distinct legislative and ideological orientations within which Muslim immigrant cultures are reconstructed, not only problematizes essentialist and static conceptualizations of Islam, but also underlines that each 'national' context produces its own opportunity structures. In the Netherlands, the combined tendencies of pillarization, ethnization and integration makes for a different field than in Britain with its predominant discourse of racialized cultural difference, while in France secularism and *laicité* make for yet another arena of difference. These sites of diaspora each provide different opportunity structures and generate novel combinations. In all, migrant Islam articulates with the host society to generate new, hybrid cultural forms. But Nederveen Pieterse underlines that Muslim diasporas are simultaneously caught in the vortex of a contradictory current: as the dynamics of economic restructuring generate high levels of unemployment, Europe's immigrant workforce is progressively entrapped in economic and cultural enclaves. Hence the questions of whether the boundaries constructed between Muslims and non-Muslims in European metropolises will solidify or become increasingly fluid, or whether the mix of cross-cultural influences specific to each locality will yield hybrid identities, remain uncertain.

In elucidating how experience of being a Muslim gains meaning in time and place, these chapters move beyond the rhetoric of unity, essentialism and homogenization which currently underpins most discussions of Islamic revivalism. They also forewarn against representations of Islam as passive resistance and reaction to globalization. Rather, Islam is actively constructed as a viable political and cultural identity through the daily struggles for *lebensraum* in the cosmos of the contemporary metropolis. Far from being a manifestation of the erosion of national boundaries, it is a response to the practices of the state elite in their attempts to inscribe their own visions upon the physical and cultural map of the city.

What the chapters in the present volume collectively suggest, is that processes of 'localization' entail place-based power struggles among relevant social actors who are differentially located within, or seize upon new, opportunity spaces engendered by global movements. Global circuits and flows can both reinforce and undermine existing power relations; which is not to say that they produce them. To reiterate our earlier point, it is only from the optics of the global, from a position of social distance, that 'other' metropolises, in various regions of the world, appear to be a *tabula rasa*, their inhabitants cast adrift from their moorings in time and place amidst the complex assortment of cultural icons and symbols which circulate around the globe. The complexity of social reality, from within the cultural frames of distinct groups located in the metropolis, is of a different order. It is a complexity associated with the diverse cultural projects, strategies and practices of contending groups, one which cannot be reduced to the 'power geometry' of global flows, but needs to be taken into account as a separate focus of understanding and research.

References

Amin, A. (ed.) (1994) *Post-Fordism: A Reader*. Basil Blackwell, Oxford.

Appadurai, A. (1990) 'Disjuncture and Difference in the Global Cultural Economy', in M. Featherstone (ed.), *Global Culture*.

Bauman, Z. (1991) *Modernity and Ambivalence*. Polity Press, Oxford.

Behar, R. (1994) *Translated Woman: Crossing the Border with Esperanza's Story*. Beacon Press, Boston.

Bird, J. et al. (eds) (1993) *Mapping the Futures: Local Cultures, Global Change*. Routledge, London.

Boyarin, J. (ed.) (1994) *Remapping Memory: The Politics of Time and Space*. University of Minnesota Press, Minneapolis, MN.

Budd, L. and Whimster, S. (eds) (1992) *Global Finance and Urban Living: A Study in Metropolitan Change*. Routledge, London.

Castells, M. (1989) *The Information City: Information Technology, Economic Restructuring, and the Urban-Regional Process*. Basil Blackwell, Oxford.

Drennan, M. (1992) 'Gateway Cities', *Urban Studies* 29 (2), 217–35.

Eickelman, D. F. and Piscatori, J. (eds) (1990) *Pilgrimage, Migration and the Religious Imagination*, University of California Press, Berkeley, CA.

Ekholm-Friedmann, K. and Friedmann, J. (1995) 'Global Complexity and the Simplicity of Everyday Life', in D. Miller (ed.), *Worlds Apart*. Routledge, London.

Fainstein, S., Gordon, I. and Harloe, M. (eds) (1992) *Divided Cities: New York and London in the Contemporary World*. Basil Blackwell, Oxford.

Featherstone, M. (1991) *Consumer Culture and Postmodernism*. Sage, London.

— (ed.) (1990) *Global Culture*. Sage, London.

Fischer, M. and Abedi, M. (1990) *Debating Muslims*. University of Wisconsin Press, Madison, WI.
Fiske, J. (1987) *Television Culture*. Methuen, New York.
Friedland R. and Boden, D. (eds) (1994) *NowHere: Space, Time and Modernity*. University of California Press, Berkeley, CA.
Friedmann, J. (1986) 'The World City Hypothesis', *Development and Change* 17 (1), 69–83.
Fujita, K. and Hill, R. C. (eds) (1993) *Japanese Cities in the World Economy*. Temple University Press, Philadelphia.
Giddens, A. (1990) *The Consequences of Modernity*. Stanford University Press, Stanford, CA.
Glick Schiller, N., Basch, L. and Blanc Szanton, C. (1992) *The Transnationalization of Migration: Perspectives on Ethnicity*. Gordon and Breach, New York.
Hall, S. (1991) 'Old and New Identities, Old and New Ethnicities' in A. D. King (ed.) *Culture, Globalization and the World System*. SUNY, Binghamton, NY.
Hannerz, U. (1987) 'The World in Creolization', *Africa* 57 (4): 546–59.
— (1991) 'Scenarios for Peripheral Cultures', in A. D. King (ed.), *Culture, Globalization and the World System*. Macmillan, London.
Harvey, D. (1989) *The Condition of Postmodernity*. Blackwell, Oxford.
Jain, M. (1990) 'The Curry Eastern Takeaway', *Public Culture* 2 (2), 121–8.
Liebes, T. and Katz, E. (1990) *The Export of Meaning*. Oxford University Press, Oxford.
Manuel, P. (1993) *Cassette Culture*. University of Chicago Press, Chicago, IL.
Marcus, G. E. (1995) 'Ethnography in/of the World System: The Emergence of Multi-sited Ethnography', *Annual Review of Anthropology* 24, 95–117.
Massey, D. (1993) 'Power-geometry and a Progressive Sense of Place', in J. Bird et al. (eds), *Mapping the Futures*.
Naficy, H. (1993) *The Making of Exile Cultures: Iranian Television in Los Angeles*. University of Minnesota Press, Minneapolis, MN.
Phillips, R. (1995) 'Why Not Tourist Art? Significant Silences in Native American Museum Representations', in Gyan Prakash (ed.), *After Colonialism*. Princeton University Press, Princeton, NJ.
Rouse, R. (1991) 'Mexican Migration and the Space of Postmodernity', *Diaspora* 1 (1), 8–23.
Sassen, S. (1991) *The Global City: New York, London, Tokyo*. Princeton University Press, Princeton, NJ.
Soja, E. (1989) *Postmodern Geographies*. Verso, London.
Stokes, M. (1992) *The Arabesk Debate: Music and Musicians in Modern Turkey*. Clarendon Press, Oxford.
Straberny-Mohammedi, A. (1991) 'The Global and the Local in International Communications', in J. Curran and M. Gurevitch (eds), *Mass Media and Society*. Edward Arnold, London.
Watson, S. and Gibson, K. (eds) (1995) *Postmodern Cities and Spaces*. Basil Blackwell, Oxford.

PART I

Global visions and changing discourses of power

2

Between economy and race: the Asianization of Singapore

Beng-Huat Chua

In 1995, Singapore was thirty years old as an independent nation. In its brief history, collective memory regarding the nation is relatively shallow and is still in its formative stages. Its political formation as an 'unintended' nation has imposed an overwhelming, indeed desperate, preoccupation with forming itself as a 'nation' and its population as a 'people'. This is manifested in highly self-conscious attempts to 'fill-in' the new but empty terms of identity.

The People's Action Party (PAP), which has ruled, even before independence, without a break, has sought at different times to define the nation using certain 'national' characteristics and values, and to inscribe the same on the population. The inscription exercises constitute a part of the political practices that are discursively glossed over by the modernization concept of 'nation-building'. In each attempt, the single dominant party regime has never failed discursively to thematize, and thus transform, the ontological presence of race into a socially and politically relevant element to be given explicit central attention; the population has never been allowed to forget that it is hewed from three different races: namely, Chinese, Malay and Indian. The discursively transformed 'race' has been foregrounded in different ways at different points in the 'nation-building' enterprise.

Taking the social production of 'race' as the base-line from which to theorize, broadly speaking, so far three inscription attempts can be identified. These are: first, political reduction of race to 'festival' cultures and the privileging of the economic; second, delineation of race as the bond that binds the different constituent population groups and using this as the basis of social welfare organization; and, third, concurrent homogenization of the races under the label of 'Asians' and the continuing maintenance of racial divisions.

Substantively, instead of evolving from one to the next in a linear, temporal manner, the trajectories of these attempts slide into each other and mingle. They constitute part of the ongoing ideological formation of the Singaporean state. They reflect the current political purposes and the responses of the managers of the state to changing economic and social conditions, as the new island nation embarks on the path of capitalist development. The following discussion will flesh out these instances and draw out the political effects they have in the self-definition of the Singaporean identity.

Singapore: an absence

Singapore as an independent polity was, at one time, inconceivable. Granted self-government of its domestic affairs by the British colonial administration in 1959, it was nevertheless difficult for the population to take the obvious next political step because an independent Singapore was thought by Lee Kuan Yew to be 'a foolish and absurd proposition' for several reasons (Drysdale 1984: 249). Economically, under the then prevailing belief in import substitution as the best development strategy for decolonized states, an island without a large domestic market was deemed to be non-viable; demographically, the population consisted almost entirely of immigrants (even the island's Malays were immigrants from neighbouring areas); culturally and ideologically, these immigrants were oriented to the nationalisms of their China, India and Malay 'homelands'. Consequently, the population could see its continuing existence only as part of peninsular Malaya, of which it was a part until the latter's independence in 1957.

Then, in 1963, the possibility of communist rule on the island prompted the Malayan political leadership, which had been unenthusiastic about a 'merger' with Chinese-dominant Singapore, to move quickly to form a Malaysian Confederation with Singapore and the British colonial territories of Sarawak and North Borneo, renamed Sabah. Membership proved difficult for Singapore, leading to its separation from Malaysia after two brief years. In 1965, political independence was thrust upon the population by fiat, under the PAP government. The 'absurd' had become the reality.

Until 1965, a politically independent Singapore was, therefore, an 'absence'; it was not an idea which the population was trying to realize. This 'absence' accounts for the need and the successive attempts to 'define', to 'substantiate' and eventually to 'realize' a national identity in social and political life. Unlike economic development, however, success in identity-building is elusive because the ontologically real appears able to slip out cunningly from under attempts to represent it.

Multi-racialism and the privileging of economics

Political independence dismantled the supra-racial governmental structure, which was originally provided by the British colonial administration and subsequently by Malaysian federalism. An alternative arrangement for the races had thus to be found. The Chinese, though numerically dominant, morally had no proprietary right to the new island nation. Also, the geopolitical condition of archipelagic Southeast Asia placed them in a region populated by an overwhelming number of Malay-speaking Malaysians and Indonesians, who were unlikely to accept a Chinese nation in its midst with equanimity. On the other hand, the island's Malays, though regionally indigenous, were unable to dominate Singapore politics because of their numerical minority. Finally, the Indians were both immigrants and the smallest minority. Given these conditions, constitutional separation of citizenship from racial identification was, perhaps, the least troublesome solution. Furthermore, so long as the conditions hold, as they have for the last three decades, the solution will be in place.

The separation of citizenship from race gave rise to an ideological commitment to 'multi-racialism' as the 'rational' basis for other social policies.[1] Multi-racialism is thus unavoidably a discursively produced phenomenon which makes reference to, but goes beyond, the ontological existence of race in its political effects. It requires at its base the elaboration of a discourse of race whose production will serve to rationalize specific ways of disciplining the social body in Singapore. The analytic issue is: how is the ontological given of different races discursively thematized and in the process transformed as a relevant phenomenon in political discourses which serve to rationalize strategies of social administration?

Race is discursively produced in the following manner: officially, race is defined strictly by patriarchal descent; racial descent supposedly defines a person's culture (multi-culturalism); this race-culture is assumed to be embedded in the language of the race, thus, the latter is assured continued existence through compulsory school instructions as a 'mother-tongue' language (multi-lingualism), as a second language, after English.[2] In this set of discursive processes which locate individuals as members of distinct racial groups, differences within the population are radically reduced. For example, in the discursive formation of Chinese individuals as a 'single' group, dialect differences which had sharply divided them were suppressed by abolishing dialects in the mass media and the promotion of Mandarin as the 'language of the Chinese'.[3] Similarly, dialect differences among Malays are reduced under a common 'Malay' language and, in this particular instance, the 'group' is additionally defined by Islam. Finally, the south Indian language, Tamil, spoken by more than 60 per cent of the Singapore Indians, was initially privileged as the official Indian 'group' language. Other Indian languages were made available subsequently as official 'mother-tongues', including Hindi, Punjabi and Bangladeshi, in response to protests from these language-speakers. This reduction of differences is, of course, tantamount to the suppression of some constitutive components of individual and collective identities within the population itself. The three discursively-produced groups of 'Chinese', 'Malays' and 'Indians' in turn became the relevant administrative racial categories that are used to rationalize public policies and political practices (Siddique 1989).

In practice, these three groups are made 'observable' through their 'cultural' activities. For example, annually two public holidays are dedicated, respectively, to Hindu (Indian), Muslim (Malay) festivals and for the Chinese new year (multi-religiosity). The officially sponsored racial/cultural categories in turn generate activities organized by the racial groups themselves, giving an impression that the 'cultures' of Singaporeans are frozen in three respective 'traditions'. While such a conception may be considered deeply mistaken from an anthropological viewpoint (Benjamin 1976; Clammer 1985), it is an effect of official 'multi-culturalism' and one which is very much promoted by the government for precisely its political and ideological returns.

This intentional discursive production of race has at least two clear political consequences. First, it undermines 'race' as a political currency. What multi-racialism promotes is 'cultural equality' between groups; each is assured the 'group right' to cultural maintenance and continuity. By promoting 'group equality' in a cultural sphere which is circumscribed by racial boundaries, the state is able to claim for itself a 'neutral' stance towards all racial groups, without prejudice or preference (Kuo 1985; Siddique 1989). Thus, except for 'protecting' the 'mother-tongues' in schools, the responsibility for promoting racial/cultural activities is entirely dependent on volunteered individual and/or collective efforts of each officially constituted racial group.[4] The cultural vibrancy of each group is dependent entirely on its members, with the state providing an equal administrative support role; no preferential claims can be made on any state agencies on the basis of race.

Significantly, within cultural discourses of developed Western nations, the conventional belief is that multi-racialism is a mechanism for 'empowering' minority race/ethnic groups, a mechanism for redressing discriminatory practices against them. The Singapore case shows that this 'empowering' argument holds only against a background of prevailing racism on the part of the numerical majority race in the nation. Without extant majority racism, multi-racialism can be used strategically to erase the grounds on which a racial group can make claims on behalf of its own interests without ostensibly violating the idea of group equality that is the foundation of multi-racialism itself. In Singapore, multi-racialism pushes race out of the foreground of politics while according it very high visibility in the cultural sphere.[5]

The second political consequence lies in the economic sphere. The capitalist success of Singapore is now well documented (Rodan 1989). This success requires as one of its necessary conditions the active transformation of a population into a disciplined workforce (Offe 1987: 94), which in turn is dependent on developing certain cultural traits. Cultural development has to abide by the dictates of the logic of the economy. For example, self-discipline must be maintained at the workplace and, by extension, there must be generalized social discipline (Quah 1983); a generalized orientation to the constant upgrading of education, skills and productivity; a deep sense of competitiveness that is sustained in part by an individual's desire for comparative advantages in material consumption against others; a belief in merit as the basis for the attainment of appropriate rewards (Chua and Kuo 1992). Indeed, 'meritocracy' underpins the entire developmentalist orientation of the state. Above all other cultural sentiments, these cultural prerequisites of capitalism are the predominant values and anxieties that today characterize the everyday life-world of the Singapore population.

Significantly, these values were not extant on the island at the time of political independence. Then, high levels of unemployment gave rise to a life-style that left an individual with very significant degrees of freedom *vis-à-vis* work-related activities; albeit a freedom accompanied by very substantial material deprivation (Chua 1989a).[6] The cultural requirements of the industrial regime had, therefore, to be actively established with government interventions. The promotion of a disciplined workforce was given precedence over other practices from the very outset of independence. For example, job-creation became a priority in the agenda of the new nation in view of the very high population growth rate of more than 4.3 per cent (Lim and Associates 1988: 6). It was ideologically linked to the people's daily struggles with 'making a living'; 'survival' of the new nation and its people became one. What emerged is a new social order characterized by instrumental rationality and a population with strong achievement motivation and fundamentally subjected to the compelling logic of a capitalist economy which determines their daily life. The bulk of the population's shared experiences is derived from this everyday life and its attendant patterns of class stratification, within an expanding capitalist economy.

To avoid the potential political thematizing of these 'shared' experiences, as for example in the discourses of class, they are ideologically under-conceptualized by the state as the 'culture' of the people.[7] Capitalism is 'naturalized' and its attendant values ideologized as basic necessities for the physical survival of people in the world; 'survivalism' becomes an ideological corner-stone. Such values are thus placed in an absolutely hegemonic space, outside the realm of preferences, hence outside the 'cultural' sphere. This ideological side-lining of the value entailments of capitalism is made easier by precisely the foregrounding of the 'cultures' of the three races in the political discourse of Singapore.

Multi-racialism and competition entwine further to devalue race as political currency. To the extent that it is believed that the economy operates with open competition and that racial equality is the norm, then, the very possibility of racial discrimination is rendered ideologically unintelligible. Hence, no moral recourse and no institution for redressing racial discrimination exist in Singapore.

The concurrent processes of privileging of capitalist economics and the reduction of race to 'festival' cultures manifest themselves physically in the urban landscape of Singapore. Corporate architecture, the physical embodiment of capital, jostles for space in the financial district, itself an important regional financial centre of the Asia–Pacific (Chua 1989b). The same spatial competition is seen in the tourist belt of Orchard Road which, in addition to corporate structures, contains five-star hotels and where designer goods and their imitations crowd the display windows. The consumers of these internationally-styled, up-market goods are no longer only tourists but also an increasingly affluent Singaporean population. The 'internationalization' of the physical environment extends to the residential sector. In the government's salutary effort to improve the housing conditions of the population through rehousing people in comprehensively planned high-rise, high-density public housing estates, racially exclusive rural and urban villages of vernacular architecture were demolished to make room (Chua 1991).

By the early 1980s, the total rebuilding of Singapore, itself a symbolic representation of national capitalist economic success, began to threaten thriving tourism. The 'Manhattanized' Singapore was beginning to look like all international cities and becoming 'culturally' uninteresting as it shed its 'Asianness'. This led to a concerted effort by the planning agencies, along with the Singapore Tourist Promotion Board, to 'conserve' the 'historic districts in the central area': namely, the 'traditional' racial settlements of the Chinese, Malay-Arabs and Indians.[8] These areas are now 'gentrified'. The buildings have been rebuilt, rather than 'restored', to their original designs but with a proliferation of new colours. The interiors are reworked into offices or trendy restaurants and bars. Finally, houses along more residential streets at the margin of these areas are redesigned to house high-income professionals.

The life of the racial communities has all but disappeared. Their identites as 'racial' areas are maintained tangentially in their names such as Chinatown, Little India and Kampung Glam, the 'village' of Malays and Arabs. In the cases of Chinatown and Little India, identity with their respective races is more substantial because they remain the commercial centre for everyday and ritual commodities traditionally used by those races. With reference to the 'festival' culture, each of these areas is decorated, by the Public Works Department, in the same manner with similar strings of lights across the main thoroughfare, on the annual major festival for each race: Chinese New Year for Chinatown; Diwali, the Hindu 'festival of lights' for Little India; and Hari Raya Puasa, the end of Ramadan for Islamic Malays. Ironically, this idea of 'lighting-up' was first introduced for the tourist belt in celebration of Christmas and to encourage the annual buying spree.

Race and the organization of social welfare

The hegemonic economy is thus apparently allowed to operate without moral restraints. However, part of the legitimacy of the modern state is based on its ability to ameliorate the inevitable social inequalities that result from the market processes. The Singapore state is no exception.

In 1981, in recognition of the structurally determined disadvantaged economic position of Malays (Zoohri 1990), the government sponsored the establishment of Mendaki (the acronym of a Muslim organization), under the leadership of Malay MPs.[9] Ten million dollars of public funds was donated as the inauguration fund for the institution. Its aim is to enhance the academic performance of Malay students, so as to improve the long-term employment and financial prospects of the Malays as a whole. In 1989, a similar organization, the Singapore Indian Development Agency (Sinda), was set up by Indians to help their own 'low achievers'. Given the logic of multi-racialism, a Chinese agency was inevitable; the Chinese Development Assistance Council (CDAC) was established in April 1992. In these latter cases, no funds were provided by the government.

The racial basis of these agencies lies in the way they are funded: every Singaporean worker contributes respectively to improve the educational performance of children of needy families in his or her 'own' racial group. The state lends an administrative hand. Contributions are deducted monthly from the employee's compulsory social security savings in the government-managed Central Provident Fund. No cross-racial contribution is permitted in this basic deduction. These agencies are officially called 'community self-help organizations'; obviously, the term 'community' is narrowly drawn around the discursive boundaries of the three official races.[10]

Politically, these organizations achieved their articulated rationalization only after the explicit promotion of a national ideology, in 1990, by a government that vehemently considers itself as 'pragmatic' and beyond ideologies (Chua 1985). The background and significance of this uncharacteristic promotion of an explicit national ideology will be discussed in the subsequent section. For now it should be noted that precisely because of its avowal of being non-ideological, the national ideology came to be given a less politically emotive name as the 'Shared Values'. A White Paper on Shared Values was adopted by Parliament on 2 January 1991 as the guiding principle for the ongoing governance of the nation. These 'values' are: nation before community and society before self; family as the basic unit of society; regard and community support for the individual; consensus instead of contention; racial and religious harmony.

The social base of the 'community self-help' agencies can be rationalized in terms of 'regard and community support for the individual'. In principle, contributions are voluntary. However, in contrast to the conventional practice of charity, a contribution is presumed unless one deliberately opts out. Given the obvious good cause and the paltry monthly contribution, few opt out. Some who do are against the 'opt-out' practice, preferring to preserve the right to decide whether and how much to contribute. Others argue that this strategy of care for the less able will intensify racial divisiveness, which is detrimental to the generation of a Singaporean identity and national unity. They prefer a national institution for the needy which defines 'community' in national rather than racial terms; adding often that the formation of 'self-help' organizations is but a state's means of reducing its commitment and responsibility to the social welfare of the people.

With the institutionalization of these racially-constituted self-help organizations, each caring for the education of its own needy, race occupies a prominent place in the management of certain aspects of the overall social welfare of the nation. This is a significant change from enclosing race, with high public visibility, in the private spheres of religious and festival practices while keeping it politically ineffective. The trajectory of the elaborate ideological work of initially side-lining race from political discourse and subsequently reframing it so as to invoke and use it for certain aspects of social welfarism, is a consequence of a larger ideological framework formulated by the government.

It should be obvious that the 'Shared Values' privilege the 'collective' over individuals. This privileging of the collective is crystallized and represented in what the government calls the 'communitarian' cultures of Asia. The 'community self-help organizations' find their ideological justification within the auspices of this 'communitarianism'. [11] However, logically, their emergence and inscription as a ideological frame lie beyond the organizations themselves.

The 'Asianization' of Singaporeans

A significant effect of thematizing multiple racial/cultural traditions to the exclusion of the economically-determined culture of everyday life is to place the population on a constant search for an encompassing 'Singaporean' culture. A rather humorous and semiotically interesting example is the forsaken search for a 'Singaporean' costume, which in the past had driven fashion designers into frenzies of pastiche of different elements drawn from traditional Chinese, Indian and Malay costumes; instead, the orchid is now being promoted as the motif of 'national' fabrics. The search for a 'Singaporean' culture took a politically consequential turn in 1990 with the re-initiation of the deliberate ideological effort to 'forestall' the allegedly corrosive effects of the Westernization of Singaporeans.

The 'West', used inclusively, is discursively cast as an ideology which embraces liberal individualism at its cultural core. To this individualism are attributed all the perceived ills of contemporary Western capitalist nations. Among these alleged social ills are relatively high rates of divorce, crime and unemployment, and a high level of social welfarism which allegedly undermines the work ethic while generating expanded demands, based on claims of citizenship rights and entitlements, on the largesse of the state; the state in its attempt to satisfy these demands is in turn forced into a rapid expansion of state institutions and ruinous fiscal deficits, as each successive government irresponsibly over-extends its promise in order to win electoral office (Chua 1992). The PAP government argues that to avoid similar outcomes in an increasingly affluent Singapore, liberal values must be kept in abeyance, without jeopardizing continuous economic expansion.

It is in this ideological context that a conscious effort to inscribe a set of values to check the insidious penetration of liberal individualism in the social body was initiated in the early 1980s. Initially, this consisted of an attempt to instil a counter-individualistic ideology through religious education. This experiment was abandoned when it was discovered that such education heightened religious commitment and rigidified religious/racial divisions (Kuo et al., 1988). Subsequently, an 'integration' of selected elements of supposedly traditional values of the Chinese, Indian and Islamic cultures was proposed and consecrated as the cultural essence of 'Asia'.

In the latter exercise, the state distilled the 'three' traditions and appropriated them for its own ideological reinscription of Singapore as an 'Asian' society (White Paper 1991: 1). The appropriated values were reformulated into the earlier-mentioned set of five 'Shared Values'. Ideologically, these 'Values' obviously privilege a specific definition of the 'collective' welfare over individual rights and entitlements. It is further argued that this privileging of the 'collective' is the essence of 'Asian' cultures, and if consciously inculcated by individuals it will ensure continuing economic success and social cohesiveness in Singapore.

This 'Asianization' of Singaporeans, which refers to the intentional discursive distillation and reformulation of vast traditions and their respective histories into a simple 'cultural' formula, constitutes the current ideological conjuncture in the PAP government/regime's attempt to 'fill-in' the absence of a defining, if not definitive, 'national' character that may ideologically homogenize the differences among the population and unify them as a 'people' in the collective imaginary. The government's ability to inscribe the 'Shared Values' in the population remains to be seen, and perhaps is even dubious in the long term.[12]

However, against a background of prolonged recessions in the North American and European developed economies and the contemporary rise of Asian capitalism, this 'Asianization' discourse has met with immediate ideological resonance in some segments of the population, not only in Singapore but elsewhere in the region. The rise of capitalism in Asia has generated a new confidence in Asian 'cultures' that are supposedly essential to economic growth, inciting political leaders in some of the Asian nations to 'insist' on and justify their differences with the liberal 'West'. The redefining of Singaporeans as essentially 'Asian' is an astute move; not only does it seek to re-present the population but, in its inclusiveness, it also places Singaporean leaders in a position to 'speak for', that is, to represent, Asia. It is to the double effect of this Asianization discourse that this analysis must now turn.

Asianization as difference

As suggested earlier, the discursive Asianization of Singaporeans is grounded in a particular construction of Western liberalism. Liberalism is read as a culture within which individual rights and civil liberties are highly privileged because it is assumed that the individual is best disposed and singularly able to make rational choices regarding his or her own interests. Beyond the individual are 'interest groups' constituted of people who share similar corporate interests. The political arena is constituted of interest groups competing for their respective advantages, in which the state is merely the 'umpire'.

The state is therefore conceived of as 'minimal and neutral'. It is minimal in terms of intervention and neutral both in that it is supposed to be unbiased in terms of the interests of one group over another, and that it is without interests of its own. As umpire to the contests, the state is the guardian of 'public interests' only in the limited sense. It serves as a guardian where a dispute between two parties, such as employers and employees, has negative repercussions on the public at large. Every social intervention thus requires that the threat to public interests be demonstrably present; where such demonstration fails, the state is held to be in violation of the rights of individuals. Overall, the state is viewed as a necessary inconvenience. This liberal democratic discourse may be said to be globally ideologically hegemonic in the present conjuncture, such that it subjects all states to its moral injunctions (Wallerstein 1992).

The discursive move of the Singapore regime towards a communitarian ideology begins with a conceptual and substantive critique of liberalism. Conceptually it is suggested that liberalism embodies an imaginary hyper-independent, unencumbered 'individual', without substantive social attachment or entanglement.[13] Within its conceptual space, the 'social' is seen negatively as a moral injunction against the pursuit of self-interest at the expense of others' interests. It is, therefore, difficult to develop positive concepts of 'collective interest' and 'collective responsibility' in the social and political body. Substantively, in practice, the injunction against jeopardizing the interests of others often goes unheeded. Furthermore, with the entrenchment of individual rights, the civil society appears to be no longer constituted morally; instead, it has been reduced to one which is defined and determined by the competition for rights among individuals, settled only by litigation. The general thrust of the critique is that the absence of social responsibility accounts for the current state of declining civility and economic health in public and private spheres in the West.

The criticisms not only serve to reject liberalism but also make room for the insertion of 'Asian' traditional values as its Other. The ideological divide, indeed the ideological battle line, is drawn between the declining/individualistic/liberal West versus the ascending/communitarian/non-liberal Asia (East).[14] Against the centrality of individual self-interest is placed the 'collective' well-being. Against individualism is placed communitarianism. The terms 'Asia/Asian' and 'West/Western' are used with their maximum inclusiveness, intentionally eliminating the vast differences that exist within peoples in geographic Asia and those within the nominal West, which spans three continents: North America, Western Europe and Australia and New Zealand. This inattention to the differences is maintained for its ideological purchase.

To the extent that 'Asianization' is an attempt at a discursive self-definition of Singaporeans, it is a strategy that is 'productive'. In particular, for Singaporeans, it is a formulation of the post-colonial subject. It did not seek to reproduce itself in the image of the colonial past, which often leads to self-alienation, if not self-hate. Nor did it seek to construct itself by negation of the colonial subject without recourse to alternative substance to develop a new identity. Instead it seeks to construct itself in affirmation, to mould itself in substance that is recovered, albeit in reinvented fashion, from its own mixed traditions.

At the general level, in elevating 'communitarianism' as the Other of liberalism, a possible entry into the moral critique of liberalism is gained.[15] This is particularly significant at the current global conjuncture when the liberal democratic West appears to have no political opponents, when its arch-alternative, state socialism, is in retreat, when liberal democracy is hailed as the 'end of history' (Fukuyama 1992). 'Communitarianism' may be able to preserve a concept of the 'social' which had motivated 'socialism' and 'communism'. The insistence of the 'social', as in the conceptualization of human individuals as 'species' beings, provides socialism with the basis for a moral critique, and offers itself as an alternative to the rapaciousness of the market. It is the market that requires for its proper functioning, among others, the concept of a 'free' individual, the better to commodify the social exchange between capital and labour as an activity contracted between 'free' worker and capitalist.

Ironically, the PAP regime has always been staunchly anti-communist. Yet, the possible conceptual shading of communitarianism into socialism was revealed by the re-invocation of its own social democratic roots by the current Minister of Information and the Arts and 'ideas-man' of the party itself, George Yeo. Consistent within the concept of 'Asian communitarianism' and the 'Shared Values', he argued: 'Socialism will never die, of course, because it springs from the very nature of man as a social animal. At least, the family will always stay socialist' (Yeo 1994). Thus, according to him, the social welfare policies of Singapore are aimed at strengthening the family and not at replacing it with agencies of the state as in the extensive welfarism of Western developed nations.

Asianization as self-identity

As a discourse of the self, Asianization has a different set of effects within the domestic sphere. Central to communitarianism is the idea that collective interests be placed above those of individuals. The immediate questions are: how is the collective that it implies to be constituted? How are its interests to be defined? Finally, how is it to be represented and by whom? Given the technical difficulties of enabling all interested parties to engage in the process of arriving at a discursive consensus, the elected government tends to constitute itself as a singular voice which articulates the collective/national interests. There is thus a conflation of regime and society through a concept of 'national interest'. The government's role is to define and implement community needs, and 'it needs to be efficient and authoritative, capable of making the difficult and subtle trade-offs' (Lodge and Vogel 1987: 20). All its interventions may now be rationalized and justified as pre-emptive actions which 'ensure' collective well-being and, by extension, the national interests, and as such they are deemed measures of good government rather than abuses of power or of individual rights. The interactive, closed logic of communitarianism and national interest is consistent with the PAP's interpretation of its mandate to govern; once elected, it is its duty to govern in the interests of a single people rather than as representatives of the multiple constituencies that voted for its member MPs. The interventionist regime has thus arrived at a new ideological threshold through 'Asian communitarianism'.

It is the conflation of state and society, and of representation and governance, behind the 'communitarian' face, that need to be deconstructed. These conflations provide room for the elected to slip into authoritarianism, either in the genuine belief that they are acting in the collective welfare or by merely using it in a self-serving fashion. Thus, while logically not privileging any form of government, in practice 'communitarianism' often spawns authoritarianism. The question that faces Singapore's political development under a single-party dominant government with a communitarian ideology is, therefore, one of developing political institutions that can hold off the possible imposition of authoritarianism. There are three obvious candidate institutions.

First is, of course, election as the means of selecting political leadership within a multi-party political system. Ironically, it took the recent decline in PAP's electoral support to convince sceptics that election in Singapore is more than a veil for authoritarianism. Observers have marvelled at the seriousness with which the PAP takes every percentage point lost, since the losses did not translate into proportional oppositional representation in Parliament. This reaction to every small shift of electoral sentiment is partly the result of its communitarian ideology. As non-PAP votes constitute protests against the party, their increased volume stands as an indication of the 'absence' of consensus, thus weakening the PAP government's claim to be the embodiment of the 'collective interests'. Electoral support is thus not about how well the opposition parties do but how united the nation is behind the PAP leadership and the party's self-characterization as a 'people's movement'.

Second may be called the 'right to be consulted'. Within communitarianism there is little conceptual space for individual rights. Constrained within the conceptual space of collective interests, no individual or group can assert its own right as a basic condition of existence, lest the assertion be read as unacceptable self-interest, potentially detrimental to the whole. However, as consensus is required, legitimate interest groups have the right to be consulted in consensus formation. This right differs from liberal concepts of individual rights, which are conceived as 'transcendental' and 'natural' rights to be protected against state infringement. In contrast, it is constituted pragmatically, on grounds that consensus can emerge only when all identifiable interested parties are consulted and differences accommodated where possible. Similarly, and not on liberal premises, the rights to interest group formations and representation have to be institutionalized.

As the inscription of communitarianism is a recent phenomenon in Singapore, the right to be consulted is not yet firmly institutionalized. This is reflected in the government's continuing refusal to pay equal benefits for female and male civil servants. However, it is a step from which the PAP government cannot retreat because failure to consult obvious groups on actions that are prejudicial to them will potentially cause further erosion of electoral support. The actions were not satisfactorily normatively justified.

Third is the institutionalization of an independent press. That incumbent leadership may be more keen on retaining power than on furthering collective interests is always a possibility, hitherto clean leadership notwithstanding. A pro-government press is therefore not synonymous with pro-consensus and nation-wide interests. Furthermore, contrary opinions do not disappear through their absence in the press; instead, they bide their time for the right opportunity. Consequently, the lack of published information about contrary opinions renders the incumbent leadership unresponsive to opposition, neglecting to diffuse it until its effects are manifested.[16] The potential negative consequences demonstrate that an unquestioning pro-government press and the government mutually constitute a monologue, rather than a conversation required for a strong consensus on national interests. Communitarianism thus pragmatically needs an independent press, which remains absent in Singapore.

Conclusion

The history of Singapore as an independent nation goes back barely thirty years, and the circumstances under which it 'gained' political independence left it devoid of an identity as a 'nation' of 'one people'. The single-party dominant regime of the last three decades has worked consciously to 'fill-in' the absence with different 'substances' at different historical conjunctures. These ideological efforts, coupled with direct legalized interventions, have enabled the regime to reduce potential racial tensions while transforming the population into a disciplined workforce that has achieved impressive economic development in the island city-state.

Having successfully integrated the population into the global capitalist structure, the government is now seeking to redefine and reinscribe the population with an imaginary collective character through the reinvention of the Singaporean culture as essentially one of 'Asian communitarianism'. Such a reformulation has, very significantly, enabled the political leadership to open up an avenue for a general critical engagement with the developed nations of the West, especially the ex-metropolitan colonizing nations, rather than continue subjugation to the moral/ideological injunctions of the latter.

This is ideologically all the more important because of the demise of state socialism in Eastern Europe. Behind the indisputable globalization of capitalism lurk the attempts by Western ideologues to translate it into an ideological phenomenon as well. The most notable of these are theories that announced the 'end of ideology' or its variation, the 'end of history' (Fukuyama 1992), and, more generally, those which insist that capitalist economic growth will inevitably spawn a middle class who will be the harbinger of liberal democracy in developing nations. The thrust is ideologically to globalize liberal individualism along with democracy; the hegemonic desire of liberal democracy is to suppress arguments for democracy with a different value-base, such as conservatism or socialism.

The reinvention of 'Asian communitarianism' by the PAP in Singapore is aimed at confronting this presumption of the inevitability of liberal democracy. By insisting on the conceptual and substantive difficulties in liberalism's conceptualization of the 'social' and its negative effects, 'Asian communitarianism' is ideologically explicitly anti-liberal. By privileging the 'collective' welfare over individual rights, it rejects the basic liberal ethos. This confrontation is difficult to dismiss by liberal democracy precisely because Singapore (along with other East Asian nations) has been capitalistically successful; indeed, conjuncturally more successful than the liberal democratic nations themselves. That this confrontation is being taken seriously is encapsulated in the following statement: 'the most significant challenge being posed to the liberal universalism of the American and French revolutions today is not coming from the communist world ... but from those societies in Asia which combine liberal economies with ... paternalistic authoritarianism' (Fukuyama 1992: 241); 'paternalistic authoritarianism' being the code of critiques for what the PAP regime calls 'communitarianism'. The unfolding of this ideological contest, of course, remains to be seen.

However, in the political sphere of Singapore itself, this reinvented communitarianism bears the risks of the continuation of a highly interventionist state; indeed, it is now even better able to rationalize the interventions behind a reading of communitarianism as 'ensuring the national and collective interests'. Analytically, one must not lose sight of the desire of the population to have greater democratization within the political sphere. There is, therefore, a need to be vigilant about the possible slippage of 'communitarianism' into authoritarianism. The best safeguard against this possibility remains the demand for the establishment of democratic institutions, perhaps without liberalism, depending on the outcome of the critical engagement between Singaporeans and their liberal 'Others'.

Notes

1. Substantively it may be argued that the political experiences of the PAP leadership, in the brief period of membership in Malaysia, might have predisposed them to the cause of 'multi-racialism'. This would be consistent with their championing of a 'Malaysian Malaysia' in contrast to the model of Malay dominance promoted by the United Malay National Organization.

2. Only a brief statement will be made about language policy in Singapore due to limitations of space. It is argued that in order to tap into global capitalism, the population must be familiar with the English language, the language of international commerce, science and technology; repeating the 'universalization' theme. The overwhelming economic advantage of English effectively wiped out education in other languages. The 'natural' demise of community-based 'vernacular' schools was made complete by the institutionalization of a 'national' education system in 1987, with

English as the primary medium of instruction and the languages of the different races as 'second' languages.

3. Reflecting the multi-racialism policy, Mandarin in Singapore is known as the 'language of the Chinese' (*huayu*), in contrast to being known as the 'national language' (*guoyu*) in Taiwan and 'the common language' (*putonghua*) in the People's Republic of China.

4. It should be noted that the fixing of the 'mother-tongue' of a child is often a difficult issue; for example, a child with a Chinese father and Indian mother is generally given Mandarin as his/her mother-tongue language in school because of patrilineal descent criteria in the fixing of one's race (Purushotam 1989).

5. This political side-lining of race reaches a high point in the intentional dispersion of the Malay population, through a quota system, in the public housing estates (Chua 1991).

6. Indeed it has been suggested that the absence of a workforce accustomed to the industrial regime was the prime reason why American semiconductor industries chose Hong Kong over Singapore as the first offshore base for the internationalization of semiconductor production in the early 1960s. The flight of industrial capital from mainland China because of political instability since the 1930s had led to the industrialization of Hong Kong for more than two decades by then; it thereby possessed the prerequisite proletarianized labour force (Henderson 1989: 77–80).

7. Ironically, evidence of the overwhelming significance of this emergent culture of capitalist industrialism can be readily found both in self-congratulatory celebrations of the 'new' Singaporeans and, conversely, in conservative critiques of the same 'new' Singaporeans as mindless consumers in a 'cult of materialism' (Ho 1989).

8. In this connection, the Urban Redevelopment Authority, which also houses the state planning office, produced three manuals for the conservation of these areas, respectively.

9. Zoohri asserts: 'the inescapable fact is that the Malays have found themselves trapped within a definite vicious cycle. The absence of the right education had made them incapable of associating themselves with modern trade and commerce. They, therefore, had to opt for occupations of low economic status. This inevitably made them poorer than the other communities. It is this vicious cycle syndrome that had entangled them for over a century' (Zoohri 1990: 9).

10. David Brown (1993) has read this process of the constitution of racial groups as equivalent to the government-sponsored formation of interest groups which can then be given proper operating space within the inclusive sphere of the PAP regime.

11. It should be noted that even Mendaki, which was founded before the institutionalization of the 'Shared Values', was justified by Prime Minister Goh Chok Tong in terms of its potential contribution to the welfare of all Singaporeans. According to him: 'If the money is seen to be in aid of communal ends, then no party, governing on the basis of one man, one vote, will be in a position to go out of its way to give more to a group which says it is going to be more loyal to its ethnic ties than to Singapore society' (Zoohri 1990: 82).

12. For example, the lament of those who are older and in relatively better economic positions is the absence of concern for the collective among the younger who are supposedly too self-centred in the pursuit of their own interests (Fong 1994).

13. This hyper-independent character of the individual in liberalism is fully criticized in Bell (1993).

14. In the words of the Second Minister of Foreign Affairs, the last few centuries of global politics, culture and economy have been characterized by Western domination

but, 'Now, after 500 years, the pendulum is inexorably swinging back to Asia, first to East Asia and eventually to South Asia as well' (Yeo 1993).

15. In the formulation of a communitarian ideology, Singapore is a late-comer in a trio of ASEAN nations; both Indonesia and Malaysia have enshrined a communitarian national ideology in their constitutions, namely *Panca Sile* and *Negara Ku*, respectively. However, Singapore is the most vocal in promoting this ideological definition of the differences between 'Asia' and the 'West' in international meetings.

16. Arguably, in 1991, the failure of the national press compounded the failures of other feedback mechanisms to give the PAP an accurate reading of the electorate's sentiments, leading to a snap election that resulted in a further slide of popular support for the PAP government (Singh 1992).

References

Bell, D. (1993) *Communitarianism and its Critics*. Clarendon Press, Oxford.

Benjamin, G. (1976) 'The Cultural Logic of Singapore's Multiculturalism', in R. Hassan (ed.), *Singapore: Society in Transition*. Oxford University Press, Kuala Lumpur.

Brown, D. (1993) 'The Corporatist Management of Ethnicity in Contemporary Singapore', in G. Rodan (ed.), *Singapore Changes Guard*. Longman Chesire, Melbourne.

Chua, B.-H. (1985) 'Pragmatism of the PAP Government in Singapore: a Critical Assessment', *Southeast Asian Journal of Social Science* 13, 29–46.

— (1989a) 'The Business of Living in Singapore', in K. S. Sandhu and P. Wheatley (eds), *Management of Success: Moulding of Modern Singapore*. Institute of Southeast Asian Studies, Singapore.

— (1989b) *The Golden Shoe: Building Singapore's Financial District*. Urban Redevelopment Authority, Singapore.

— (1991) 'Not Depoliticized but Ideologically Successful: the Public Housing Program in Singapore', *International Journal of Urban and Regional Research* 15, 24–41.

— (1992) 'Confucianisation in Modernising Singapore', *Social Welt* (in German) 8, 249–69.

Chua, B.-H. and E. C. Y. Kuo (1992) 'The Making of New Nations: Cultural Construction and National Identity in Singapore', Working Papers, Institute of Culture and Communication, East–West Centre, Honolulu, Hawaii.

Clammer, J. (1985) *Singapore: Ideology, Society, Culture*. Chopmen Publishers, Singapore.

Drysdale, J. (1984) *Singapore: Struggle for Success*. Times Books International, Singapore.

Fong, X. (1994), *Straits Times*, 2 April.

Fukuyama, F. (1992) *The End of History and the Last Man*. Penguin Books, London.

Henderson, J. (1989) *The Globalization of High Technology Production*. Routledge, London.

Ho, W. M. (1989) 'Value Premises Underlying the Transformation of Singapore', in K. S. Sandhu and P. Wheatley (eds), *Management of Success: The Moulding of Modern Singapore*. Institute of Southeast Asian Studies, Singapore.

Kuo, E. C. Y. (1985) 'Language and Identity: the Case of Chinese in Singapore', in W. Tseng and D. Wu (eds), *Chinese Culture and Mental Health*. Academic Press, New York.

Kuo, E. C. Y., Quah, J. and Kiong, T. C. (1988) *Religion and Religious Revivalism in Singapore*. Ministry of Community Development, Singapore.

Lim, C. Y. and Associates (1988) *Policy Options for the Singapore Economy*. McGraw-Hill, Singapore.

Lodge, G. and Vogel, E. (eds) (1987) *Ideology and National Competitiveness: An Analysis of Nine Countries*. Harvard Business School Press, Boston.

Nair, C. V. Devan (ed.) (1976) *Socialism that Works*. Federal Press, Singapore.

Offe, C. (1987) *Contradictions of the Welfare State*. MIT Press, Cambridge, MA.

Purushotam, N. (1989) 'Language and Linguistic Policies', in K. S. Sandhu and P. Wheatley (eds), *Management of Success: The Moulding of Singapore*. Institute of Southeast Asian Studies, Singapore.

Quah, S. (1983) 'Social Discipline in Singapore', *Journal of Southeast Asian Studies* 14, 266–89.

Rodan, G. (1989) *The Political Economy of Singapore's Industrialization*. Macmillan, Basingstoke.

Siddique, S. (1989) 'Singaporean Identity', in K. S. Sandhu and P. Wheatley (eds), *Management of Success: The Moulding of Singapore*, Institute of Southeast Asian Studies, Singapore.

Singh, B. (1992) *Whither PAP's Dominance?* Pelanduk Publications, Petaling Jaya.

Wallerstein, I. (1992) 'Liberalism and the Legitimation of Nation-states: an Historical Interpretation', *Social Justice* 19, 22–33.

White Paper (1991) *Shared Values*. Singapore National Printers, Singapore.

Yeo, G. (1993) 'East Asia Must Not Fuel Insecurity of the West', *Straits Times*, 6 December.

— (1994) 'Democracy and Socialism, East Asia Style', *Straits Times*, 17 June.

Zoohri, W. H. (1990) *The Singapore Malays: The Dilemma of Development*. Singapore Malay Teachers' Union, Singapore.

3

On two conceptions of globalization: the debate around the reconstruction of Beirut

Suzanne Kassab

The seventeen years of civil war drained much of the energy and productive forces of Lebanon and the Lebanese and produced a landscape of both mental and physical devastation. Civil war disconnected the country from the rest of the world and threw it into the isolation of an obscure periphery. Since the end of the fighting in October 1991, Lebanese society seems to have been caught in a troublesome stagnation, its destiny inexorably embroiled in the regional so-called 'peace process' and thus exposed to its risks and pitfalls. Despite various signs of some elementary economic recovery, including monetary stability and a limited cultural revival, the country remains without a healthy democracy, without a serious political agenda, without a genuine peace-building dialogue and without any wound-healing work. It is as if a curtain was lowered over the years of war, and peace simply announced by decree. People were and are too exhausted to inquire about true political questions – those for instance concerning the causes of the war and their true remedies, or the fears and grievances of various social sectors and the constructive answers to them. Caught up in a tough struggle for economic survival, vulnerable to anxieties inspired by the precarious atmosphere of 'no war – no peace' in the volatile regional context, Lebanese society has been drained of the energy and constructive imagination needed to envision a credible and confidence-inspiring future.

The urban physiognomy of Beirut betrays this disorientation of Lebanese society. Today it consists of a number of confessionally identified, more or less isolated, suburbs surrounding an empty centre: a constellation that reflects very well the fragmentation of society and the absence of a focal centre. It is true that, contrary to the years of war, people can now move around freely and circulate from one quarter of the city to another, but no real meeting point has yet been found, either political or urban. The question is: to what extent can the planned reconstruction of Beirut reclaim the civitas together with an economically active centre, thus serving as a true meeting ground for the Beirut residents and for the Lebanese?

My aim in this chapter is to discuss the envisaged scenarios regarding the future of Beirut which underpin the current debates surrounding the reconstruction of the city. My concern is not with issues of planning as such, but with the visions which seem to inspire the planners. Hence, rather than offer a detailed assessment of planning efforts, I shall focus upon the nurturing visions of Beirut's future role in a globalized world, or, perhaps more accurately, on the absence of new visions. Since it is the pre-war role of Beirut which seems to inform the reconstruction of the city today, I shall begin by sketching a profile of Beirut in the 1960s and 1970s. Then I shall turn to the post-war political and economic landscape of Beirut, against which the Hariri government's plan to integrate the city into global networks was unveiled in the course of 1992. Last, I shall turn to the debates and criticisms surrounding the inaugurated plan and the real estate company founded for its realization, to discuss the lack of connection between the physical and the political reconstruction of the city and the country.

Let us begin by considering the pre-war functions of Beirut, since it seems to provide the main inspiration for planners in the reconstruction of the city today, without, however, raising the serious question of whether or not that role can still be upheld in the years to come.

The global profile of pre-war Beirut and the vision that nurtured it

It was in the course of the nineteenth century that Beirut as a city started to grow, benefiting primarily from the transit of goods through its port into the Syrian hinterland. This function was enhanced by the building of the Beirut–Damascus road in 1860. However, it was challenged a few decades later by the railway constructed between Damascus and Haifa, Beirut's main competitor on the Levantine coast. A railway line connecting Beirut to Damascus soon followed.

This regional function of Beirut, based on its port activities, was reinforced after the First World War under the French Mandate, when the French authorities chose it as the regional centre for their activities. They developed the basic infrastructure in the city and its surroundings and constructed a number of buildings which today are among those chosen for reconstruction and preservation in the destroyed downtown area. The growth of Beirut was increased by this additional regional function.

The independence of the Lebanon in 1943 was followed by a number of important regional events that were to have an impact on the further expansion of the city. On the one hand, the creation of the state of Israel in 1948 neutralized the role of Haifa in the Arab world and provoked the exodus of many Palestinian families, and their capital, who fled to Beirut. On the other hand, unstable military and protectionist regimes succeeding one another in Egypt, Syria, Iraq and Jordan caused further flows of the entrepreneurial elite middle classes together with their capital towards Beirut. The flow of capital led to a considerable growth in the Lebanese banking sector, a growth that compensated for the decrease in the port activity in the 1950s, when the borders between Lebanon and Syria were closed, permitting only a very limited exchange in the following decades. The activity of the banking sector reached its peak in the 1960s and early 1970s with the inflow of capital from the Gulf oil dividends. Their owners found in the free and relatively stable Lebanese economy – and more particularly in the Lebanese banking system – a safe place in which to deposit and invest their money. The developing oil countries offered in turn highly lucrative work opportunities for Lebanese skilled and semi-skilled labour as well as for managerial and business know-how. All these regional factors contributed to the development of a regional and even a global sector in Beirut that could be seen in the following phenomena:

1. The expansion of the banking sector and its integration into the global banking system, contributed strongly to a surplus economy based on international trade and services.
2. Along this central sector there prospered a number of other related economic activities such as business services, regional and international financial transactions, advertising, accounting and insurance activities.
3. A number of transnational corporations made Beirut their centre in the region.
4. The tourism sector flourished quickly, opening the country to Arab and non-Arab visitors. This expansion was reflected in the development of a new business centre outside the old downtown centre, namely the Hamra street and its surroundings, representing the global, most modern and cosmopolitan part of the city, housing alongside the economic institutions, fashionable cafés, exquisite boutiques and entertainment centres such as cinemas, art galleries, nightclubs and restaurants.

5. This development rapidly started to attract workers from the suburbs, local Palestinian camps and the mountains on the one hand, and from Syria and Egypt on the other hand.
6. It also contributed to the growth of a considerable middle class in almost all confessional groups of Lebanese society (less within the Shia community perhaps), a social class that characterized the socio-economic landscape of the Lebanon in the 1960s and 1970s.
7. Furthermore, Beirut, together with the summer resorts surrounding it, became an attractive entertainment centre for the neighbouring rich Arabs who would eagerly take advantage of the liberties permitted in Lebanon and banned in their own countries and often invest in Lebanese real estate.
8. Finally, and on account of this same climate of freedom, Beirut became the refuge for many Arab dissidents, intellectuals and journalists, ensuring most of the publishing activity of the Arab world and attracting students from many Arab and third world countries to its good universities. Foreign scholars, on the other hand, found in Beirut a convenient base for their research in the region.

However, these developments brought about a number of conflicts that eventually contributed to the aggravation of the social tensions in the country by the early 1970s. It is true, for instance, that economic prosperity helped to raise the educational level in general and that more people had access to higher education, but the economy could not accommodate all of them, thus giving rise to a wave of frustration and anger. On the other hand, the climate of freedom was often transformed into a climate of chaos and *laissez-aller* more than of *laissez-faire*, and the liberal state became a pseudo-state, producing a city and a country run by wild mercantilism and the neglect of public welfare and order. The urban landscape of Beirut with its wild construction style reflects very well this chaos and lack of public urban planning. It is not the purpose of this chapter to analyse the socio-economic causes of the war of 1975, notwithstanding the importance of such an analysis. For our concern here, I would like to look instead at what enabled Lebanon to take advantage of the above-mentioned regional developments, and to argue that it is a certain vision of itself and the choice of a number of values that made this regional (and almost global) role of Beirut possible.

This vision is well illustrated in the thought of Michel Chiha, principal author of the 1926 Lebanese constitution and co-maker of the Muslim–Christian so-called 'National Pact'. His thought was to shape to a large extent the general project of the 'First Republic', although it was never accepted unanimously. It was rejected on the one hand by those

Christians who preferred to have a smaller Lebanon but with a guaranteed Christian majority, and on the other by the majority of Muslims who contested from the beginning the very existence of a Lebanese state separate from Syria and from the Arab world in general. Chiha's idea of Lebanon was a response to Arab Nationalism and emphasized its distinctive character with respect to the rest of the Arab world. Lebanon, according to him, was a Phoenician, Mediterranean country, at the crossroads between East and West. Its precariousness, of which he was aware, needed international guarantees and links with the East as well as with the West. Lebanon was viewed as a refuge for the oppressed in the area, housing multiple groups of people, and hence as a pluralist country. This pluralism, according to Chiha, called upon respect for the various traditions on the one hand and their assembly into a harmonious unity on the other hand. It consequently necessitated a representative parliament, a confessional division of higher employment, minimal legislation and a maximum guarantee of liberties: in other words, a minimal state. Moreover, the small refuge needed to be open to the outside world and to ensure liberty of movement as well as liberty of trade. After all, the Lebanese were, according to this view, the heirs of the historical Phoenician trading nation. And as a trading country, Lebanon needed a sound currency, a liberal foreign exchange and a liberal economic system. Under various governments this *laissez-faire* ideology was transformed into a *laissez-aller* principle, making the country a 'Merchant Republic', proud of the weakness, if not the absence, of the state. The country was run, especially between 1943 and 1958, by a business oligarchy from and for the merchant city. In 1958, the country experienced its first serious crisis and Chiha supported the idea of a stronger state and sided with the government of General Chehab who tried to introduce some elements of planning in the governing of public affairs, especially socio-economic ones.

Again, an assessment of these attempts at planning falls beyond the scope of this chapter. What is relevant here is that this opting for liberalism as well as for the cultural and economic openness that it implied, allowed the Lebanese to be in contact with developments in the West, enabling it to acquire know-how, skills and languages and to engage actively in trade and economic exchange. In other words, it was this preference for liberalism and openness that made possible the cosmopolitan and regional, if not global, profile of Lebanon and Beirut in particular. Moreover, its choice of pluralism guarded it against inner hegemony projects and thus offered it a relative stability. These are the conditions that enabled the Lebanese to take advantage of regional circumstances and to play this distinctive role in the region through Beirut.

What are the regional givens today ? And what is the vision of the so-called 'Second Republic'?

The post-war socio-economic, political and urban landscape of Beirut

After becoming a regional centre for business, finance, tourism and culture, Beirut became a centre for global, regional and local violence, and Lebanon began its decline into peripheral obscurity. The 'First Republic' collapsed and the vision that had nurtured it was seriously shattered. The downtown centre that had epitomized that vision was destroyed; the conviviality between the various Lebanese groups as well as between East and West turned into violent confrontation. The free trading centre, based on individual initiative, was burned down. The quasi-global Hamra sector became an obscure district in a provincial suburb. From the ruins of the downtown centre there emerged peripheral centres characterized by the religious and often political homogeneity produced by the protracted civil war. The governmental plan of 1991–92 was to remedy this situation. Its nature was not unrelated to the circumstances under which it was prepared and presented, nor to those who were promoting it. Hence a brief description of those circumstances and actors is required.

The two decades of civil war, which fed on the local tribalism that the First Republic had not managed to subdue, exacerbated that tribalism, compromising the chances of the so-called Second Republic of being safe from it, especially in the political climate after the ending of violent hostilities in the autumn of 1991. It is an obvious fact that the fighting did not end as the result of the inner maturation of the conflict among the Lebanese, nor as the result of their resolution to start dealing with their conflicts by means other than the military. An end was put to the fighting by the force in the region that emerged victorious from the second Gulf war, thus ushering Lebanon into a new era of Pax Syriana. Hence this post-fighting period was the expression of a clear change in the regional balance of power, with the Lebanese allies of the victorious taking over the apparent means of power in the country. On the basis of these givens, any fair or free exercise of power was ruled out and this state of affairs was to determine the kind of political activity that could be undertaken in the country.

Their first impact was on the implementation of the Taef agreement which was supposed to provide an equitable legal and political basis for the new, peaceful Lebanese Republic, now referred to as the Second Republic. Obviously, its incomplete and biased implementation was to serve the interests of the victorious. Among the flaws in this implementation was, for instance, the non-disarming of the Hizbullah militia (for its possible use by Syria in its negotiations with Israel), while other militias were almost dismantled. The Taef agreement itself was accepted by most parties in the civil war as a common platform for the ending of the fighting. However, if the agreement stopped the fighting, it did not provide a very convincing ground for the making of real peace. For one thing, it consecrated the confessional nature of the political system legally and in writing, a matter that was earlier only an oral national pact, and at a time when most Lebanese politicians called for the abolition of political confessionalism as a prerequisite for a democratic, just and peaceful Lebanon. Contested elections, moreover, came to reinforce the alienation of important sectors of society and to exclude some warlords, while others, happening to be in the right alliance at the right time, were called upon to hold some of the most humanitarian posts in the government. Censorship, partisan and obscure arrests as well as more or less subtle forms of repression (particularly concerning the press) contributed to the creation of a climate of alienation, discontent and suspicion as to the fairness and legitimacy of the power in control. More recently, the amendment of the constitution for the prolongation of the mandate of the President of the Republic in power was a further manifestation of the absence of real political life in the country. Finally, the tutelage of Syria over Lebanon in the conflict-resolution negotiations with Israel confirmed the considerable marginalization of the Lebanese government as a real agent.

It is perhaps for this reason that the Hariri government, in the autumn of 1992, offered an essentially economic agenda, addressing very timidly, if at all, political questions. In any case, the popular hopes attached to Hariri's becoming Prime Minister were mainly related to the economic recovery of the country, at a time when people were (and are still) caught up in a tough struggle for economic survival, in a country suffering from severe inflation. The appointment of Hariri was in fact welcomed with mixed feelings of optimism on the one hand, inspired by his impressive financial power and his profile as a successful multi-millionaire businessman, and of suspicion on the other hand as to the dangers of this very power and profile. There was also fear of seeing the fate of the country, at least economically, tied to the life of a single individual, as well as fear of having the private interests of the latter confused with the public interests of the country. People were in fact too exhausted to inquire about highly intricate political issues, absorbed as they were by the difficult task of making ends meet. The priorities and needs of the country, the necessary requirements for a healthy democracy, were not addressed by the government or by a society exhausted by two decades of civil war. Successive ideological disillusionments, the moral bankruptcy of almost all the political parties and militias had given rise to a tendency for a nihilistic lack of interest and a disbelief in politicians and politics in general. This apathy was reinforced by the post-fighting givens of power described above as well as by the idea that the fate of the country in any case did not lie in their hands but in powers outside its boundaries.

It was in this atmosphere of political paralysis and apathy that the Hariri government, soon after its formation, presented its plan of reconstruction for the downtown district of the capital. Colourful sketches of a modern, clean and grandiose centre were distributed throughout the city, and big posters appeared in public places. At first people in general reacted with a mixture of enthusiasm and scepticism: enthusiasm for the rebuilding of their capital, for the start of an economic recovery and for a long-awaited better future; and scepticism as to the hidden agenda and hidden partners of Hariri, especially given his tremendous financial power and connections with the Saudi royal family. Soon, strong protests started to be voiced by the union of engineers, the bank association, the property and rights owners of the centre, the association for the preservation of old buildings, urbanists, architects, sociologists and others. Controversy about the project within political circles became important and popular unrest about this project could be sensed. Several television debates were set between the defenders and opponents of the project, numerous newspaper articles were written, seminars, conferences and lectures were organized, all this manifesting, in spite of the general disarray, the presence of a healthy and active civil society, aware of and concerned with public issues and capable of engaging in free and rational public debate.

The Hariri plan and the private real estate company found for its execution

The Hariri plan of 1991–92 was not the first government plan for reconstruction. Two others had preceded it. The first was elaborated in 1977 under the direction of the governor of Beirut by a joint French–Lebanese team. It was conservative in its overall approach in the sense that it aimed at preserving as much as possible what had remained from the old urban, social and economic structure of the centre. It encouraged the owners and tenants of the place to come back as quickly as possible and participate actively in the reconstruction work, except for the heavily damaged areas where the state would intervene. According to it, the role of the state was also to be extended to a number of important tasks, namely the legislation of new laws facilitating and regularizing the process of reconstruction, the improvement of car traffic, including the development of better road networks, tunnels and public transportation, the construction of parking lots, the designing of pedestrian zones, the preservation of historical monuments and old souks as well as the financing and insuring of a basic infrastructure, such as a new sewerage canalization, electricity and communication cables. The plan could not be executed because of renewed fighting in 1978. In 1986 a second reconstruction plan was elaborated adjusting the first one to the new dimensions of destruction caused by the ongoing war. This plan incorporated within its scope the totality of the capital city including its suburbs. Fighting broke out again and it was only in 1991 that reconstruction could be envisaged anew.

However, the plan of 1991, promoted by the multi-millionaire and newly appointed Prime Minister Rafik Hariri, differed in many important respects from the two preceding plans. First of all, it focused on the downtown business district and did not have any substantial plans for the area of the city outside the centre or for the rest of the country, at a time when destruction and damage had continued to affect a wider and wider area. Secondly, and again contrary to the other plans, it was non-conservative: its approach was that of the *tabula rasa*, that is, a new centre was to be built on the ruins of the heavily damaged old one. More than two-thirds of the remaining buildings were to be destroyed to make room for modern, sparkling buildings as well as wide and imposing boulevards (some of which were to be 80 metres wide, that is 10 metres wider than the Champs-Elysées). Huge tower blocks were to house a world trade centre, international businesses and the necessary hotels, luxurious furnished apartments and entertainment centres to service them. All this was to be ornamented with some folkloric cosmetic touches. The idea was to replace the old Beirut with a modern and global one obviously inspired by Manhattan, Hong Kong and Arab oil cities. To the centre was to be added land reclaimed from the sea. And thirdly, this plan was to be carried out by a private real estate company.

The need for such a company was justified as follows:

1. The extreme fragmentation and entanglement of property rights, involving owners, tenants and lease-holders required, according to the promoters of this project, a unified organization which could make decisions and act upon them within reasonable spans of time, thus minimizing legal complications and enhancing the chances for a rapid start and a rapid progression of the reconstruction work. Property- and rights owners would become shareholders in this company and

shares would be allotted to them on the basis of an estimation of their property lots.

2. The financial and administrative inability of the state to carry out reconstruction made necessary the delegation of this work to a private company that would avoid the pitfalls of corruption and lack of public funds. Through a call for subscription, considerable capital could be raised and the means ensured for such a wide enterprise. It was stipulated that no one (individuals or companies) could buy more than 10 per cent of the shares. The subscription would be open to the property- and rights owners of the centre, to Lebanese and Arab investors as well as to the Lebanese state.

The obligations of this private real estate company were to involve the installation of a basic infrastructure, including roads, public squares and gardens in the business district centre as well as in the reclaimed land. These works were to be performed on behalf of and at the expense of the state, on the basis of a budget presented by the company and approved by the state. As for the construction of private buildings, at first the law did not mention anything about it, but following public protest some vague provision was made in this respect. Indeed, people had started to get more and more upset about the creation of a company that would take over the properties of tens of thousands of people, but would not pay for the infrastructure or be required to undertake any construction of private buildings. Moreover, no specific deadlines were set for the various phases of the work and no way of ensuring quality and standards was foreseen. However, the company was to be exempt from state taxation for a period of ten years.

With Hariri as both the promoter of this project and the company and as Prime Minister, laws were quickly passed to found and legalize the company, notwithstanding some resistance inside Parliament. It was named Solidere: Société Libanaise de Reconstruction.[1] Property lots were estimated and subscriptions raised; everything was then set to start the work for a modern business district centre, fully equipped with the latest communications technology and thus fulfilling all the requirements of a modern global economy. Experts from various fields of specialization were recruited and it was hoped that the project, once started, would generate employment and have an overall positive economic impact on the country. The first spectacular act of the company was the destruction through dynamite of a whole range of buildings in the downtown area on the grounds of public safety, each time causing new damage in neighbouring buildings by the blast of the explosions.

A critique of the Hariri plan and the counter-proposals

The central question raised by the plan's opponents was the following: who is constructing what, for whom? For many the project seemed to be a massive privatization, showing disrespect for private property as well as for the historical and human elements of the centre and ignoring the importance of popular participation in the planning and implementation of the reconstruction. Criticisms were voiced about the legal, political and financial aspects of the project, about its aims as well as its means, about its overall approach and spirit, its presuppositions and priorities.[2]

On the legal level, protests were formulated against the imposed expropriation of the rights owners and their forced transformation into shareholders of a company, which in their majority they rejected. This was regarded as a serious violation of the right to private property, a right that was a corner-stone of the country's wealth and liberal economy. On the political level, this implied an imposed exchange of actors on the scene of the city centre: middle-class rights owners were sent away and room was made for anonymous big capitalists whose interest in the place could only be that of a real estate speculation. This was regarded as a further blow against the Lebanese middle class that was already damaged by the heavy losses and destruction of the war as well as by the acute inflation and devaluation of the Lebanese currency. By favouring the private real estate company to the detriment of the middle class, the government was contributing to the dismantling of a class of people who were known to be the carriers and defenders of liberal and democratic choices. How could a city centre be vivified without its thousands of active inhabitants and actors of various religious, social and geographic origins, for whom that city had been, often for generations, a busy space for interaction and exchange, especially since its centre was and still is the heart of the country with all its wounds and need for healing? Fighting and war destruction had emptied this space of its original actors; the reconstruction policy was obviously doing the same. The potential for the democratic revival of the country was thus jeopardized. Also, by alienating these citizens, the reconstruction task could not mobilize the productive forces of the people and bring them together into the reconciliation and healing process which they badly needed after two decades of civil war. But this reconstruction policy did not alienate only the citizens, it also marginalized the state. By putting most of the prerogatives in the hands of the private company, the state, as a defender of public welfare, was considerably deprived of its control over the reconstruction of the centre of its capital city. A monopolistic private real estate company was now supposed to become the defender of the public good: could this be consistent with the very logic of such a company? Even if this could be granted for the sake of argument, which authority was to control and evaluate its accountability? This brings us to the financial aspect.

If the creation of the private company was justified on account of the lack of public funds, it could certainly not help to remedy this situation: the state was to pay the company for its work and, in addition, to collect no taxes from it, at least for a period of ten years. This arrangement would definitely not strengthen the financial position of the state; on the contrary, it could only perpetuate its weakness. On the other hand, the opponents of the project considered the estimated budget for the work to be done by the company to be seriously inflated: up to five times their estimate of the reasonable costs to be incurred. As to the estimation of the property lots made by the company, it was often held to be below a fair market price. Also, the idea that this unique private company was the only possible way to finance such a big reconstruction enterprise was seriously questioned. The opponents offered a counter-proposal of creating, among other financing channels, a reconstruction bank in which the Lebanese banks and the property-owners as well as other investors could be actively involved. Such a financing model would be less gigantic and less anonymous, and definitely not monopolistic, thus more encouraging for small investors. It would also be more accountable to its participants and to the state, the involvement of which was regarded as essential, in spite of its poverty. In fact, the very idea of a monopolistic privatization was strongly criticized.

Two visions of globalization and two sets of priorities

By focusing exclusively on the business district and failing to connect it to the rest of the city and to the rest of the country, the promoters and defenders of the project made clear their interests and priorities. What they wanted to build was a global business centre for global capital and they did not care about the distortion of the local identity in this centre, or about its original inhabitants, or about relating the centre to its immediate surroundings. Obviously, the possible reconciliatory and healing effect of reconstruction was not a priority for them. The centre was not to have any local significance or function. It was to be built at the expense of the city instead of being built for it. It was intended as an island for the rich in the middle of an undeveloped city and a neglected country. It was to display modernity in the form of architectural façades without producing any social or political modernization, that is, without developing a middle social class and without designing a centre to serve as a real public space where people from all regions, religions and social strata could meet and mix.

For the opponents of the project, true modernity lay in the interacting, communicating and participating of active citizens and not in their exclusion. For them priority was to be given to the logic of life over the logic of strict capitalist economic profit. Instead of imposing a monumental and rigid Master Plan, the reconstruction management had to respect the natural rhythm of a reviving city. Instead of promoting luxury in the midst of a poor periphery and displaying physical modernity in an environment of social archaism, the social and political dimensions of the reconstruction process had to be ensured and the local function of the centre had to be respected. Only then could this centre and, for that matter, the whole city and country open themselves gradually and modestly to the global economic networks, in a way that would not paralyse the rest of the country in favour of an isolated city centre.

The public debate surrounding the governmental project has thus brought forth two very different conceptions and cultural visions of reconstruction. The Hariri government's plan was obviously based on the assumption that Beirut would resume its pre-war regional position and fulfil again its old regional functions. Such an assumption, according to its opponents, ignored the many economic and political changes that had occurred in the region in the last three decades. The oil boom was over and the Gulf countries were no longer open for Lebanese labour, as they had been in the 1960s and the 1970s. Moreover, these countries had no further need for Lebanese middlemen in their transactions with the West, having developed their own mediating structures. And most importantly, the ongoing Middle Eastern peace process was to open the way to a whole range of possible scenarios concerning the division of labour among the various cities and countries in the region. Where were the anticipatory studies of the possible regional economic role of Beirut that could justify the construction of those hundreds of business offices? In other words, a whole set of structures were envisaged on the basis of highly questionable assumptions about the external (that is, regional) role of Beirut within the givens of the new, globalized power games.

After almost four years since its launching, the official plan for the reconstruction of Beirut has not been substantially modified and continues to divide the Lebanese. So, a city is being built without building its society and a city centre is being projected as essentially an anonymous apolitical business centre – a centre whose economic feasibility and prospects of success are highly questionable. Is it possible to plan for the rehabilitation of buildings and roads, without addressing the rehabilitation of the socio-political human tissue of a city and a country?

Given the absence of a political agenda, and the kind of political power represented by the post-war Hariri government, the physical and political reconstruction of the city and the country remain disconnected. The vision of the so-called Second Republic remains blurred, reflecting the nature of the political power governing (rather, not governing) the country today and its manifest lack of imagination and freedom. As Lebanon continues to be more than ever captive in the regional power games and unable to think freely itself, Beirut's chances of rehabilitation remain bound to an uncertain future. In a city used to being shaken by neighbouring turmoils and used to feeling impotent in the face of uncontrollable forces of destruction, this is not news, provided that the years of captivity do not erode its creative capacities.

Notes

1. The viewpoints of the promoters of the project outlined here have been elaborated in Solidere's numerous brochures.

2. A detailed elaboration of the various criticisms of the Hariri project can be found in N. Beyhum et al. (1995) *Beyrouth: Construire l'avenir, reconstruire le passé?* published by the authors.

4

The myth of the 'ideal home' travels across cultural borders to Istanbul

Ayşe Öncü

> Istanbul ... The legendary city of splendid architecture which has inspired songs, poems, books ... The gate across continents and the cradle of ancient civilizations ... But unfortunately a city which has lost much of its former beauty to become a metropolis of ten million today ...
>
> Istanbul's pollution has become oppressive ... It contaminates not only the air, water, soil of the city, but its traffic, its people and its culture ... Those who have to continue working in this polluted environment are moving away to escape its influence in their living spaces. They are searching for clean, happy, peaceful settings ...
>
> And in Istanbul's hinterland new towns are emerging to answer this need ...
>
> But GARDENCITY is very special among them ...
>
> • Luxury villas in gardens with 500m²
> • Only 20 minutes to Istanbul
> • Swimming pool, tennis courts, sports club, children's park, Country Club
> • Entries and exits guarded by special security systems
>
> (from a glossy advertising brochure)

Over the past decade, Istanbul's middle classes have rediscovered the city they live in through the optics of the global. In the profusion of photogenic images, from advertisements to televisual media, they have come to perceive the exotic beauty of the city's old neighbourhoods, the romanticism of its indigenous wooden architecture, the splendour of its historical monuments. The more historical a city, the more it falls prey to the tourist gaze. And it is through the tourist gaze that Istanbulites have come to realize the profundity of their loss: the disappearance of 2000 years of history.

In the political juncture of the mid-1980s, this awareness of loss and disappearance gave urgency to a series of massive urban renewal projects designed to re-create Istanbul's past glory in the present. Thus, large tracts of the living city's nineteenth-century urban core were bulldozed to resurrect times and places no longer in existence. Ancient mosques and churches were restored to 'timeless glory' by clearing away the unsightly buildings and activities which had accumulated around them over the centuries, and replacing them with green lawns and flowerbeds. Back streets with dilapidated old wooden structures were redesigned as pedestrian walkways, lined with picturesque houses in freshly painted colours to serve as restaurants or boutiques selling oriental kitsch. The legendary beauty of the Golden Horn, with its proverbial blue waters and green surroundings, was brought to life by demolishing some 30,000 buildings along its shores, and replacing them with freshly-laid-out parks and newly planted trees, as well as a parallel corniche wide enough to accommodate two-way traffic along the waterway. In the selectiveness of their preservation, these projects, intended to preserve Istanbul's disappearing past, blotted out from local memory what were once thriving areas of the city, re-creating them as historical sites and scenes to view. This was history as decoration and display, and as nostalgia for a distant past free from the anachronisms of more recent events.

In the feverish clearance operations undertaken between 1983 and 1990, Istanbul's historical peninsula was re-created as an open-air museum, now within easy reach of different parts of the city on the newly constructed throughways, underpasses and overpasses. The internationalized business centre towards the north of the Golden Horn, with its deluxe hotels, modern office towers and wide avenues, was to host global functions, welcoming conventions, businessmen and tourists. Visitors to Istanbul could thus use the new highway network from the airport to bypass the congestion, noise and traffic of the inner city and reach their hotels, later touring the open-air museum or driving along the Bosporus. Amidst frenzied construction activity, rumours of fortunes changing hands in the awarding of lucrative municipal contracts, and of unprecedented corruption in city hall, Istanbul emerged as the showcase of Turkey's new era of integration into the global scene.[1]

Paradoxically, however, the optics of the global through which Istanbul's middle classes rediscovered the aesthetics of their city's historical heritage, giving overwhelming political support to the dramatic clean-up operations which transformed the physiognomy of the city, also rendered visible how disorderly, contaminated and polluted the familiar fabric of Istanbul's everyday life had become. The middle classes of Istanbul discovered, in the accelerated cultural flows of the 1980s, the chemical, social and cultural pollutants which threatened their daily lives.

My concern in this chapter is with the ways in which the

'homogenizing' optics of global consumerism have transformed the lives and practices of Istanbul's middle classes by rendering them visible in novel ways, thereby 'fragmenting' them spatially and culturally at the local level. On the following pages, I will narrate how diverse segments of Istanbul's 'middle strata' were initiated into the fantasy world of the 'ideal home', as the quintessential dream, symbol and embodiment of middle-class identity, and who were inspired to depart for progressively quartered lives – 'quartered' both in the sense of 'drawn and quartered' and also of residential 'quarters' – on the outskirts of the city. This is a story which begins in a style reminiscent of the post-Second World War suburban exodus from North American cities, which progresses towards an ending which evokes the hyper-real images of contemporary Hong Kong's huge residential estates (Abbas 1994). Be that as it may, it is still a unique story, one that involves a distinctive set of historical mediations which have to be attended to, and which require consideration in terms of the politics of space as well as the politics of identity.

Ways of thinking about a 'global' culture of consumption

Istanbul has always been a major consumer city, cosmopolitan in flavour throughout its history. It has always been a divided city, diverse in its cultural and social geography. Hence the question of *what is new* in the era of globalism seems to require some conceptual clarification before proceeding.

There are various ways of approaching and/or understanding consumer culture and its 'globalization' (Featherstone 1991). One way of thinking would be to begin with the universal language of money, interpenetrating, as it were, into an ever larger sphere of meanings, adding a new level of signification to 'local' habits, standards, beliefs or practices, by attaching to them a monetary sign. To invoke Simmel (1971), the notion of money standardizes the objective existence of disparate things thereby valued. Or to invoke Marx (1967), it establishes a universally valid equivalence, undermining a plethora of local logics by drawing them into the sphere of exchange, thus 'commodifying' them. Proceeding from this line of reasoning, globalization of consumer culture would mean the expansion of the process of commoditization, bringing 'the local' into its fold.

A second line of thinking would be to begin with the symbolic significance of consumption practices, classified and classifying, to invoke Bourdieu (1984). It is by claiming distance from vulgar considerations of money that symbolic hierarchies of taste and style legitimize themselves.

Via taste and style, consumption practices are linked to class-specific codes, meanings and competencies. But the symbolic worth of taste and style derive from ' disavowing', 'repudiating' or 'negating' any attempt to assign monetary value. Hence the elaborated system of distinction and difference embodied in consumption practices depends upon defining and creating a realm of 'cultural goods' which are outside the realm of the economic: a consecrated, sacred realm with its own producers, vendors and institutional bases.

Following this line of thinking, it is possible to think of 'globalization' as the erosion of referential hierarchies from which cultural goods derive their meanings. As distinctions between high culture and low culture, the original and the reproduction, the 'sacred' and the 'banal' or the 'vulgar' become increasingly slippery, the referential system from which cultural goods derive their meanings is blurred. Consumption practices lose their anchoring in the class system, become foot-loose so to speak, ceasing to signify categorical differences. Globalization, in this sense, implies a pastiche of styles and tastes (Baudrillard 1981), creating a world of movement and mixture, to invoke the 'global ecumene' of Hannerz (1989), in which the global and the local are moments of the same process; a blending of disjunct and different cultural forms which yields new diversities, that is, hybridization.

Last, it is possible to begin thinking about consumer culture as the realm of contemporary myth-making, to invoke Barthes (1972). A culture of consumption would mean, in this sense, a culture wherein goods become the embodiment of desires, dreams, emotions; wherein subjective experiences of love, excitement, cleanliness, pleasure or freedom are objectified in goods (for example, cars denote speed, connote excitement; the movement of meanings between them creates a natural unity). Such 'mythical' properties of goods, generated in the lexicon of particular societies, classes and sub-groups, are universalized in contemporary global culture, and come to operate as myths in a diversity of 'local' contexts. Contemporary advertising and audio-visual media are the institutional contexts of this 'myth-making' process.

These different ways of understanding consumer culture and its globalization need not be thought of as mutually exclusive. In Istanbul of the 1990s – where business tycoons are avidly 'buying' Ottoman history in international antique auction houses, where young executives are pursuing the distinctions of internationalized yuppiedom in aerobics centres, and where stalls in open-air markets of low-income neighbourhoods are featuring electronic goods from Taiwan and tableware from Germany – the 'money sign' and 'cultural pastiche' are everywhere. But for Istanbul's middle strata, I would suggest, it was initiation into the fantasy world 'ideal home' through the accelerating cultural flows of the past decade which has proved critical.

The myth of the 'ideal home'

As a historical construct, the 'ideal home', with its imaginary associations of comfort, well-being and status, as the locus of a middle-class identity and culture, can be traced back to the late nineteenth and early twentieth centuries, an era when values and ideals began to fuse with the actual purchase of commodities. It was associated with the steadily growing cities at the turn of the century, when in Western Europe as well as in the United States, the processes of professionalization and bureaucratization of public as well as private administrations gave birth to a new stratum of 'salariat' (white-collar groups) who wanted to distinguish themselves from the lower social strata, especially the working classes. Within this stratum the desire for social status was translated into consumerism, shaping a distinctive culture wherein ideals and desires and status symbols centred upon purchasing. This fusion of middle-class identity and culture with consumerism followed somewhat different paths in Western Europe and the US. In Europe, the formerly dominant aristocratic culture was emulated by the newly rising bourgeoisie and the urban petty bourgeoisie, whereas in the US the absence of such models meant that the constitution of the middle-class family and the housewife as the home-maker coincided with the rise of the advertising industry and shaped its distinctive ethos. In the post-war era, cultural spaces emblematic of the middle class – family and neighbourhood – were translated into the physical space of mass-produced suburbs and transposed on to television.[2]

As a 'global myth', however, the 'ideal home' belies the historical mechanisms of its construction to acquire the status of a timeless and placeless truth. Contemporary myths are not expressed in long, fixed narratives of the primitive epic, but in visual images, phrases and forms of speech whose meanings appear self-evident and hence natural. In the global consumer culture of the present, dominant-hegemonic meanings which are historically specific to particular class- or interest-linked discourses travel across national boundaries to acquire the privilege and moral authority of universal truths, that is, they assume the status of global myths. The 'ideal home' is thus a global myth in the sense of discursive construct which claims for itself the moral superiority and legitimacy of a timeless and placeless truth.[3]

But while global myths are timeless and placeless, the optics of the local through which they are mediated is always historically grounded.

Hence complexities of historical juncture have to be taken into account at the level of the local. For Istanbul's middle strata, the introduction to the dreamland of the 'ideal home' as a mythical construct came through colour television, beginning in the early 1980s. It was in this decade, concomitantly with Turkey's economic opening to global flows of capital and finance, that the Turkish advertising industry became internationalized, gaining access to techniques and technologies of multinational advertising through joint ventures. Public investment in new information technologies, coupled with the increasing domestic production of television sets, meant that within less than a decade roughly 6 million households in Turkey (out of a total of 11 million households) had acquired colour television sets. In Istanbul, 90 per cent of households owned colour television sets by 1990.[4]

Thus Istanbulites were initiated into the global myth of the ideal home as the embodiment of a middle-class way of life through the landscape of the television screen, in the abundance of representations offered by cheap films from the Hollywood archives of the 1950s, in the weekly instalments of series and serials from the global bestseller market, as well as in slick advertisements featuring gleaming kitchens, antiseptic bathrooms and healthy foods. But the abundance of consumer goods emblematic of the 'ideal home' on the television screen held little novelty for Istanbul's middle strata. For in the expansionist wave of the 1980s, riding on capital inflows from abroad and fuelled by double-digit inflation figures, Istanbul was flooded with goods from different parts of the world, to be bought on cash or instalment basis, from opulent shopping arcades or from street vendors. In this boom-town climate, televised images of conventional consumer goods held little fascination.

What captured the imagination of Istanbul's middle classes and became the focus of their desires was the homogeneity of a life-style cleansed of urban clutter – of poverty, of immigrants, of elbowing crowds, dirt and traffic – a world of safe and antiseptic social spaces where the 'ideal home' signifies clean air, clean water, healthy lives; a homogeneous setting and a cultural milieu where adults and children lead active lives, engage in sports, socialize with each other around their barbecue sets in the gardens. The ways in which this 'dreamland' is discursively constructed in contemporary advertisements in Istanbul's lucrative home market is remarkably similar, despite the wide range in quality and prices.

Marketing 'dreamland'

In the current residential market of Istanbul, what is promoted as 'your ideal home' or 'the home of your dreams' can range from 100-square-metre flats in high-rise, high-density blocks advertised in the daily newspapers, to the more spacious flats in upscale apartment complexes pictured in full colour on the pages of glossy magazines, to the most exclusive garden-homes illustrated in sophisticated watercolour designs in brochures which are mailed to a selected few prospective customers.[5] Irrespective of size, type and cost of dwelling, two common features of these new homes are reiterated in almost identical phrases in the texts of advertisements. Whether a small flat or a garden-home, they are all 'outside Istanbul' but 'very close', and can be reached 'within minutes' by car on the 'expressway'. Furthermore, they all possess 'the necessary accoutrements of modern way of life', described in terms of new opportunities for 'parking', 'children' and 'sports'. However different the actual list of possibilities may be, ranging from car parks to helicopter pads, or from volleyball to golf and canoeing, the necessities of a modern way of life are articulated in terms of parking facilities, playgrounds for children and opportunities for sports.

But what conjures and defines the 'dreamland' is the way in which these buzzwords are interwoven into a particular narrative, both a story with a beginning, a middle and a promised ending, and also a way of telling it. The story is that of Istanbul, which begins with a return of memory to the past, a past-without-pain. Most frequently, this is nostalgia for childhood days in Istanbul:

> I am now forty years old. I remember childhood days when we used to collect pine cones with friends. Istanbul was green. Now there are only a few pine trees left. I have been working and toiling for so many years. Now is the time for a home. But where to buy a home in this huge city?
>
> (newspaper ad for SERAkent, *Hürriyet*, 30 December 1995)

Depending on the ingenuity of the advertisers, nostalgia for the ancient Istanbul of legends, nostalgia for picnics under the shade of fruit trees, nostalgia for days of fishing in the clear waters of the Bosporus, are all possible. Or it could be simple phrases such as 'I miss my Istanbul'.

> Some of us miss our homes in gardens, some of us those selective five o'clock teas, some of us our childhood parks … Yes, each age is wistful for a different Istanbul … Now there is ALKENT which combines all these beauties with modern comfort, brings back together what everyone misses, and protects its environment.
>
> (weekly magazine ad, *Nokta*, 5 June 1993)

Remembrances of Istanbul's past in terms of its natural beauties – green trees, flower smells, fishing – serves to underline its current plight, described in terms of 'pollution', a word whose only synonym in the Turkish lexicon is 'dirty-fied'. In advertisements, 'dirty-fied' connotes, in one word, everything that is wrong with contemporary Istanbul and requires little elaboration. Hence lyrical descriptions of the past are immediately followed by statements such as, 'to be away from Istanbul's traffic, its noise, the degenerate behaviour of its people and yet remain in the city', condensing the middle part of the story about current sufferings, with the prospect of a happy ending. The contrast between the natural beauties of the past and the pollution of the present inevitably moves the story towards a happy ending: healthy lives, clean air, beautiful homes in natural surroundings. Thus nearly all new residential estates surrounding Istanbul have names which denote 'back to nature', such as SERAkent in the advertisement quoted above which translates as 'greenhouse city'. At SERAkent, the high-rise, high-density apartment blocks are named after flowers; 'Magnolia, Lilac, Honeysuckle, Jasmine, and Lily Blocks' are described as 'the last flowers of SERAkent' available for sale.

The texts of the advertisements which accompany and frame the visual representations of 'the ideal homes' in Istanbul's residential market all narrate the same three-part story, discursively constructed through the metaphors of 'nature' and 'pollution'. Unless we assume that Turkish marketing agencies are totally lacking in imagination (and the illustrations above prove the contrary), or that they are capable of manipulating consumers (which current theoretical literature argues is not the case), then the repetitiveness of this narrative, and its appeal, can be explained only in terms of a 'global myth' which prospective customers and advertisers share alike. To put it more simply, these advertisements appropriate meanings from a repertoire of signs, symbols and images which Istanbulites are already familiar with, the global myth of the ideal home.

It is also apparent that this is a global myth which acquires meaning through the optics of the local, specific in time and place. In the narrations of the ideal home, in Istanbul of the 1990s, it is no longer possible to sort out the local and the global, the historical and the contemporary, the traditional and the modern, the mythical and the real. Was there ever a point in time when Istanbul was 'green' and 'clean'? Did middle-class Istanbulites have a 'traditional' way of life, original and authentic cultural spaces, which have now become contaminated by traffic, crowds and pollution? The answers to these questions are obviously ambiguous and equivocal, but not particularly relevant, perhaps, since it is the past as constituted through the optics of the present which informs the practices of Istanbul's middle strata as they depart for new lives on the outskirts of the city.

On changing social spaces and the cultural geography of Istanbul's middle strata

Emphasizing the social and cultural fragmentation of Istanbul's middle classes in the 1990s runs the risk of reading undue homogeneity and continuity into the recent past. One way of avoiding this might be to begin with the spatial divisions of the present, focusing upon groups which have departed for residential estates on the outskirts of the city, to try to capture what is 'new'.

The new suburban villages of Istanbul: 'garden cities' For the corporate executives and top professionals in the upper ranges of the middle strata, whose aspirations as well as incomes have risen meteorically during Istanbul's integration into global markets over the past ten years, acquiring 'the home of your dreams' means investing in one of the single-home suburban villages towards the Black Sea coast in the north of the city. More than twenty such exclusive suburban complexes are currently under construction, aggressively marketed at prices beginning at $150,000, all the way up to $500,000 or more, depending upon size and luxury of homes as well as the surrounding acres. Most of the major construction companies have ventured into this highly lucrative and competitive market for suburban homes, selling 'not only a home but a whole new life-style'.[6]

None of these dream suburbs, offering a taste of country life within easy reach of Istanbul, is as yet inhabited. A visit to any one of them entails a long drive of more than an hour on bumpy roads, only to reach a giant construction site. Invariably, one model home from each price range is available for potential customers to see. And on Sundays, families who have already made downpayments come to the site to see how the construction is proceeding. The number and size of such giant construction sites portend the exodus of the city's executive-technical-professional elite in the near future. But for moment, the 'dreamland' with its promise of tennis courts and golf courses, with entertainment and shopping facilities, to be reached within minutes, exists only in expensive brochures.

For most families in the upper reaches of Istanbul's middle strata, investing in a suburban garden-home means pouring a lifetime's savings (in the absence of long-term home-mortgage schemes)[7] into a life-style of which they have had little experience. Since the turn of the century, inner-city apartment dwelling has been the sign and symbol of modernity and westernization for Istanbul's upper- and middle-income families. The significance of apartment dwelling as the *sine qua non* of middle-class status and respectability was enhanced by the successive waves of immigrants from the countryside beginning in the 1950s. In the broader social and cultural geography of the city, the distinction between residential neighbourhoods of apartments and the peripheral sprawl of squatter districts housing recent immigrants has become, over the past thirty years, emblematic of the cultural divide between a peasant way of life and 'genuine' urbanism, between white-collar occupations and manual work. Among apartment residents, however, finer distinctions of financial worth and symbolic hierarchy are defined in terms of proximity to the Bosporus. Thus for the managerial-technical-professional elite of the city, until very recently, residence in one of the prestigious luxury apartments overlooking the Bosporus was the main locus of aspiration and symbol of upward mobility. In Istanbul, whether a flat has 'a view of the sea' or not, and how broad, close and beautiful a view it commands, were, up to a few years ago, the most important symbolic markers of distinction between the wider segments of the city's salaried and its managerial, professional elite. Currently, the prices of flats on the market still depend on a view of the sea as much as on size or quality, if not more. But the aspirations of the city's corporate elite and top professionals have shifted elsewhere.

Istanbulites currently investing in suburban homes, then, will be leaving behind a view of the sea shared with neighbours living in the same apartment block, or friends next door, abandoning the familiarity of everyday life mapped out by proximity to the corner grocery store, and leaving the street life of an accustomed neighbourhood, to live with acquaintances (not total strangers) of similar background and social status in the countryside. But anxieties over the move (rarely admitted and by women only) seem to be compensated for by the promise of rambling lawns, barking dogs and social spaces cleansed of cultural pollutants. For according to the 'customer profile' targeted by marketing agencies, these are busy executives or professional men who dream of relaxing at the weekends by working in the garden and who plan to buy a dog immediately after moving in; but who also have 'educated wives' desiring to escape the pollution of the city: air pollution, traffic pollution, noise pollution and, most important, *cultural* pollution.

In its broader contours, this is a story reminiscent of successive waves of suburbanization which occurred in North American and European cities after the Second World War, when single-family houses, cars and consumer durables became symbolic of a new life-style.

***The new high-rise suburbs of Istanbul: the* site** For the broader segments of Istanbul's middle strata – managers and upper civil servants as well as employees from the lower rungs of numerous public bureaucracies and quasi-public organizations – the pursuit of 'a new home and new way of life' entails moving to one of the new residential developments which have rapidly sprung up along the major new throughways into and out of Istanbul.

Site[8] is the word currently used to designate such uniform clusters of high-rise, high-density residential blocks, most of them organized as cooperatives, either by the developer firm or associations of employees, retirees and so on, and located on sites designated for mass housing development by the metropolitan government. Subsidized by the Mass Housing Fund (MHF), ownership in such cooperatives entails the payment of instalments from the ground up for a flat not exceeding (in theory) 100 square metres.[9] The mortgage, with a maturation period of fifteen to twenty years, is owned by the MHF and the developer is directly reimbursed in full by the MHF upon completion of the building. In Istanbul more than 1000 such cooperative housing projects (entailing roughly 100,000 dwelling units) were launched, catering to mid-range professionals, civil servants and military personnel as well as employees from the lower rungs of numerous public bureaucracies and quasi-public organizations.

On the city-scape of Istanbul, the *site*s are a novel phenomenon, both architecturally and as a way of life. Built according to stringent state regulations to minimize cost per dwelling, upon land designated for mass housing along major expressways, these are clusters of concrete blocks which often seem to be in the middle of nowhere, often without public transportation (that is, dependent upon private car ownership, and/or employers' bus services), and homogeneous in terms of the social composition of their inhabitants. Those which are closer to the city are equally striking in their height, which separates them, like walled villages, from surrounding settlements of squatter housing and commercial use.

In the cliché of city planning manuals and architecture textbooks, such high-rise residential blocks are infamous for sacrificing communal values in the name of utility and cost-effectiveness. They are frequently described as concrete slabs which segregate residents, alienate them from each other by sterile and coldly forbidding hallways, serve to isolate them behind closed doors in the absence of community walkways and residential meeting areas. Hence the new *site*s of Istanbul have become a favourite PhD research topic for Turkish city planning and architecture students. Based upon the achieved wisdom of the disciple, and fashionable concepts borrowed from environmental psychology, a variety of questionnaire surveys have been conducted, attempting to measure levels of dissatisfaction, feelings of isolation, lack of feelings of community and so on, among the new residents. Some of the general findings of these studies are of interest, primarily because they reveal the discrepancy between the mindset of researchers/outsiders and the residents themselves.

When asked about their 'ideal home', the universal response appears to be 'an independent house in a garden', which seems to be farthest away from the actual situation of *site* residents. Yet at the same time most residents express themselves to be very satisfied with *site* life and environment, choosing to describe it through adjectives such as 'airy', 'light', 'refreshing', 'clean', 'orderly'. This is true for residents of the more upscale developments where individual flats are larger than 100 square metres (despite MHF regulations, more than 50 per cent of cooperative housing is of this type) as well as the downscale apartment developments with 65–100 square-metre flats; and regardless of the adequacy of playgrounds for children, green space between apartment blocks and so on. 'A clean environment' seems to be the most frequently used phrase to describe *site* life. Often, however, this phrase is modified to emphasize 'a clean *social* environment', referring to similarities in the social and occupational backgrounds of residents. Responses to survey questions which probe what residents would wish to change, given the choice – with precoded answers on alternative design possibilities to break the monotony and sterile uniformity of identical flats; to create common spaces to enhance neighbourliness and community ties – seem equally unanticipated. What the residents actually complain about, time and again, and express as their most desired wish, is a shopping centre. What they desire most, it would seem, is to be able to 'go shopping'. Hence it is not park benches, greenery, trees, playgrounds (spaces of neighbourliness of the sort Turkish urban designers have in mind) that residents articulate as lacking. Indeed, when available, such spaces seem to be rarely used. Furthermore, most inhabitants seem to suffer from a dearth of imagination on alternative interior design possibilities, beyond enclosing balconies to acquire more space. Instead, collective imagination seems to centre upon 'shopping', not simply to buy things but equally important as a way of seeing people, strolling, having something to do.

However limited and/or questionable the findings of such survey research may be, they suggest that the experiences of *site* dwellers themselves are far more complex and varied than the architectural uniformity of the high-rise residential blocks initially suggests. To the outside observer, whether a flat is slightly smaller or larger than 100 square metres may be trivial, distinctions among clusters of high-rise blocks inconsequential, yet for families who decide to invest in such a flat, beginning to pay instalments from the ground up and waiting for a minimum of two years (provided the developer firm does not collapse in the meantime or become embroiled in legal disputes with MHF which cause interminable delays, or economize by using building materials of much lower quality than originally promised – all of which are likely scenarios) before finally moving in, gradations of size and quality are of enormous significance. Not only are the costs of flats highly variable, depending upon size, bathroom and kitchen installations, availability of lifts and so on, but also the symbolic worth and cultural significance of moving to a *site* changes according to the backgrounds of the inhabitants themselves.

For groups such as policemen, municipal employees, primary school teachers whose limited savings are susceptible to continuous erosion under inflation, managing the initial downpayment and monthly instalments towards a small flat entails a major effort. And the actual move to a *site* often signifies upward mobility, away from one of the informal neighbourhoods of the city. For this group, the very uniformity and orderliness of high-rise apartments articulates and symbolizes the cultural distinctiveness of *site* residents, distinguishing them from the inhabitants of 'informal' neighbourhoods. The so-called informal neighbourhoods of Istanbul are by no means the shanty towns of Africa or the *favelas* of Latin America. Indeed, Istanbul's informal housing markets provide considerable opportunity for capitalizing on increasing land values, and have been a channel of accumulation for waves of immigrants flooding into Istanbul over the past three decades.[10] But refrigerators, washing machines and kitchenware require 'modern' bathrooms and kitchens; matching living-room furniture and television sets demand rooms to display them in. Thus moving from informal housing with its cramped spaces, to a regular flat, with a standardized plan – two bedrooms, one living room, with a separate kitchen and bathroom – provides space for a host of consumer goods already purchased on instalment.

For managers, higher civil servants, or professional employees who are already apartment-dwelling Istanbulites, *site* residence means a homogeneous, safe, orderly environment, distant both spatially and socially from the heterogeneous populations of Istanbul. The appeal of moving into a brand-new, spacious flat with gleaming kitchens and up-to-date bathroom fixtures, decorated with ceramics of assorted colours and designs, is considerable for this group. Leaving behind old, ill-assorted accumulations, to redecorate living rooms ('salons') with matching furniture, new curtains and crystal chandeliers is part of the ritual of moving. Hence architectural standardization is accompanied by other signs and symbols of cultural homogeneity and social uniformity, in the acquisition of new furniture, new tableware, new matching towels and bed-sheets commensurate with the dazzling cleanliness of new flats. But equally important, if not more so, is the cultural and social homogeneity of *site* life, which connotes 'order' rather than sterile uniformity for the inhabitants themselves. For these families, the emergent culture of the 1980s in Istanbul, with its 'mixed' forms of music, grammar and dress, represents a half-bred world of pseudo-urbanism, one which contradicts and pollutes the cherished purity of their own 'Westernized' way of life. Bureaucrats, professionals, managers constitute a stratum of people for whom the global pastiche of styles and tastes in contemporary Istanbul threatens to erode the sanctity of their 'modern', 'Western' way of life. Symbolic markers of what was barely a decade ago a distinctively middle-class life-style, appear to have lost their cultural moorings in the Istanbul of the 1990s, polluted and contaminated by hybridization. *Site* life, with its antiseptic social and cultural spaces, thus represents an escape from pollutants, but it would seem to be a mixed blessing in the absence of a 'shopping centre' with its associated pleasures of looking and wandering around, transforming the contemplation of visual displays into leisure activity, fusing buying-pleasure-leisure.

Concluding remarks

My intention in this chapter has been to describe how the experiences and perceptions of Istanbul's middle classes have been crucial in the negotiation of global cultural flows, and have in turn shaped the course of historical events. In embracing the global myth of the ideal home, in the variety of their own phenomenal experiences, the middle strata of Istanbul have departed for progressively fragmented and quartered lives on the outskirts of the city. They have thus been crucial social agents in shaping the course of historical events which have altered the physiognomy of Istanbul, remapping its social and cultural topography. It was through the 'globalized' optics of Istanbul's middle classes, I have emphasized, that the familiar fabric of Istanbul, with its intermingling of social and cultural spaces, came to be perceived as disorderly and polluted, and the political will to transform it was mobilized.

Two analytical points which emerge from this descriptive account seem worth reiterating by way of conclusion. The first point has to do with global myths in general, and the myth of the ideal home in particular. The global circulation of myths is not equivalent to the globalization of meanings. But they are directly involved in the production of the cultural frames within which life strategies of various social groups are negotiated. A global myth such as 'our ideal home', for instance, whose meaning appears to be self-evident and natural, connotes an ensemble of diverse elements, the relationships among which have to be actively constructed by social agents – advertisers as well as prospective customers. In this sense, consumer myths which circulate across the globe acquire facticity in response to different sets of circumstances, in different historically specific sites. What is consumed as 'our ideal home' is contingent upon the spatial/ideological context in which it is reproduced. But this is not to suggest that the 'locals' are happy bricoleurs assembling their own 'ideal homes'. On the contrary, 'our ideal home' has a money sign attached to it. The significance of contemporary global myths resides, I would suggest, in conjuring dreams as commodities, to be bought and sold. What has travelled across cultural borders to Istanbul is the ideal home as a commodity, laden with mythical content through the language of an increasingly globalized advertising industry.

My second analytical point has to do with the so-called 'crisis' of the middle classes in the context of globalization and liberalization, variously referred to as 'shrinking' or 'disappearing'. As several recent book titles (and their contents) such as *Fear of Falling* (Ehrenreich 1989) and *Falling from Grace* (Newman 1988) suggest, the middle classes feel threatened, in one country after another, by policies of liberalization which erode their economic as well as their social standing. Integration into the global economy often strengthens the upper segments of the middle strata at the expense of worsening conditions for the lower middle class who are faced with the prospect of downward mobility. Global cultural flows which erode distinctions of high and low culture progressively undermine the symbolic capital upon which a distinctive middle-class way of life is based.

But this general tendency of globalization to undermine the capacity of the middle classes to reproduce themselves, does not mean that future outcomes at the level of particular metropolises are obvious. In the competitive economic and political environment of the globalizing city, the middle classes actively pursue a variety of social strategies and cultural practices to maintain or rebuild markers of distinction which define a distinctive way of life. To understand the ways in which these variable strategies succeed, survive and fail, it is important to move from the space-time of the global economy to study processes of social and cultural reproduction in the space-time of particular metropolises. In the context of Istanbul, the strategy of survival of the middle classes has chiefly centred upon the domain of consumption symbolized by the ideal home. For the majority, their new lives in huge residential estates on the outskirts of the city remain far from what an outside observer, from a position of cultural distance, may judge to be the fantasy world of the ideal home. In the awareness and understanding of their own standing as 'middle class', however, Istanbul's middle strata have been successful in reconstituting the locally distinctive cultural markers and boundaries which separate them from other groups in city space, by embracing the global consumer myth of the ideal home.

Notes

1. For a broader account of Istanbul's transformation in the 1980s see Keyder and Öncü (1994).

2. There are numerous studies which trace this process, such as Lynn Spiegel's (1992) book on television and the family ideal in post-war America; Fishman's (1989) analysis of suburbia as a bourgeois Utopia; or Ewen's (1976) study on the social roots of advertising.

3. Roland Barthes's mythologies were part of his earlier project of a critique of French bourgeois culture. In talking about 'global myths' I am obviously stretching his mythologies beyond the original intentions of the author.

4. According to the PIAR-Gallup national consumption patterns survey conducted in 1991, 60 per cent of 11 million Turkish households owned colour television sets. The 1990 'Euro' average (17 countries) quoted by Gallup International is 90 per cent. For metropolitan Istanbul, the 1993 consumer survey of the Istanbul Chamber of Industry reports 90 per cent colour-TV ownership.

5. The advertisements I draw upon in this section come from a larger archive compiled for comparative purposes across different segments of the residential market as well as to illustrate changes over time in the past decade. In the brief summary provided here I have simply ignored changes over time which are significant in their own right but remain tangential to the current discussion.

6. The significance of a globalized advertising language in rendering the home a commodity laden with mythical content is obvious. Turkey's advertising sector has been among the most rapidly globalized sectors of the economy. Since the mid-1980s, many of the global advertising agencies – such as Saatchi and Saatchi, Young and Rubicam, Lowe, McCann-Ericson, Lintas – have established partnerships with local firms. Currently, the top fifteen advertising firms which hold 80 per cent of the advertising market all have international partners. Hence both the buzzwords and the formats of home advertisements in Istanbul's residential market are remarkably similar to what Caroline Mills (1993), for instance, describes in the context of a gentrified neighbourhood in Vancouver, where the experience of gentrification has been recast as a myth. What is being sold as 'a new home and a new way of life' is obviously very different in the two contexts, that is, specific in time and place.

7. The Turkish financial system has been overwhelmingly dominated by commercial banks. The role of private pension funds, savings and loan associations, and building societies is negligible. Commercial banks are legally prohibited from using their own resources for long-term home mortgages. Hence individual home-ownership is either directly financed by private savings or by short-term commercial and suppliers' credit.

8. The Turkish word *site* is adapted from the French word *cité*, which refers to outsize housing projects in France's suburbs or *banlieues*. In France, however, residents

of such projects or *cités* are often multi-ethnic immigrant populations. The word *site* connotes residential estates for the Turkish middle classes.

9. The MHF was initially established in the mid-1980s to provide preferential credit for low-income groups, but it rapidly evolved into a mechanism for subsidizing middle-class housing in large cities, especially in Istanbul where more than 50 per cent of the dwellings subsidized are larger than the 100–square-metre eligibility requirement.

10. Successive waves of immigrants to Istanbul in the 1950s and 1960s, having once acquired a foothold in Istanbul's informal land markets, were often able to legalize their ownership rights; they took advantage of high inflation and rising property values to become owners of rentals, multi-storey buildings and so on. Concomitantly, the vast opportunities for capitalization in this market attracted outside investors and developers. Thus by the mid-1970s, it was no longer possible to 'squat' in the time-honoured fashion. Once the land grab bonanza of the 1950s and 1960s was over, fresh waves of immigrants were forced to buy split-deeds in unserviced, agricultural land. See Öncü (1988) and also Seufert in this volume, chapter 10.

References

Abbas, A. (1994) 'Building on Disappearance: Hong Kong Architecture and the City', *Public Culture* 6, 441–56.

Barthes, R. (1972) 'Myth Today', in *Mythologies* (selected and trans. by A. Lavers). Hill and Wang, New York.

Baudrillard, J. (1981) *For a Critique of the Political Economy of the Sign*. Telos Press, St Louis.

Bourdieu, P. (1984) *Distinction*. Routledge and Kegan Paul, London.

Ehrenreich, B. (1989) *Fear of Falling: The Inner Life of the Middle Class*. Pantheon, New York.

Ewen, S. (1976) *Captains of Consciousness*. McGraw-Hill, New York.

Featherstone, M. (1991) 'Theories of Consumer Culture' in M. Featherstone, *Consumer Culture and Postmodernism*. Sage, London.

Fishman, R. (1989) *Bourgeois Utopias: The Rise and Fall of Suburbia*. Basic Books, New York.

Hannerz, U. (1989) 'Notes on the Global Ecumene', *Public Culture* 1(2), 66–75.

Keyder, Ç. and Öncü, A. (1994) 'Globalization of a Third World Metropolis: Istanbul in the 1980s', *Review* XVII (3), 383–421.

Marx, K. (1967) 'The Fetishism of Commodities' in *Capital*, Vol. 1, ch. 1. International Publishers, New York (originally published 1863).

Mills, C. (1993) 'Myths and Meanings of Gentrification', in J. Duncan and D. Ley (eds), *Place/Culture/Representation*. Routledge, London and New York.

Newman, K. (1988) *Falling from Grace: The Experience of Downward Mobility in the American Middle Class*. Free Press, New York.

Öncü, A. (1988) 'The Politics of the Land Market in Turkey: 1950–1980', *International Journal of Urban and Regional Research* 12 (1), 38–64.

Simmel, G. (1971) 'Exchange' and 'Prostitution' in D. N. Levide (ed.), *Georg Simmel*. University of Chicago Press, Chicago. (Trans. from *Philosophie des Geldes*, 1970.)

Spiegel, L. (1992) *Make Room for TV: Television and the Family Ideal in Postwar America*. University of Chicago Press, Chicago.

PART II

The symbolism of space and the struggle for *lebensraum*

5

Culture shock and identity crisis in East German cities[1]

Ulrich Mai

Urban symbols and social identity

As part of their social interaction, individuals appropriate the social and material environment in the sense of ascribing 'meaning' to it. Meaning can be both individual and collective in character, that is it may refer to specific experiences in human biographies or it may refer to incidents in local or regional history (or, in fact, to both at the same time).

Urban symbols play a relevant role in the process of socialization, as their unreflected presence stands for the continuity of acquired social norms and roles within a network of more or less stable everyday relations. In fact, a 'meaningful' environment corresponds with a high degree of the individual's social identity which, through the ability of social and spatial orientation, is likely to include feelings of familiarity and security (Buttimer 1980; Greverus 1979). Consequently, losing one's home results not only in the loss of familiar social links in the neighbourhood and the loss of the familiar view through the kitchen window; it may also entail a critical identity crisis, reflected in symptoms of disorientation which have often been depicted as homesickness (Fried 1963).

The quality of homes in East Germany prior to the political changes

Until 1989 social life in East Germany was, for a number of reasons, very much restricted to local networks. Car-ownership was scarce and there was only a small degree of mobility compared to that in Western societies. The locality of social life was also enhanced by the socialist idea of linking various aspects of life – not simply the ordinary production process – with the factory and its employees. For instance, health services, kindergartens and even family holidays were widely integrated into the factory's provisioning scheme.

Social life in East Germany has often been characterized as life in social niches of close friends, neighbours and relatives which, on the basis of mutual trust in a repressive and authoritarian system, provided some shelter from control, but also offered informal possibilities of overcoming the economy of scarce consumer goods so typical of the socialist period.

In more theoretical terms, social networks functioned as a more or less locally oriented system of individuals who engaged in pooling and transacting social capital and resources such as information, trust, physical and emotional aid, and thereby strengthened the feeling of collectivity, but also of belonging to a specific place or neighbourhood. Hence, social networks prior to the political overthrow in East Germany bore a strong element of locality and contributed to the intensity of local identity.

What is more, life took place in a social and material environment that hardly underwent any changes: social advancement for the individual was as scarce as, for lack of monetary resources, the construction of new buildings in the neighbourhood. In fact, the stability and strength of local and social identity was a major attribute of East German society.

Reconstructing the urban landscape: from uniqueness to uniformity

Since the political changes in 1989 the reconstruction of East German cities has been carried out with breathtaking efficiency and speed, leaving the ubiquitous and obtrusive traces of the new economic system (Mai 1993). Buildings under repair disappear behind scaffolding to receive new paint, roofs and windows, not to speak of the many new buildings which have already been constructed: hotels, department stores, videothèques and so on. Interestingly enough, immediately after unification considerable attempts were made to support the enjoyment of car-ownership, which after the long years of scarcity was widely considered a central symbol of a higher standard of living. There was not only an immense invasion of car traders, garages and service stations, but also complementary swift action was taken to replace the old bumpy cobblestones with new tar pavements, and even the government was eager to replace almost overnight the old traffic signs made of plastic with solid, Western-style ones with a new colour and design, while on the outskirts and in the countryside many an attractive side-street was sacrificed for the sake of wider roads in order to carry more traffic.

Most obtrusive, however, are the changes of the urban landscape in the central business districts (CBDs). While in socialist times CBDs used to be hardly more lively or colourful than any other part of the city, within a few years they have come to abound with all the signs and symbols of the capitalist commodity world and its multiplicity of colourful and promising gimmicks. Nowhere else has the change in the environment been more drastic or faster. No wonder local residents often express difficulties in spatial orientation, in 'finding their way'. In fact, until recently, the East German city, and especially the historic city centre, was unique in the sense of bearing its unmistakable individual face. Swift modernization with its equalizing universal standards that are indifferent towards spatial idiosyncrasies has, however, destroyed uniqueness and imposed uniformity. Within only four years, cities in East Germany have come to resemble their universal Western model.

Strange symbols, alienation and symbolic expropriation No doubt, the reconstruction of the East German home meets with the wide cognitive approval of the population, as it reflects above all the overthrow of an unpopular political system. This does not, however, exclude a deep identity crisis and feelings of suffering elementary losses, even feelings of alienation and expropriation.

The issue seems most plausible in the depletion of the old social environment. First of all there has been a remarkable deterioration in the social infrastructure: kindergartens were closed down for reasons of 'economic effectivity', and the same happened to youth clubs, recreation centres, even pubs, small retail shops and post offices which all also used to serve a social and communal purpose (Heitmeyer 1992). In a characteristic case an old community hall, where virtually all private and public festivities used to take place, was turned into a more profitable furniture depot, leaving the community with no place to hold celebrations.

Of course, unemployment, an experience hitherto virtually unknown, represents the most drastic impact on local identity, as it cuts off familiar social links that used to go far beyond mere work relations to strengthen group solidarity and integration in locally-based interaction (Nissen 1992).

Also, there is a noticeable change in the construction and composition of personal networks. After the political overthrow their major purpose – to pool and transact resources in order to acquire scarce goods – has become obsolete in the market economy. Instead there is a continuous need for information on job opportunities, cheap credit and, of course, for reliable assistance on how to learn many modern skills, such as how to fill in the unavoidable tax-return forms and how to identify the better of two competing offers from different health insurance companies. Evidently, as the type of social capital in social relations changes, personal networks spread in terms of competence represented by members and in terms of the space over which members in networks are connected. Thus, as networks are restructured under the new political and economic conditions, the old quality of locality becomes less important. Only with the losers in unification – the jobless and the old – do the locally focused personal networks, spatially confined to neighbours, relatives and close friends, survive, mainly for the purpose of emotional and to some degree manual support. Generally speaking, however, personal networks in East Germany now reflect the erosion of local identity and, in fact, contribute to its crisis.

Strange symbols have invaded virtually all spheres of life in East Germany so fast and overwhelmingly that people often feel themselves strangers at home (Schmidtchen 1991). There is, of course, not only the metamorphosis of the urban landscape, the many new façades, commercials, and traffic signs; social and political changes are accompanied by the shock of unfamiliar tastes (food) and even smells (especially of the cleansing agent applied in public places), thus contributing to the loss of sensual orientation or at least causing unknown problems of sensual adjustment in spatial orientation.

What really aggravate the difficulty of readjustment are the invisible symbols and signs of strangeness, such as the innumerable new laws and regulations necessary to register a private car, to receive the rent or tax refund you are entitled to, to claim on an insurance policy (after the many cases of fraud) and so on. Almost overnight there are entirely new bureaucratic rules and institutions and running them, usually in superior positions, are 'experts' from the West, representatives of the new system, whose consciousness of their superior experience and competence often makes them appear arrogant and presumptuous.

To many, this strangeness constitutes a threat of eviction or homelessness when it appears in the guise of straightforward claims by Westerners to legal ownership of flats and houses. Presently there are around a million still undecided claims to no fewer than three million dwellings in East Germany (Kirchner 1992: 4). In these cases expropriation as part of social change takes, of course, a more existential than symbolic form. No wonder the social and economic aftermath of unification is, with some bitterness, being characterized by many as the 'big sellout' or 'colonization'. It should be taken as a valid indicator of the way East Germans perceive their own role after unification, namely as the helpless victims of a superior strange power.

The victory of 'the other' political system is, in a subtle way, reflected in the many symbolic gestures of triumph which leave no doubt which side is the winner after the East–West confrontation and the long competition between societal and political systems. There are indeed striking examples: in an act of unreflecting and undiscussed retaliation, conservative majorities in the city parliaments swept away many old street- and place-names that carried a socialist meaning, making no distinction between local communist heroes, Karl Marx or anti-fascists. I do not here question the necessity for a critical moral dispute about history or the role of individuals in it, provided it *is* a dispute. In any case, however, one cannot totally ignore the psychological consequences in terms of alienation; in the process of socialization the individual learns symbolically to 'appropriate' the environment by being able to *name* it, so that it becomes a part of his or her identity. Consequently, the strong feeling of being 'at home' is undermined when the old familiar place-names become obsolete.

But, of course, there are other symbols of political overthrow, many of which attract more collective attention. A case in point is the reconstruction of the Garnisonskirche (Garrison Church) in Potsdam which had been pulled down by the communists directly after the Second World War as a pre-war symbol of the historic coalition between the Nazis and the bourgeois conservative forces in the country. Of similar symbolic value are the reconstruction of the baroque Dresden Frauenkirche, the ruins of which many would rather preserve as a war monument, and, above all, the plans to remove the socialist Palace of the Republic in Berlin, a popular multi-functional paliamentary building during the socialist period, and to reconstruct in its place the old city palace of the former Prussian dynasty.

Culture shock: new collectivity and scapegoating

What we have described so far reveals all the signs of a massive culture shock, that is, of psychological reactions to a sudden encounter with a different culture. Normally, individuals experience a culture shock of this quality only in a strange social environment, and only through a long process of acculturation is there a chance to overcome disorientation, instability and isolation (Schütz 1972; Mai 1991). In this case, however, the culture shock is experienced at home, thus aggravating feelings of inferiority.

How then do East Germans react on and perceive the invasion of strangeness? Obviously there is a whole range of possibilities for handling the new situation and it is still hard to generalize, as the ambivalence of cognitive acceptance and feelings of alienation will prevail for some time.

Watching West German television programmes, with their enticing and fictitious world of better living, may have stimulated and accelerated the process of political change but it was certainly an inadequate preparation for coping with the manifold aspects of social change in everyday life.

First there is a discernible, widespread and, in a way, self-destructive feeling that individuals have lived 'on the wrong side'. This rejection of one's own history, understandable as it may be, seems very much congruent with the old attitude of passivity and internalized experience of life in an authoritarian society. In any case, this feeling of being a victim of uncontrollable historic forces now nourishes a widespread resignation and paralysis.

Not necessarily exclusive to this is the creation of a new sense of collectivity among East Germans, and it is only seemingly paradoxical that this should appear *after* unification. But there is in fact a new type of solidarity noticeable in factories, offices and universities, wherever 'Wessies' and 'Ossies' get together, sometimes intruding into public disputes about the relegation of East German ice-hockey or soccer teams from the first division, or in other cases about people suspected of collaborating with the former communist secret police. Even the remarkable renaissance of East German consumer goods among East Germans is not just a sign of nostalgia but reflects the will to support firms from the region which almost all experience problems of survival.

There are, however, also signs of a more critical type of collectivity. In times of the sudden breaking-in of modernization many seem to give in to the temptation of finding compensation for alienation and insecure identity by excluding the weakest in society: foreign workers and asylum seekers. It is indeed a tragedy that those who themselves are made strangers at home through alienation processes seek to improve their status by rigidly ascribing the quality of strangeness to the weakest. Although only among a few is this transposed into violent action, it is very likely that latent xenophobia will remain a threat as long as people feel they are strangers at home. Hence the basic principles of the Western-dominated process of unification should have been modified in such a way that individuals had a chance creatively and self-determinedly to mould and construct their lives and homes; in such a situation strangers and foreigners would then more easily be included.

Note

1. This chapter presents empirical findings from a research project on social networks in East Germany financed by the Thyssen Foundation.

References

Buttimer, A. (1980) 'Home, Reach, and the Sense of Space', in A. Buttimer and D. Seamon (eds), *The Human Experience of Space and Place*. Croom Helm, London.

Fried, M. (1963) 'Grieving for a Lost Home', in L. J. Dahl (ed.), *The Urban Condition: People and Policy in the Metropolis*. Harper & Row, New York and London.

Greverus, I. M. (1979) *Auf der Suche nach Heimat*. Beck, Munich.

Heitmeyer, W. (1992) '"Der einzelne steht im Wind – ohne Nischen": Der doppelte Transformationsprozeß in den neuen Bundesländern', *Frankfurter Rundschau*, 25 September.

Kirchner, K. H. (1992) 'Wir sind eine Bevölkerung: In Deutschland wird auf hohem Niveau gelitten', in Arbeitsgemeinschaft Jugend und Bildung (ed.), *Das nicht mehr geteilte Deutschland ... Zwei Jahre danach!* (PZ Extra/Wir in Europa, No. 16), 4–5.

Mai, U. (1991) 'Die Wahrnehmung des Fremden: Über Möglichkeiten und Grenzen des Versehens', in J. Hasse and W. Isenberg (eds), *Die Geographiedidaktik neu denken: Perspektiven eines Paradigmenwechsels*. Bensberger Protokolle der Thomas-Morus-Akademie No. 73, Bensberg, 65–75.

— (1993) 'Kulturschock und Identitätsverlust: Über soziale und sinnliche Enteignung von Heimat in Ostdeutschland nach der Wende', *Geographische Rundschau* 45 (4), 232–7.

Nissen, S. (1992) '" ... das Schlimmste ist die Ungewißheit": Der Siegeszug des Ökonomischen führt zu Bindungsverlusten', *Frankfurter Rundschau*, 15 September.

Schmidtchen, G. (1991) 'Die Ostdeutschen als Fremde in ihrem eigenen Land: Sozialpsychologische Anmerkungen zur Lage in Deutschland nach der Einigung', *Frankfurter Rundschau*, 9 September.

Schütz, A. (1972) 'Der Fremde: Ein sozialpsychologischer Versuch', in A. Schütz, *Gesammelte Aufsätze II, Studien zur soziologischen Theorie*. The Hague, 53–69.

6

Gendered lives in global spaces

Petra Weyland

The globalization of urban spaces in the metropolis is the result of capitalist market integration; it is also an outcome of local people translating global flows into their local urban social geographies. Globalization provides for them new opportunity spaces which may be exploited according to their potentials and capacities. This becomes most obvious in the construction of the 'hardware' for the global capitalist city, by clearing away from inner-city space those communities and their built environment which are seen as an obstacle to the needs and interests of global business. In the same vein, new meaning and use is inscribed to the built environment and its inhabitants. In many cases this involves the expulsion of those residential groups who are seen as dysfunctional in the new economic context. In turn, other people move in, with different socio-cultural and economic characteristics. These migrants have been referred to as 'global personnel', engaged in the 'production of management, control and service operations' in the global city (Sassen-Koob 1985: 231). The question thus arises of the ways in which the newly created global space in the metropolis becomes a new opportunity space for these new residents, the global migrants to the city. How, then, is the local global space socially and culturally constructed by the people who have come to live and work there? What 'third cultures' are developed in this specific district?

Any attempt to understand how global corporate executives and their staff are involved in the creation of the global city immediately prompts a second question. What about women and the issue of gender? How is global space gendered? What is the relevance of women in the global district of a city, and of what relevance is this space to women? These questions are at the centre of this article.

The growing number of women in the transnational flow of migrant labour to global cities has been remarked upon by a series of authors in recent years (Feagin and Smith 1990: 73; Lin 1987; Sassen-Koob 1984; 1987: 63). As the gap between poor and rich strata continues to widen, cheap female labour seems to be on the increase. In addition to increasing numbers of women employed in 'sweat shop' production, there is a conspicuous demand for cheap female labour in the lower rungs of the service sector, as waitresses, cleaners and as domestic helpers. In the context of the Middle East and the Gulf region cities, for instance, immigrant women from Southeast Asia, and especially from the Philippines, have begun to reach substantial numbers. Cruz and Paganoni (1989: 15), drawing on statistical data from the Philippine Overseas Employment Administration for 1986, give the following numbers for domestic helpers and nursing staff: Hong Kong 30,000; Singapore 16,000; Japan 28,000; Italy (especially Rome) 30,000; Spain 10,000; USA 7000; Middle East (especially Jedda) 70,000. It appears that women from Southeast Asia are beginning to replace their migrating husbands, as international labour migration becomes increasingly difficult for men under conditions of prolonged recession in the world economy. What is of immediate relevance here is that the rising number of Filipina women working in Middle Eastern cities over the past decade has been based upon and articulated with the demand for domestic help in the households of corporate executives.

As is to be expected, perhaps, a large portion of the global managerial personnel, rotating in a two-to-five-year rhythm from one global city to the next, move together with their households. The domain of the household is where all the services essential for the reproduction of their 'executive labour' is provided by women, be it women who are employed as housekeepers and are remunerated for that in cash, or their wives who are compensated with a life of luxury in a global city. Hence my interest lies in the women of multinational corporations' (MNCs') executives' and experts' households, women whose presence is indispensable for the smooth functioning of the 'production of management, control and service operations' for global business (Sassen-Koob 1985: 231).

With these considerations in mind, I contacted women who had accompanied their manager husbands to Istanbul, the city where I was living and working at the time. I soon discovered the existence of a large network of women whose husbands were working for global businesses. They were all housewives, many of whom had worked themselves before joining their husbands in the global city. Many of them were mothers. All of them had employed some form of domestic help, often a live-in housekeeper, sometimes a maid who came for work during the day, or less frequently a cleaning lady who came several times a week. Usually, these were immigrant women from rural Anatolia who lived in the vast shanty towns encircling Istanbul. But I soon discovered that some of the households employed female labour from a different ethnic background: women from the Philippines. I therefore began simultaneously to trace networks of Filipina women in Istanbul, women who had travelled across the globe to work in private households.

It may be misleading to suggest that the 'global space' of Istanbul can serve as an example for other metropolises across the world, since the global arises out of the intersection of global flows and particular local givens. In this sense, Istanbul is a particular local global space. Nevertheless, it provides clues about the dynamics through which global spaces are constructed. In particular, it reveals how the services provided by global corporate executives and experts are dependent to a very large degree on the articulation with domestic service labour, which is predominantly female labour, performed by domestic helpers or/and by accompanying wives. This empirical case shows that informal sector labour is not a residual category in the economy of the global city, but a basic precondition. However, what I am interested in here is not to develop further the notion of an articulation of modes of production in the global city;[1] rather, and along the lines of the questions I raised at the beginning, I want to deal with the cultural dimensions of this problem. I am investigating here the question of a gendered construction of global space. I want to shed some light on how these two groups of global women construct and make sense of the most global of all globalizing spaces in Istanbul.

Istanbul's female global space

Different as accompanying wives and female domestic helpers are with regard to status, they share the same space: domestic space. A number of reasons account for this. First of all, men are conspicuously absent from the home. Managers tend to have long working hours, are obliged to appear frequently at evening meetings or receptions and they are often away on business trips. While they are working at their corporation's office, their accompanying wives spend their everyday lives at home:

> My husband almost from the first day of our arrival in a new city returns to his job where he finds everything prepared: his office, his company car, the driver, colleagues awaiting him. When he has left in the morning I find myself alone in the house, wondering where I am and how to get to know somebody. (Mrs S., accompanying wife)

Under such circumstances, to have a place where one feels at home becomes ever more important. Accompanying women stress the emotional and existential importance of their homes as the only stable, known and controlled places in a periodically changing and each time newly alien setting. In Istanbul this means being confronted with an unfamiliar language, chaotic traffic and heavy pollution. For many of these women, and especially for those who have had little experience with a 'third world' environment, venturing into local Istanbul is not a nostalgic trip into the mysterious city of the 1001 Nights as advertised by the tourist agencies, but into an incomprehensible and exhausting urban jungle.[2] The result often is a search for a mediator to the local, such as the company's driver, the husband's secretary, the doorkeeper. While this is definitely of help it also restricts women to the household where the alternative is to engage in home-centred activities.

Restriction to the global household is still more evident with regard to the Filipina domestic helpers. Having crossed the globe to work in Istanbul they find themselves in a global local domestic space with very little chance for self-determination, with their passports and earnings taken away, prohibited from using the telephone and allowed very little free time. Most of them do not have fixed working hours and are on duty from the early morning until late at night. They usually get a day off only on Sundays, though many of them have to work even on this day. Another important reason for their restriction to domestic space is that most of them are working illegally in Turkey, which makes them fear being apprehended when venturing into public global space. In such a situation the global household amounts to a kind of global prison.

One other reason for the feminization of domestic space is that women of both strata have practically no chance of finding a job on the local labour market, given the very restrictive Turkish labour legislation and extremely low local wages. Women often claim that they want to work, but given their situation they find it more appropriate to stay where they are. While they often complain about the restrictions life in the global city places on them, domestic helpers and accompanying wives also stress the advantages: 'Yes, I want to work in different countries because I want to learn about the life of other people, I want to associate with different people … and is not everyone looking for a greener pasture?' (Mrs R., domestic helper).

Global domestic space is a luxury space where all the menial household chores are performed by domestic helpers, with facilities such as swimming pools, children's playgrounds and so on belonging to the housing compound. The emergence of global space in the city evidently involves the feminization and privatization of domestic space. Female global space first of all is domestic space. Its foremost function is to secure all aspects of the reproduction of the male executive's labour force. Global space, therefore, is composed and created out of gendered space with men and women fulfilling different functions.

Gendered space also finds expression in the built environment which is deeply engraved with male and female symbolism. Global Istanbul is increasingly designed in the fashion known from other global spaces: glassy office towers and five-star hotels reaching into the sky definitely speak a male language. Global domestic space, on the contrary, is often well hidden in a dead-end street on a hill overlooking the Bosporus. Surrounded by high walls, situated in a park-like landscape and protected by guards, it is not accessible from, nor even seen by, the outside world. Female global space is hidden, enclosed, protected, secret, but luxurious.

Female global space is privatized space because women retire – and are made to retire – from their waged, formal sector jobs to become housewives or paid helpers in the household; because they withdraw from public sector or production-related formal jobs and engage in the person-related reproduction of the labour force; because women have scant chances of finding other employment opportunities in the realm of the production of global management and control functions.

Female global space and symbolic capital

The privatization of female global space also results from its status-related functions. The private home of a manager and its inhabitants, inaccessible to all but a small number of admitted persons, is an important asset in the competition over symbolic capital within the local global community. This can already be derived from the fact that global enterprises invest in their representatives' prestigious private addresses, size of Bosporus view and living rooms.

In this context, the amount and nature of paid domestic labour a global household disposes of becomes an important signifier of status. This symbolic hierarchy ranges from those households which hire a Turkish cleaning lady for a few hours a week only, to those households which dispose of the labour of several live-in Asian helpers. It is relevant whether domestic help is local or international, as Turkish helpers are often described as 'uncivilized', 'illiterate' and 'ignorant' women with a rural or shanty town background:

> I now have a couple from darkest Anatolia working for me. One has to tell them everything time and again, time and again. ... I am polite, I say 'please', I say 'thank you' because I want them to learn this, too. Because not all of them know this. And one has to be very firm with them, because otherwise they do not learn anything and then they are not effective. I

mean, the one who has still swept the earth at home does not know how to deal with parquet and tiles. (Mrs W., accompanying wife)

Domestic labour from the Philippines, on the contrary, is regarded as providing good labour services. This assessment is reflected in the following quotation by a Filipina maid:

> And then they [the employers] said they like Filipinas more than the Turkish housekeepers. Because Filipinas are very clean, they are honest with their employers, and, then, even if the employer is away, they are performing their role in the house, unlike the Turks who are also on holiday when their employers are away. So they do their work only if their employer has an eye on them, but if they are not watching them they don't. ... They do not know to perform all the jobs coming up in the house, that is what I heard about the Arab and Turkish helpers. They are lazy. [She laughs.] And not trustworthy. And I heard from a Filipina friend that sometimes they steal when the employers are away. So this is what the employers do not like. (Mrs R., Filipina housekeeper)

Filipinas are obviously easier to exploit than local women because of their far more vulnerable position as illegals and live-in housekeepers, but also because of the higher quality of their labour in terms of education and experience with foreigners. Many of them went to high school and have worked for international employers in Manila or other cities before coming to Istanbul. Exploitation of the labour force is one thing; the other thing is that perfection in the performance of housekeeping, proficiency in the English language, 'modern' clothing, and around-the-clock presence in the household also are useful as a source of status. Labour from the Philippines involves an extra symbolic profit. This two-fold profit clearly also derives from competition in the sector of cheap female Turkish and Southeast Asian labour. This competition can easily be seen in the above quotation.

The Filipina maid's mistress is also an asset in the struggle over symbolic capital within Istanbul's local global community. As the representative of the global privatized space, she is its most precious asset. Being diametrically opposed to the global 'public' and identified with the manager's private home, she can be made use of in the more informal business meetings:

> Large companies invite large companies, this is a never-ending circle. Women have to join in. One is not obliged to, but one should. ... If there are only men I try not to go. Only then. In all the other cases I join in. I think, this is part of my duty. And I like to go, not always very much, but generally I like to go. I belong to my husband. That is it. Why should he go alone when both of us are invited. People do not invite Mrs G., they

> invite Dresdner Bank, that is logical. I always say we are a visiting card. Do you think anybody would invite Mrs G.? Only my friends. But not Is Bank, Crédit Lyonnais. Why? Because they want to make business. It is only a pretence, but we have to live like that. I cannot refuse. And I don't want to refuse. But we are always a visiting card, this is all. ... And I have a good life and there is an unwritten law: the woman joins in. I mean, I cannot take all the advantages that such a big company like that of my husband offers me, a huge apartment, they pay the whole rent, they take over the costs. Me, who likes to live in different countries, I cannot say, no, I do not go this evening. (Mrs G., accompanying wife)

The women's role as 'visiting cards' becomes even more accentuated when the company's representative invites his business partners to his home. Wives and maids, carefully prepared and arranged home-made food, a hospitable and comfortable atmosphere, precious carpets and furniture, the size of Bosporus view, are all shown off before the global representatives:

> Inviting home is appreciated more here. Because it has a more informal and a more intimate touch. Probably this is the reason. Because one takes much trouble. Everyone with money can invite, this is easy. But to invite home – this costs far more trouble ... It is my husband's most important clients who are invited home. (Mrs I., accompanying wife)

> Yes, he invites business partners home because his interest is to have nice relations with the big businessmen here in Istanbul. (Mrs R., domestic worker)

It is precisely the private nature of the domestic space with its non-market-related, home-made hospitality which makes such an invitation more precious than that to a five-star hotel where hospitality can only too easily be recognized as a professional simulation in a market-related, monetarized context. Belonging to the inner circle of the global community is hereby confirmed: only the most important, the most distinguished, those whom one wants to belong to the inner circle of business and friendship, are given the honour of an invitation to the private sphere. As Mrs G. puts it, she, too, has to fulfil her obligations towards the company. As female domestic space is privatized, it becomes an informal space where social, economic and cultural capitals are converted. In this sense, the households' women, the helpers as well as the wives, can be put to use as an indirect sign of global power in the local global context.

The line between privatized female space and male global business space is ideologically drawn because the more domestic space is represented as private, the more it is valuable as a sign of local global status. The global household can be put to use only in the local global community when it is constructed as the bipolar opposite of global business. But this line is also practically drawn as women simply do not have the chance to find a job and many have given up their initial endeavours and instead decided to become mothers. Filipinas estimate that being a global housekeeper is more profitable than working in a factory in the Philippines, and the accompanying women state that, after all, being a housewife in a luxurious global household is not the worst of all possible destinies. It is, therefore, that all involved see the advantages for themselves in this constellation and that domestic space is associated with the female. This should not mean we overlook the fact that domestic space is dominated and determined to a large degree by men (see, for related discussions, Grosz 1995 and Wilson 1995).

Global women mapping local Istanbul

Beyond all ideological and practical bi-polar fragmentations of local global space, for a global person it would hardly be possible to restrict his or her life to the local global socio-cultural sphere. It is, however, difficult to establish rules as to the degree and quality of interaction of a global person with local Istanbul. Whether one actively tries to get to know the local or whether one restricts oneself largely to the global is also a question of mentality and interests. One could perhaps hypothetically argue that managers do so less because of their heavy involvement in their global jobs. This is why wives often seem to acquire comparably better knowledge of the local, of the language, of the locations of cinemas and grocery stores, of the opera's programme. This is why women often become the organizers of their husbands' leisure time. How, then, do women view the local Istanbul lying beyond their own global place?

For the Filipina maid, as for the foreign representative's wife,[3] local Istanbul to a large extent remains an alien cosmos they are unable – and often also unwilling – to enter and to get to know. One important reason is that they generally speak only a little Turkish. For many of them local Istanbul is identical with the space of the rural migrants and the shanty towns, territories where local systems of meaning, in terms of language, of Islamic or rural-Anatolian culture remain not only incomprehensible, but potentially threatening. This bi-polar mapping of global and local spaces is clearly expressed in the following quotation:

> Istanbul is international. Unless you go to a quarter as the one where my people [her Turkish domestic helpers] live. In Istanbul there are quarters I do not know at all. I once got lost in such a quarter on my way back from Galeria [one of Istanbul's most prestigious shopping centres]. What I saw

there … I would not like to live there. I must say you like to live in Istanbul if you live nicely, in a tidy quarter and a nice apartment. … Like in Cihangir or in Nişantaşi, or on the Asian side though I know this less. These are nice places to live in. … As a woman in Istanbul you can move in all these quarters, and also in Pera and Şişli. It is perhaps more difficult in the satellite towns around Istanbul, which are inhabited by villagers. There they must still walk around with a headscarf. They take care about that very much. But otherwise you can move in Istanbul as in any other city, like in Europe. And therefore, I wouldn't say, that Istanbul is Turkey. (Mrs W., accompanying wife)

Public local Istanbul is also often associated with male domination. This means that (foreign) women may only intrude into male space when being familiar with and conforming to the local rules of behaviour:

I wanted to attend the lecture, but my husband is on a business trip, and so he could not accompany me. And his driver did not have the time to drive me home after the lecture. I do not want to take a taxi late in the evening, especially as our house is situated up the hill and the road leading to it goes through a small wood. I certainly would not do this alone in a taxi. I am too afraid. And even more so if there is no man who puts me in the taxi and tells the driver where to bring me. This is better for a woman than standing alone at the roadside. (Mrs M., accompanying wife)

For the Filipina maid venturing into male public space is a still more ambiguous enterprise. As women from Southeast Asia they are notoriously stigmatized as prostitutes, and they often complain of being harassed in the streets and on public transport, especially if they are out alone or are out after sunset. How best to protect and defend oneself is often part of their conversations:

I never tried to go to cinema, because I am afraid if only us women will go there. I am afraid that the Turks come and grab us, so we never go. We go for a walk only during daytime but at night we should have to come home. I am also scared of the taxi drivers, some are thieves. Some Turks are bad. Sometimes even during daytime. When we are walking in the street cars stop and they invite us for a ride in their car although we do not know them. … We never ride in their cars because we know they are bad. I heard from a friend that a Filipina once did so. And they said that they would take her where she wanted. And then they took her to a hotel and they raped her. According to the Filipina friend that really happened, but the woman herself never complained because as an illegal she is afraid to report to the police. (Mrs R., domestic helper)

Another important reason for the Filipinas' avoidance of Istanbul's public space is that most of them are illegally in Turkey: any step outside the house therefore turns into a highly dangerous enterprise, as they run the risk of being apprehended by the immigration police which at the very least would mean spending a night in a prison cell. This might lead to deportation and, consequently, to the destruction of their life strategies. There are places in Istanbul which are assessed to be particularly dangerous while others seem to be safer. Filipinas therefore map public Istanbul in terms of no-go areas, usually the busy Westernized middle-class areas with their self-service restaurants, cinemas, moderately priced shops and discotheques. Besides these no-go areas there are the safer places, typically the residential areas of the rich and the Asian side of Istanbul. If inside the global household they are virtually under total surveillance, in public Istanbul they have to control their own movements and try to conceal themselves. As they also have very little free time, this leads to a situation where most of them hardly ever go beyond their living quarters and never have a chance to develop more than a vestigial spatial awareness of the city they live in.

In all, local public Istanbul is not a space the global women feel they can use for their own interests, where they can manifest their presence, where they can leave traces. Rather, local Istanbul remains a heavily polluted place with notorious traffic congestion, an alien and potentially hostile male territory through which they must move quickly, where they must do their best to remain unnoticed. This, to a certain extent, may not be very different from how local women experience Istanbul. What are different, however, are the strategies and means employed by global and local women to create and negotiate their presence in the local public space.

Creating a female global space in Istanbul

The consequence of all this is that female space in Istanbul is first of all domestic space where both the domestic helper and the mistress spend a considerable part of their everyday lives. This is also the only place which mistress and helper jointly occupy, and if they entertain a friendly relationship one might even now and then find them together in the kitchen for a coffee and a chat. Still, domestic space is shared in a hierarchical order along status, class and ethnic lines. As the manager of the global household, the accompanying wife has the privilege of delegating the hard and menial household chores to the Filipina – a privilege which is also a signifier of status. Thus, the mistress also regards it as her prerogative to determine in what ways and when her maid is to use the domestic space. The Filipina's realms are the kitchen and her own room where she spends her free time, but where she will often also carry out some household chores such as ironing or darning. For her, the household is her working place and her home. Also here, it is the virtue of a good housekeeper to make herself invisible. On the other hand, the degree to which a housekeeper is conceded freedom of action and movement inside the house also determines the quality of her employer in the eyes of the maids, as the best employer is the one who 'treats her helper as a family member', as the Filipinas express it.

Female global space consists of domestic islands articulated into a female informal network. These are the domestic spaces of their female friends and acquaintances, usually women who share nationality, status, family roles and stages in their life-cycles. They meet for coffee mornings, bridge sessions or children's playgroups. These networks do not include men:

> We do this among women only. Right now we are trying to organize an evening where the parents go out together, without the children. So that the men can also get to know each other. This is a funny thing here. We are always half of a family who know each other very well ... but the men are excluded because they don't join in. And sometimes this is a pity. Especially when you already know somebody so well. Then it would be quite nice to get to know the husband also ... But we probably would not be able to integrate the men into our groups, even if we wanted to. It is clear to us that this is Utopian. It is because of their jobs which do not release them at one or two o'clock p.m. (Mrs Sch., accompanying wife and mother of a small daughter)

Nationality and status are important lines along which female networks are organized. Thus, Mrs Sch. (actually the wife of a manager working for an important German bank) remembered how a German woman invited her to join her local-global female networks when she was still new in the city:

> She was a cute woman and she tried to introduce me here ... but this was naturally a slightly different standpoint. I say this in quotation marks. So I hope you understand me right if I say this now. They were predominantly the wives of teachers, you can say teachers' spouses. They have totally different expectations in life. (Mrs Sch.)

Another example of this is a Filipina housewife married to an MNC's general representative who would never think of including her Filipina helper within the network of her female friends.

Networks are further determined by the length of stay in Istanbul. Women who stay permanently in the city and those who are there for a limited number of years form separate groups:

> One now and again makes new friends, you know, but gradually one gets

> tired of always looking for new ones. One sort of ties oneself down to those who are here permanently. … I must say it wasn't always like this. Formerly? There is a newly arriving person? One immediately tried to contact her. Now, I must say, I am tired, I don't want that any more. … Now we want to concentrate on those who are here for a longer time. (Mrs W., accompanying wife)

Making friends is a process involving much time and energy. The experience of frequently losing a precious friendship through rotation from one global job to the next eventually leads to a deliberate decision to socialize only with those who are not expected to leave; or, in the case of the sojourning women, to build up only superficial relationships while investing emotional energy in their old friendships in their home countries.

Filipina maids map their global living place in a similar way. They largely stick to their own group of Filipina housekeepers, integrating the few helpers from other Asian countries living in Istanbul, but never Turkish domestic helpers. They meet on Sundays in the homes of those Filipina maids whose employers are absent or allow them to bring friends home. These meetings are not only a rare occasion to socialize, to make friends with other Filipinas, and to have fun. It is here, too, that a secret subversiveness and opposition to their employers is lived out, as stories are passed around about their employers' private lives, their little quirks and quarrels. This is the time and place where they compensate themselves for all the drudgery they suffer during the week. This of course is also the time and place for consolation, to listen and give advice to those Filipinas who suffer from their employers' ill treatment, to think about strategies of how best to help them by spreading information about good and bad employers, about hiding places and job vacancies. Sunday's parties are a place of resistance inasmuch as they are an occasion to regain strength for the working week ahead of them. Perhaps still more important in this respect is the Sunday sermon given in English at one of Istanbul's Catholic churches attended by most of those who are legally in Turkey.

Women of both groups actively engage in the establishment of their informal female networks. But the practical realization of these places in time is to a high degree not determined by the women themselves, but by others. While the Filipina helpers can meet their friends only with the permission of their employers, the wives usually organize their meetings according to the times of absence of their husbands. They want to be home when their husbands are present, to fulfil their roles as the organizers of a nuclear family life.

Conclusion

Discussing the roles and status of women, and their spatial organization, in the global city (that is, those urban sectors where global control and management functions are spatially located), we have a sense of *déjà vu*. In the global city of the late twentieth century, as in the industrial city of the eighteenth and nineteenth centuries, urban space is ideologically and practically constructed as bi-polar and gendered space (Ryan 1994). In both settings, the ideals of the family and domestic space are reified along a gendered division of labour, attributing to men and women different domains and tasks. Here, as then, women are first of all mothers and spouses, and the representatives of a privatized domestic realm, a kind of peaceful haven where the male heads of household can retreat to from the pressure of competition reigning 'out there' in the capitalist economy (Frevert 1986: ch. I). Among these female representatives of the domestic sphere there are also, now as then, the domestic helpers.[4] Unpaid and paid female labour within the privatized household in both historical settings is a signifier of male status. Ideologically and practically constructed as the representatives of the private home, women of the bourgeois as well as the global household are the signs of male achievement, finding expression in the degree to which the women become the administrators of goods purchased from male earnings. The more the luxurious domestic space is represented as female, private and enclosed, the more it becomes the 'other' of capitalist business space, and the more it serves as a signifier of status for the husband's corporation. Talking about status, one should not forget, however, that female paid and unpaid labour in the household first of all reproduces the male labour force. In both historical settings, the 'privatization' and feminization of domestic space emerges as the result of social negotiation over the construction of difference (Ryan 1994). It is therefore, also, that we can interpret the emergence of the privatized domestic space of female paid and unpaid labour as a sign of a widening gap between the poor and rich of the national or global economy.

What evidently differentiates global from bourgeois female domestic space are the forms and degree of migration involved. It is true that the maids in the bourgeois households also were migrants who came from the countryside. Today, migration is international labour migration, involving all members of the global household. The global household is the practical result of a fully-fledged global labour market. Service sector labour, highly and moderately paid – or not paid at all – flows around the globe and articulates within the household. As the multinational corporation has become a synonym for global capitalism, its managers migrate from one global city to the next. And maids from the Philippines have long since established their informal global networks, always in search of a better job in yet another global city. Global female domestic space seems to be a category of some importance in the global city, yet it is not linked to particular people. Its inhabitants, like modern nomads, stay on the move, always forced to re-map their local global imagination of being at home.

Women, without doubt, until today have had few chances of getting a job in an MNC's regional headquarters, unless they become secretaries or cleaning ladies. But it would be too simple to end up with the conclusion that women are the eternal victims of patriarchy and capitalist market integration, as the emergence of global city space is concomitant to the women's renewed retreat into the seclusion of the 'private' sphere. While there are of course broken partnerships and women lamenting their destiny, many executives' wives stressed that they prefer to participate in and represent a global household's high income and status to being a wage-earner holding an averagely paid service sector job in their home country. And Filipinas deliberately accept containment in a kind of global domestic prison as a phase in their life-cycle, thereby becoming the principal breadwinners and achievers of an advanced societal status in their families back in the Philippines. Belonging to an affluent global household in one of the global cities of this world is an important matter of distinction also for them. Negotiating the structures of global capitalism with their personal situation, most of these women state that they are the winners rather than the losers. It is therefore, also, that they too participate in the construction of gendered space in the city.

Notes

I am grateful to Helmut Weber and Ayşe Öncü for their constructive suggestions on an earlier version of this chapter.

1. For a broader discussion of this topic, see Weyland (1993).
2. This seems to be the case especially with women who have been socialized in a 'first world' society where life is much more organized and regulated than in the 'third world'. It may therefore be the case that these women find it especially hard to adjust while women from certain regions in Asia or Latin America more easily accommodate themselves to the local systems of meaning.
3. I here again want to restrict my arguments to European or 'Western' women (who formed the majority of my interview partners), as women from 'third world' countries might possibly find an easier access to local Istanbul.
4. Also in Istanbul the 'lady's help' has a century-old tradition (see the entries on 'evladlik' and 'besleme' in *Istanbul Ansiklopedisi*: Esen 1961).

References

Cruz, V. P. and Paganoni, A. (1989) *Filipinas in Migration: Big Bills and Small Change*. Scalabrini Migration Center, New Manila.

Esen, M. (1961) 'Besleme', *Istanbul Ansiklopedisi*, Vol. 5, 2556–7, Koçu Yayìnlari, Istanbul.

Feagin, J. R. and Smith, M. P. (1990) 'Cities and the New International Division of Labour: an Overview', in J. R. Feagin and M. P. Smith (eds), *The Capitalist City*. Basil Blackwell, Oxford.

Frevert, U. (1986) *Frauen-Geschichte. Zwischen Bürgerlicher Verbesserung und Neuer Weiblichkeit*. Suhrkamp, Frankfurt am Main.

Friedmann, J. (1986) 'The World City Hypothesis', *Development and Change* 17 (1), 69–83.

Friedmann, J. and Wolff, G. (1982) 'World City Formation: an Agenda for Research and Action', *International Journal for Urban and Regional Research* 6 (3), 309–44.

Glenn, E. N. (1981) 'Occupational Ghettoization: Japanese-American Women and Domestic Service, 1905–1970', *Ethnicity* 8 (4), 352–86.

Grosz, E. (1995) 'Women, Chora, Dwelling', in S. Watson and K. Gibson (eds), *Postmodern Cities and Spaces*. Basil Blackwell, Oxford and Cambridge, MA.

Harvey, D. (1989) *The Condition of Postmodernity*. Basil Blackwell, Oxford.

Ibarra, T. E. (1979) 'Women Migrants: Focus on Domestic Helpers', *Philippine Sociological Review* 27, 77–92.

Karpat, K. H. (1982) 'The Population and the Social and Economic Transformation of Istanbul: The Ottoman Microcosm', in K. H. Karpat, *Ottoman Population, 1830–1914: Demographic and Social Characteristics*. University of Wisconsin Press, Wisconsin.

Keyder, C. and Öncü, A. (1993) *Istanbul and the Concept of World Cities*. Friedrich Ebert Foundation, Istanbul.

King, A. (1983) '"The World Economy is Everywhere": Urban History and the World System', *Urban History Yearbook*. Leicester University Press, Leicester.

— (1989) 'Colonialism, Urbanism and the Capitalist World Economy', *International Journal of Urban and Regional Research* 13 (1), 1–18.

Koçu, R. E. (1981) 'Evadlık', *Istanbul Ansiklopedisı*, 10. Koçu Yayınları, Istanbul, 5411–12.

Korff, R. (1991) 'Die Weltstadt zwischen globaler Gesellschaft und Lokalitäten', *Zeitschrift für Soziologie* 20 (5), 357–68.

Korsieporn, A. P. (1989) 'Female Migrant Labor: a Case Study of Filipino and Thai Domestic Workers in Rome, Italy', *Asian Review* 3, 54–68.

Lin, V. (1987) 'Women Electronics Workers in Southeast Asia: The Emergence of a Working Class', in J. Henderson and M. Castells (eds), *Global Restructuring and Territorial Development*. Sage, London, 112–35.

Mai, U. (1989) 'Gedanken über räumliche Identität', *Zeitschrift für Wirtschaftsgeographie*, 33 (1/2), 12–19.

Massey, D. (1993) *Space, Place, and Gender*. University of Minnesota Press, Minneapolis.

Rollins, J. (1985) *Between Women: Domestics and their Employers*. Temple University Press, Philadelphia.

Rose, G. (1993) *Feminism and Geography*. University of Minnesota Press, Minneapolis.

Ryan, J. (1994) 'Women, Modernity and the City', *Theory, Culture and Society*, 11 (4), 35–64.

Sassen-Koob, S. (1984) 'Notes on the Incorporation of the Third World Women into Wage Labour through Immigration and Off-Shore Production', *International Migration Review* 18 (4), 1144–67.

— (1985) 'Capital Mobility and Labour Migration: Their Expression in Core Cities', in M. Timberlake (ed.), *Urbanization in the World-Economy*. Academic Press, New York.

— (1987) 'Issues of Core and Periphery. Labour Migration and Global Restructuring', in J. Henderson and M. Castells (eds), *Global Restructuring and Territorial Development*. Sage, London, 60–87.

Toprak, Z. (1990) 'Die Expansion metropolitaner Gesellschaften: Entwicklungspolitik und die globale Stadt – Das Beispiel Istanbul', *Jahrbuch für vergleichende Sozialforschung*, Berlin.

Weyland, P. (1993) *Inside the Third World Village*. Routledge, London and New York.

Wilson, E. (1995) 'The Invisible Flâneur', in S. Watson and K. Gibson (eds), *Postmodern Cities and Spaces*. Basil Blackwell, Oxford and Cambridge, MA.

Wolff, J. (1985) 'The Invisible Flâneuse: Women and the Literature of Modernity', *Theory, Culture and Society* 2 (3), 37–46.

7

The metropolitan dilemma: global society, localities and the struggle for urban land in Manila

Erhard Berner

Globalization, polarization and localization in metropolitan Manila

It is increasingly recognized that globalization does not lead to world-wide homogenization but, on the contrary, to a world more diverse, heterogeneous and complex than ever. The globalization debate, however, often suffers from a basic misconception: it assumes that global society, economy and culture are increasingly *placeless*, and exist or at least emerge anywhere on earth. This view neglects the fact that global integration leads to a concentration of power and control and, thus, to the rise of centres. Although this process is transnational, it is spatially anchored at particular places that are located within major cities or metropolises. This close interconnection between global society and its strongholds within cities requires new perspectives for the analysis of urban social, cultural and economic change.

In this chapter I shall argue that globalization itself is a contradictory process: intensified integration on the global scale is connected with processes of fragmentation and disintegration within the world cities themselves. It is not the city as a whole that becomes part of the global society but certain strongholds and citadels, clearly demarcated social, economic and spatial parts of it. In these strongholds, the global information economy with its advanced technology and transnational corporate culture reigns supreme and dominates the physical as well as the social image of the metropolis. Professionals and managers are seen as the protagonists of the global society. This image entails, however, 'the eviction of a whole array of activities and types of workers from the account about the process of globalization which are as much a part of it as is international finance' (Sassen 1994: 9; cf. Sassen 1991). Historically, every city was dependent on its hinterland; the global economy of a metropolis is based on and articulated with non-corporate, local sectors that are regarded as backward and marginal.

The rapid expansion of these sectors can be observed in all metropolises, essentially as a result of the demands of the global society itself. The world city is marked by its dynamics which lead to extensive building activities: established business centres grow, new ones emerge and gain importance and the demand for office towers, high-rise apartment buildings, hotels, luxury residential quarters, shopping malls and recreation centres is increasing. All these have to be supplied with infrastructure and connected with roads, mass transportation and communication lines, and later cleaned, maintained and guarded. Professionals are far outnumbered by construction workers, cleaners, waiters, janitors, clerks, security personnel, drivers, domestic helpers and providers of all kinds of petty services and trade. To remain competitive in what has become a global division of labour, a metropolis has to maintain an adequate supply of these services while their price has to be kept low. The growth of the urban poor population is, thus, not an anomaly in the ascent of a metropolis but rather its very result.

The polarization of the city is the result of a fundamental contradiction in the development of a globalizing metropolis that we have described as the 'metropolitan dilemma' (Berner and Korff 1995): On the one hand, urban land becomes scarce as demand is rapidly increasing, and thus, it becomes precious as never before; on the other, a growing number of people, many of them migrants attracted by the new economic opportunities, are far from being able to pay the market price for the use of land. Skyrocketing prices for real estate and the accompanying economic restructuring of the city lead to huge movements of people, many of them through forced evictions. In the course of the Philippines' economic recuperation in recent years, foreign investments in real estate, particularly Japanese and Taiwanese, have fuelled land speculation and contributed to skyrocketing prices in Metro Manila.

For the poor, there is no longer a chance to get access to housing on the market, nor is moving out of the city a viable strategy. For those who work long hours for a small income, any increase of the time and money needed for transportation is more than they can (and want to) deal with.[1] All these groups need to 'stay where the action is' (Guerrero 1977) to remain competitive on the contested market of low and medium skilled labour. As they are not able to rent or buy a residence with access to the city – that is, to compete successfully on the likewise contested land market – they can only fall back on extra-economic means. As a result we observe the emergence and persistence of certain areas in the city – namely slums, ghettos and shanty towns – where the rules of the market apply only in a very limited sense. Land value becomes an abstract concept in squatter areas and deteriorated tenement blocks; whoever wants to use such land profitably or to sell it at a reasonable (or rather exorbitant) price has to get rid of the residents first. In Manila, as in most other metropolises, consequently, we find a high percentage of squatters and slum dwellers relatively close to the city centres. Their role is fundamental rather than marginal: Manila's metropolitan economy is heavily subsidized by the existence of squatter colonies, and cannot function without this subsidy.

In the course of globalization, coexistence has given way to open conflict. At the time when the Berlin Wall fell, the iron curtains that protect the quarters of the wealthy against the majority of the population became more and more impenetrable. The immediate juxtaposition of global and local, of rich and poor, of skyscrapers and squatter shacks is characteristic of every metropolis and at least partly caused by globalization itself. What has taken place since the 1970s is a process we call 'localization', an exhaustive emergence of enclaves and a de-differentiation of the city's population due to social differentiation of urban space. Imagined differences between cultures and classes become social and spatial boundaries that divide the city into different localities.

Our basic hypothesis is, then, that present metropolises are characterized by conflicts between globalization and localization. Globalization implies a 'tendency for a *space of flows* to supersede the *space of places* ... The logic and dynamics of territorial development are increasingly placeless from the point of view of the dominant organizations and interests' (Castells and Henderson 1987: 7; original emphasis). Localization is the search of groups among the non-dominant classes for a local identity and the creation of localities as foci of everyday life. Although apparently contradictory processes, localization and globalization are closely connected. Through globalization itself local diversity is created: Swyngedouw (1989) speaks of 'the resurrection of locality in an age of hyperspace'. Instead of a mere differentiation between world regions, the concepts of centre and periphery today indicate a differentiation between global society and segmented localities, both spatially anchored in world cities. Centre and periphery face each other in the metropolis and form the background of intensifying urban conflicts in London, Paris and Los Angeles as well as in Manila, Bangkok, Rio de Janeiro and Mexico City.

As Marcuse (1989) points out, 'dual city' is a 'muddy metaphor' for a social reality far more complex. While it emphasizes the difference between boom and decay, the boundaries between globalized universes such as Manhattan and deteriorated neighbourhoods such as Harlem, it tends to neglect the high differentiation within the latter. The modern metropolis is not only a place where the first world is directly confronted with the third; in its different districts, Korea borders on Armenia, Mexico on Vietnam, Louisiana on Samoa, and wars are possible between all these 'tribes' (Davis 1990; cf. Korff 1993). We do not find, thus, two opposing worlds, but rather a global society and 'a variety of social universes whose fundamental characteristics are their fragmentation, the sharp definition of their boundaries, and the low level of communication with other such universes' (Castells 1991: 226). The phenomenon of the quartered city has been conceptualized in urban sociology since the works of the Chicago School (cf. Saunders 1986: 52ff. for an overview); against the background of globalization, it becomes essential to grasp the dynamic and conflictive quality of fragmentation processes.

Whereas the functional necessity of self-help housing effectively precludes any comprehensive solution of the 'squatter problem', it does not ease the pressure on the actual squatter settlements which is intensified by the globalization process. Land in strategic locations has become a crucial power resource, which means in turn that those without power are evicted sooner or later and lose their access to the opportunities of the metropolis. The persistence of many slums and squatter areas close to the city centres and strongholds of globalization needs, thus, to be explained: what are the sources of power that enable the poor to defend so many pieces of precious land against global players and other strong competitors? We will show that it is the local context itself which may provide a basis of organization and, thereby, of empowerment and habitat defence. Localization is not merely a process at the 'underside' of globalization but a specific counterplay that alters the shaping of the metropolis.

Everyday life as the basis of resistance: localities and local organizations

Urban unrest and resistance have been conceptualized under the framework of 'urban social movements' (Castells 1977; 1983). While this approach meritoriously emphasizes the role of local communities as focal points of urban struggles, it seems somewhat hampered by its preoccupation with anti-capitalist societal transformation. After the abdication of the proletariat, urban movements appear as the new force of salvation:

> Urban movements do address the real issues of our time although neither on the scale nor terms that are adequate to the task. And yet they do not

> have any choice since they are the last reaction to the domination and renewed exploitation that submerges our world. But they are more than a last, symbolic stand and desperate cry: they are symptoms of our contradictions, and therefore potentially capable of superseding these contradictions. When the vocabulary becomes too restricted (a single focus on rent control, for instance) the movements lose their appeal [to whom? E. B.] and become yet another interest group in a pluralist society. (Castells 1983: 331)

In his attempt to develop a macro-sociological, cross-cultural theory of urban social change, Castells pays little attention to the problem of identifying collective actors who pursue change or react to it. Nelson (1979) points out that group building and collective action among the poor are highly conditional and precarious processes. Whether locally-based groups – if they exist at all – form a larger movement in specific places and historic situations is an empirical question that cannot be answered a priori. To formulate hypotheses about the emergence of groups among squatters and slum dwellers it is necessary to emphasize the territorial quality that is treated casually by Castells and even regarded as a distortion of the urban movement by some of his followers (for example, van Naerssen 1989: 210). In their 'Framework and Agenda for Research' (1988), Friedmann and Salguero state that the urban movement is actually a 'barrio movement', composed of a multitude of territorial communities that are the fundamental basis of group building: 'Poor people gain greater access to the bases for social (not yet political) power primarily by joining in collective, community-based efforts of struggling for survival in difficult times' (Friedmann and Salguero 1988: 8).

As a basis for this social empowerment and a however limited protection of their interests, the poor have to develop social agency and become groups themselves. It is our hypothesis that the local context – for which we propose the term 'locality' – provides multiple relations and interdependencies that can be the basis of group building and collective action. Our concept of the locality as a socially defined spatial entity is close to the Latin American term barrio as elaborated by Friedmann and Salguero:

> The barrio constitutes the space for the production and reproduction of ... life, because it is here, in the immediacy of their everyday social relations, that households are able to increase their capacity for action by gaining improved access to social power. ... As the habitat of the vast majority of the popular sectors, barrios typically have a name, a sense of their own identity, a history still fresh in the memory of its older inhabitants, dense social networks, a formal or informal structure of governance, and other attributes of a spatially defined political community. (Friedmann and Salguero 1988: 11)

Following Elias, 'social cohesion' itself is a basic factor of empowerment. Power differentials between the 'outsiders' and the 'established' may be based on nothing more than the latter's tight internal relations that enable them to act as a group:

> The social barriers dividing the two working-class neighbourhoods were at least as great, if not greater than the barriers to social relations and communications between working-class neighbourhoods and the middle-class neighbourhood in the area. ... The inhabitants of Zone 2 [the more cohesive and, thus, powerful community, E. B.] were for the greater part members of families who had lived in the area for a fairly long time, who were established there as old residents, who felt that they belonged there and that the place belonged to them. (Elias and Scotson 1965: 2)

This is precisely how we understand a locality.

Although of course spatially bound and referring to specific places, locality is not a geographic but first a social category. On the basis of Giddens's concept of 'locale' as a physical place with 'definite boundaries which help to concentrate interactions in one way or another' (Giddens 1984: 375), we are focusing on the relations, interdependencies and interactions of the people living in that place. According to Dickens, the concept of locality is linking 'the ways in which people interact with one another, with the physical environment and how they articulate their experiences' (Dickens 1990: 3). A locality, then, is the focus of everyday life; it is not merely the place where people reside but where they spend much of their life, their *Lebenswelt* (life-world). This, again, is a hypothesis that cannot simply be taken for granted but has to be tested empirically.

Most urban researchers seem to agree that the sphere of production, at least in the third world, is no longer the most important basis for the emergence of resistant groups. Even in countries where a strong labour movement existed, it failed to provide the answers to the new challenges at the global level (Castells 1983: 329). 'The effect is silence on one hand, or protest predominantly on a local level around issues directly related to material, social, cultural and psychological aspects of everyday life' (Korff 1990b: 36). To put emphasis on everyday life does not imply, however, that we restrict ourselves to the sphere of reproduction. Informal-sector activities and subsistence production are taking place in the locality and play an important role in local relations and interdependencies (Friedmann and Salguero 1988; Evers and Korff 1986; Korff 1990b: 270ff.).

In quest of localities: problems of operationalization

If it is difficult to conceptualize 'the city' as a unit of analysis (Giddens 1979: 148; cf. Saunders 1985; 1986), it seems downright impossible to define 'the locality'. Beauregard (1988) has rightfully pointed to the fact that locality research is suffering from a fundamental arbitrariness: the researcher is not informed by theory but by common knowledge when he decides what his survey 'barrio', 'community' or 'locality' consists of; it may encompass small neighbourhood clusters of fifty families, or whole city quarters of 10,000 and more. Even if he can show that the boundaries he is referring to are actually regarded as significant by the residents, the procedure is obviously circular. More than twenty years ago, Clark (1973) criticized the idea that conventional definitions of community presuppose a sense of solidarity, neglecting the actual significance for its members' sentiments that it may or may not have. Following Clark, research does not begin with localities but with interest groups that may define localities. Locality theory, apparently, has largely failed to learn this lesson which makes it prone to criticism regarding its inadequate conceptual scheme (for example, Taylor 1975; Beauregard 1988; Duncan and Savage 1989).

According to the definition proposed in the preceding section, localities are socially defined and 'created' spatial entities. Being essentially territories, they can – and have to – be defined by their occupants. Although the boundaries of the territories often coincide with streets, rivers and the like, they have to be demarcated and reinforced by social action. It is plausible to assume that individuals can hardly perform this feat, at least if they are neither financially resourceful nor politically powerful. We therefore have to look for collective actors or *groups*, and the safest indicator for the existence of groups pursuing communal interests is the existence of organizations (cf. Olson 1971). If the localities, or 'territorial communities' as Friedmann and Salguero call them, are regarded as significant – and this is a hypothesis rather than an assertion – we expect that they develop a more or less formal organizational structure.

As Nelson (1979: 254f.) points out, the precarious legal status and the lack of basic infrastructure are effective incentives to build up organizations in slums, squatter settlements and low-income quarters, with the fear of displacement and eviction as the paramount one. Although the problems are shared by all members of a local community they are not necessarily perceived as common interests that require collective action. Provided that there is such a common goal or interest, a lack of associations may, in turn, suggest that the locality itself is not a meaningful and significant entity to its residents, with loyalties attached to clans, cliques or patron–client relations rather than to the local community. By concentrating on local organizations, we are not putting forward a renewed version of the 'mythological "community-as-a-whole"' criticized by Smith (1980: 180ff.). By defining the boundaries of a locality, the organization merely claims to speak for all people living within these boundaries, be they formally members or not. Whether this claim is actually valid and the organization accepted as the representative of all residents has to be tested empirically.

For a local association, the problem of trust is crucial: people have to be confident that the activists not only care for them but articulate the needs of the whole locality. The capacity to organize is, thus, closely connected with social cohesion and the development of we-consciousness: solidarity and mutual trust may emerge on the basis of the actual concentration of social activities, relations, interactions and interdependencies in a locality. Social creativity (Korff 1988; 1990a) is a key factor for this process that is the central subject of this chapter.

On the basis of an exploration of twenty-seven slums in Manila and an intensive survey undertaken in five of them, I shall demonstrate that local groups can become an important means to achieve some bargaining power in conflicts about the use of urban space. They are often highly organized, fulfilling the conditions of order, continuity, regularity, and internal consensual purpose that Wirth (1938) set forth for social organizations but did not expect to exist at this level. We will show that local organizations can be capable of working out solutions for the problems of housing and basic services, effectively hampering and resisting the plans of land developers, city governments and corporations; we will also show that others fail and cease to exist. To investigate the conditions and means of this collective action is a sensible agenda for locality research.

Becoming urbanites: migration and the irrelevance of ethnicity

It is common knowledge that the urban poor are migrants, and that 'the influx of migrants is one major factor contributing to urban poverty' (Nelson 1979: 48).[2] Hardly any study on slum dwellers and squatters fails to mention their rural origin, frequently insinuating that a 'maladjustment' to the city is a cause of poverty. Unlike other countries in Southeast Asia, the Philippines has not (yet?) developed the economic dynamics that would attract many migrants from other countries. The newcomers to Metro Manila come from the provinces, more than half of them from the particularly poor regions of Bicol, Eastern Visayas (Samar and Leyte) and Western Visayas (Negros and Panay). For the inhabitants of the southern islands and Mindanao in particular, Davao City and Cebu City are alternative destinations and relatively few of them make it to Metro Manila.

Only 11 per cent of the respondents were born in Metro Manila, and even most of these are descendants of migrants. Asked for the reasons for their move to the city, an overwhelming majority emphasize better opportunities, especially in finding employment. Some speak, quite paradoxically, of the 'greener pastures' they hoped to find in the urban environment; others, specifically men, say that they came to 'seek adventure' and 'find their luck'. A pattern of chain migration is clearly visible: people follow their relatives after these have gained a foothold in the metropolis. The assistance of relatives is crucial when it comes to finding a place of residence. Available land for squatting or opportunities to rent in a squatter area are not advertised in Manila's dailies; for those who come directly from the provinces, relatives are virtually the only source of information. Moreover, one cannot simply walk into a slum and build a shelter: 'There is no free squatting' (Murphy 1993: vii). The fact that squatting is illegal and, consequently, not regulated by the state does not mean that it is not regulated at all. On the contrary: there is an elaborate system of 'land rights' that are bought, sold, inherited or leased temporarily, most often based on the original development of the area.

More than 70 per cent of the respondents chose their present residence on the advice of relatives, and most of the others were influenced by friends. Relatively few people stay in the first place they find after arriving from the province, often because newcomers stay temporarily with relatives until they find accommodation for themselves. Less than 25 per cent of the respondents have not moved within Metro Manila before they came to their present locality, and more than half of them have moved at least twice. Intra-city migration, therefore, provides for the bulk of population shifts. Squatters and renters are equally mobile, but for different reasons: virtually all people who had been squatters (that is, house-owners) in their former residence have only moved because of forced eviction. Those who have been tenants before and are squatters now came because they found a chance to acquire land rights and could subsequently save the rent. Renters, eventually, move for various motives: their former landlord may have thrown them out, either because they failed to pay the rent or because he needed the rooms for himself; the new place may be nicer or more conveniently located, or the rent may be cheaper.

The personalistic and kinship-based patterns of migration suggest that ethnic ties might play a significant role in the emergence of local communities. The Philippines is a multi-lingual country, with some eighty different languages spoken today, most of them in Mindanao and the Sulu islands that became incorporated into the state only in the twentieth century. Only 25 per cent of the population are native speakers of Tagalog, the basis of the national language Filipino. Yet the relevance of the concept of 'ethnicity' can be generally doubted in this country. To our knowledge, there are hardly any residential areas in Metro Manila that are ethnically homogeneous. In the preliminary survey of twenty-seven slums, we asked people where major immigrant groups came from. The standard answer was 'from all over the Philippines'; some listed places like Bicol, the Visayas and Ilocos which are the major regions of origin of most migrants to Manila and not specific to any locality.

The irrelevance of ethnicity for social distance and closeness in Manila slums is further demonstrated by residents' marriage behaviour. It is commonly recognized by anthropological theory that a high degree of in-marriage is an indicator for ethnic as well as religious identity (for example, Gray 1987; McCaa and Gray 1989; Alba 1991; McCaa 1993). A first look at our sample suggests that there is at least some preference in choosing spouses from the same language groups, as more than half of all couples are homolingual. The strong minority of mixed couples turns out to be a strong majority if we consider that many had been married already when they came to Metro Manila. There is a radical difference between countryside and city when it comes to the selection of marriage partners: while virtually all of the couples that had got married before migrating to Manila come from the same language group, more than three-quarters of those who met after arrival are mixed.

Apart from cultural patterns prevalent in the Philippines, the insignificance of ethnic identities is explained by the fact that even most of the migrants in our sample can no longer be sensibly described as provincials and would reject the label *probinsyano* themselves. Having lived in Metro Manila for an average period of seventeen years, they have become urbanites in an intricate learning process that is called 'deethnicization' by Dewan (1989). Hollnsteiner has argued that it is the neighbourhood that provides the major 'learning environment' for this process, thereby rejecting the myths of 'impersonal' life in the city:

> The urbanite is characterized as lonely in the midst of crowds, a man forced to accept both the rapid pace of city life and the slow rate at which urban institutions respond to their needs. In contrast, the countryside retains the romantic glow of a lost Eden. Convincingly though these prophets of gloom have argued their case, apparently millions of city

> dwellers have neither read, heard, or cared for their pronouncements. (Hollnsteiner 1972: 29; cf. Abu-Lughod 1973)

Our results demonstrate that it is indeed the locality that functions as the basic instance of socialization in the urban environment; a local identity is the basis, and the crucial precondition, of an urban identity.

The findings of our quantitative and qualitative survey in five Manila localities can be summarized as follows: the dense web of both personal and functional relations and dependencies allows for the emergence of mutual trust and, consequently, of relatively stable and durable alliances. The residents of a locality have developed we-consciousness and think of themselves as a group. If the fluctuation of residents is not too high, most newcomers are integrated quite quickly. A lot of ego-centred networks, based in the locality and formalized in *compadrazgo* (ritual kinship) relations, are connected and interlaced in a limited number of households, many of them long established and wealthy. It is plausible to assume that these households become cores in the process of community building, and in the formation of organized groups that are capable of collective action.

Agency and collective action: local organizations

We have stated that a locality as a socially meaningful spatial entity is defined by groups that have been formed in a settlement; and that the existence of organizations which claim to speak for the whole community is a safe indicator for such group activities. Local associations are, thus, a crucial point in this analysis. In line with an argument put up by Poethig, we see a close relation between the poor's capacity to organize and their integration into, and ability to act in, the urban environment:

> To live in the city, a person takes part in its organizations. The casualties of city life are those who are not tied to it organizationally … Organization becomes an essential factor in the participation of the poor in urban society … participation in their social, ethnic, or regional associations begins to provide the poor a sense of belonging to the city. (Poethig 1972: 42)

Based on the results presented in the preceding section, this statement can be specified: in a tedious process of local integration, ethnic and regional alignments lose much of their relevance and are submerged by the emergence of local solidarity. The necessary basis for the 'sense of belonging to the city' is a sense of belonging to a place, namely the locality. As the poor are effectively excluded from direct participation in politics and urban decision-making – in other words, cannot tie themselves up with existing organizations – they have to organize themselves to achieve some bargaining power. Our results as well as a reassertion of the literature (Nelson 1979; Schuurman 1989; van Naerssen 1989) supply evidence that locally-based associations can be much more stable, durable and efficient than anti-systemic 'movements' organized along class lines. In her comparison of 'Politics and the Urban Poor in Developing Nations' world-wide, Nelson (1979: 252ff.) makes a very useful distinction between the 'incentives' and the 'capacity' to build and maintain organizations, both necessary conditions in their own right. A common interest can become an incentive if it is perceived as such and regarded as important:

> At least a substantial core of residents must feel that some aspect of neighbourhood life creates a high-priority problem for them – a problem important enough so that they are willing to devote time, energy, and usually some money to its solution ... The most dramatic instance of a high-priority, shared problem is the threat of eradication. (Nelson 1979: 255)

As the localities discussed here are squatter settlements, this threat is always present at least latently. Another rationale is the improvement of services and facilities that, generally, leave much to be desired in Manila urban poor areas.

Very much in line with the arguments put forward in this article, Nelson sees 'social cohesion' (cf. Elias and Scotson 1965) based on a shared history as the fundamental precondition for the capacity to organize. Unlike in pure patron–client systems, there have to be intensive horizontal relations at least between the members of a community's 'core'. Urry, in his reflections on the role of space in social relations, has shown that even class-based collective action is dependent on a 'high rate of participation and of organised action within a range of spatial specific yet overlapping collectivities. Potential collective agents are thus involved in a face-to-face contact within dense, multiplex relations where there is a high certainty of the participation of others' (Urry 1985: 43). The networks of personal, social and economical interactions and interdependencies that are characteristic of a locality, although not based on a common ethnic origin or social position, can become a firm ground for organization-building and collective action. Both incentives and capacity are dependent, first, on the specific characteristics and the present situation of a locality; and, second, on the abilities, commitment and social creativity of its residents. In our survey we found a wide variety of organizations, some of them loosely structured or even dormant, others very active and successful. In most Manila squatter areas there is one association that claims to pursue communal interests and act as the mouthpiece of all residents. Each of these 'primary' organizations has a formal structure, with a president, a vice-president and a set of board members and officers, including secretaries, treasurers, sergeants-at-arms and public relations officers.

Our results supply strong evidence for the hypothesis that successful associations are deeply rooted in the local community. For most residents, the locality is the focus of everyday life. Through a multitude of social relations, interactions and interdependencies, they form several overlapping networks that become the basis of a local we-consciousness. We have shown that these networks have common nodes, namely persons and families who are involved in many local activities, and widely trusted and accepted as leaders. In all five research areas, the primary local organization was formed on the initiative of these key persons and is led by some of them. The role of the local association as core of the community is confirmed by a quantitative analysis: association officers have lived in the locality for a longer time than others, command a higher family income, and have more intensive personal relations. Non-members, in contrast, are often newcomers, renters, or belong to the dire poor; others stay outside the local networks for personal reasons.

A crucial task of local organizations is the definition of a territory that comprises all individual perceptions of neighbourhood; in other words, the definition of the locality itself. Association membership becomes a synonym for local identity and for being 'established' in the sense of Elias; people feel that they are belonging to the place and the place belongs to them. On this basis, the association can successfully claim to speak for all residents of the locality even if they are not formally members. As Laquian pointed out more than twenty years ago, the defence of contested urban land is the major incentive for building local organizations:

> Because of the insecurity involved in squatting on government land, the people have been forced to set up and join existing associations ... Interviews with many leaders, however, showed that in lobbying they did not see themselves fighting against something but rather as maintaining unity to achieve something. They want the land. By their long stay on the land, they feel that they have already earned the right to own it. (Laquian 1969: 88f.)

A place to live: localities and the social value of urban land

The diversity of slums and squatter settlements in Metro Manila is immense, and even more so is the multitude of situations and walks of life of their residents. Far from being 'representative' for the whole picture, the localities discussed in this chapter have been selected to open the view to this diversity. They have, therefore, little in common except two facts: they have survived in a principally hostile environment for twenty years or more; and they have developed a strong and durable organizational structure. The argument put forward here is that both facts are closely interrelated: by forming their own associations, slum dwellers articulate their interests as common and, thereby, become capable of collective action and conflict. They improve their bargaining position, form vertical links to potential allies, and demonstrate that they can put up considerable resistance against attempts to destroy the place they call their own.

In one study, the interrelation between a functioning organization and the capacity for resistance can be made plausible at best. Only a comparison of victories and defeats in the struggle for urban land, and the role of local associations in the respective conflicts, could supply harder evidence. Little research has been done, however, on demolitions and the affected localities. A notable exception is a research project sponsored by the Asian Coalition for Housing Rights (Murphy 1993). Murphy's team put up a list of all known demolition attempts in the years 1986–91 and went on to a closer investigation of forty-six instances. Due to obvious methodological problems – few of the victims could be interviewed as, in most cases, they are scattered all over the city – the material is far from being conclusive. Yet it illustrates that local associations often put up considerable resistance against evictions. Some successfully defended their community, others obtained at least an acceptable relocation site and/or financial compensation. Most, however, achieved nothing at all; the direct impact of local resistance against demolition, however brave it may be, is limited just because it is local.

Beyond direct resistance, localities and local organizations play a momentous role as their existence alters the land market and, thereby, the physical appearance and the image of the city. It is common knowledge that land is significantly depreciated by squatter occupation. In a considerable part of the city, the market value of land has become an abstract term; an owner can sell at this price only if he is able to establish actual control of his land.[3] If it is occupied by an established locality and defended by a strong organization, this process is both tedious and costly. A court order against the squatters has to be obtained and, much more troublesome, enforced. The Urban Development and Housing Act (UDHA) of 1992 has further enhanced the bargaining position of squatter organizations. It states that 'eviction or demolition as a practice shall be discouraged' (Article VII, sec. 28) and enumerates the situations in which demolitions are still allowable; the mandatory provision of a relocation site adds to the costs of clearing land from squatters. Politicians are doubtful allies for landowners as they can ill afford to be perceived as anti-poor; after all, the poor are the large majority of their constituency.

The 'actual' value of squatter land is a double compromise: first, the residents have to come to terms among themselves about what they are willing to pay for their land, and they can do so only if there is a functioning organization. Second, the association has to negotiate the actual selling price with the landowner who, of course, has the market value as his point of reference. An agreement can be reached only if both prices are not too far away from each other, and is, therefore, impossible for localities on prime urban land. On-site development and land transfer schemes have been quite successful in many parts of Manila because they offer a chance for a compromise between contradictory logics of action: the owners can capitalize their land, albeit at reduced prices, without the incalculable costs and risks of a demolition; the squatters can preserve their locality from the threat of eradication that has never been calculable for them.

Our results, however, indicate that such programmes always exclude a substantial part of the residents, among them the dire poor. In other words: success in the struggle for land jeopardizes the association's claim to represent all residents and, consequently, leads to internal struggles. The outcome is obviously a new de-differentiation: while the marginal segments of the population have to move on to find shelter in other squatter settlements, the former slum becomes a middle-class area; not by invasion or gentrification, but because most residents, or at least those who have the capacity to organize, have been members of the middle class anyway. The 'petty-bourgeois consciousness' of the urban poor that is deplored by many observers (for example, T. Evers 1985; Goss 1990: 520) is, thus, reflecting social reality.

Conclusion

Many observers, and city planners in particular, see slums and squatter areas as backward and marginal, pre-modern remnants of an incomplete development. Nothing could be further from reality: the localities of the poor are not 'urban villages' in an ecological sense but part of the city's diversity and heterogeneity which, according to Wirth (1938), are constitutive for urbanism and urbanity. Localities are not threatened islands in the stream of dynamic urban development, but they are produced by that stream in the first place. A locality must be seen as a response to, and an attempt to cope with, the metropolitan environment in the course of the globalization process which has changed the players and altered the arena. Many of the rank-and-file workers of transnational corporations live in informal settlements; 'self-help housing', as squatting is euphemistically called, has proven to be more efficient in terms of space and costs than all attempts of the state and the private sector. The latter's efforts are quite limited anyway; the globalizing metropolis offers much more profitable opportunities for land use than low-cost housing. The occupation of precious urban land by localities is the basis of permanent conflict and confrontations, and the outcome of these conflicts cannot always be determined in advance. Although the capacity to organize is a necessary basis for the poor's 'empowerment' and resistance against eviction, it does not make them a match for international investors and land developers who compete for the limited space in the centres. The scope of the associations is strictly parochial, reactive and defensive; there is little supra-local communication, not to mention solidarity. The local organizations in Manila, however, have found powerful allies in the emerging movement of non-government organizations (NGOs) which found their claim for power by 'representing' the poor's interests. The quite progressive legislation and the funding of land transfer schemes demonstrate the impact of this alliance which is supported by parts of the media. The NGOs, eventually, are very much global players themselves; they have access to international financial and informational resources, and their leaders join conferences in Rio, Cairo and Beijing. The protagonists of globalization are, thus, not a uniform group with common interests. For some of them, localization has become a resource in their struggle for power in the metropolis which is a struggle for the control of space in the first place.

Notes

This chapter presents some of the results of a research project which was financed by the Deutsche Forschungsgemeinschaft (DFG) and carried out by Rüdiger Korff and me. For a more detailed discussion of the situation in Manila, see Berner (forthcoming).

1. In the big cities, this group includes not only the un- and underemployed and the members of the informal sector but also people who would be regarded as middle class elsewhere: policemen, teachers, nurses, office clerks, sales personnel and so on. In Manila, for instance, a school teacher's lifetime salary is not enough to buy a 100m^2 lot (not to mention a house) in a medium-class residential area.
2. That cityward migration, at the same time, alleviates rural poverty by reducing competition for scarce resources is less often emphasized.
3. 'Considerable' is, of course, a relative term: even though far more than half of the metropolitan population are squatters, they occupy less than 10 per cent of Metro

Manila's land area. As a result of the metropolitan dilemma, however, much of this land is located not somewhere at the urban fringe but close to the centres.

References

Abu-Lughod, J. (1973) 'Migrant Adjustment to City Life: the Egyptian Case', in J. Walton and D. E. Carns (eds), *Cities in Change: Studies on the Urban Condition.* Allyn and Bacon, Boston, 112–26.

Alba, R. D. (1991) 'Intermarriage and Ethnicity among European Americans', *Contemporary Jewry* 12 (1), 3–19.

Beauregard, R. A. (1988) 'In the Absence of Practice: the Locality Research Debate', *Antipode*, 20 (1), 52–9.

Berner, E. (forthcoming) *A Place to Live in the City of Man: Localities and the Struggle for Urban Land in Metropolitan Manila.* Ateneo de Manila University Press, Quezon City.

Berner, E. and Korff, R. (1995) 'Globalization and Local Resistance: the Creation of Localities in Manila and Bangkok', *International Journal of Urban and Regional Research* 19 (2), 208–22.

Castells, M. (1977) *The Urban Question.* Edward Arnold, London.

— (1983) *The City and the Grass Roots.* Edward Arnold, London.

— (1991) *The Informational City: Information Technology, Economic Restructuring, and the Urban-Regional Process.* Basil Blackwell, Oxford and Cambridge, MA.

Castells, M. and Henderson, J. W. (1987) 'Techno-economic Restructuring, Sociopolitical Processes and Spatial Transformation: a Global Perspective', in J. W. Henderson and M. Castells (eds), *Global Restructuring and Territorial Development.* Sage, London, 1–17.

Clark, D. B. (1973) 'The Concept of Community: A Re-examination', *Sociological Review* 21 (3), 397–416.

Davis, M. (1990) *City of Quartz: Excavating the Future in Los Angeles.* Verso, London.

Dewan, R. (1989) 'Deethnicization: a Study of Language and Culture Change in the Sindhi Immigrant Community in Metro Manila', *Philippine Journal of Linguistics* 4 (1–4), 19–27.

Dickens, P. (1990) *Urban Sociology. Society, Locality, and Human Nature.* Harvester Wheatsheaf, New York, London, Toronto, Sydney and Singapore.

Duncan, S. and Savage, M. (1989) 'Space, Scale and Locality', *Antipode* 21 (3).

Elias, N. and Scotson, J. L. (1965) *The Established and the Outsiders: A Sociological Enquiry into Community Problems.* Frank Cass, London.

Evers, H.-D. and Korff, R. (1986) 'Subsistence Production in Bangkok', *Development* 4 (1), 50–5.

Evers, T. (1985) 'Identity: the Hidden Side of New Social Movements in Latin America', in D. Slater (ed.), *Social Movements and the State in Latin America.* CEDLA, Amsterdam, 43–72.

Friedmann, J. and Salguero, M. (1988) 'The Barrio Economy and Collective Self-Empowerment in Latin America: a Framework and Agenda for Research, in M. P. Smith (ed.). *Power, Community and the City.* Transaction Books, New Brunswick and Oxford, 3–37.

Giddens, A. (1979) *Central Problems in Social Theory: Action, Structure and Contradiction in Social Analysis.* University of California Press, London and Berkeley.

— (1984) *The Constitution of Society: Outline of a Theory of Structuration.* Polity Press, Oxford.

Goss, J. D. (1990) 'Production and Reproduction Among the Urban Poor of Metro Manila: Relations of Exploitation and Conditions of Existence'. Unpublished PhD thesis, University of Kentucky.

Gray, A. (1987) 'Intermarriage: Opportunity and Preference', *Population Studies* 41 (3), 365–79.

Guerrero, S. H. (1977) 'Staying Where the Action is: Relocation within the City', *Philippine Sociological Revue* 25 (1), 51–6.

Hollnsteiner, M. R. (1972) 'Becoming an Urbanite: the Neighborhood as a Learning Environment', in D. J. Dwyer (ed.), *The City as a Centre of Change in Asia*. Hong Kong University Press, Hong Kong, 29–40.

Korff, R. (1988) 'Informeller Sektor oder Marktwirtschaft? Markte und Handler in Bangkok', *Zeitschrift für Soziologie* 17 (4), 296–307.

— (1990a) 'Social Creativity, Power and Trading Relations in Bangkok', in S. Datta (ed.), *Third World Urbanization: Reappraisals and New Perspective*. HSFR, Stockholm, 168–85.

— (1990b) 'City, Trade and State: Urbanism in a Southeast Asian Primate City'. Unpublished postdoctoral thesis, University of Bielefeld.

— (1993) 'Der Nord-Süd-Konflikt in den Stadten', in B. Schafers (ed.), *Lebensverhaltnisse und soziale Konflikte im neuen Europa: Verhandlungen des 26. Deutsche Soziologentages in Düsseldorf*. Campus, Frankfurt and New York, 330–6.

Laquian, A. A. (1969) *Slums are for People: The Barrio Magsaysay Pilot Project*. UP College of Public Administration, Manila.

McCaa, R. (1993), 'Ethnic Intermarriage and Gender in New York City', *Journal of Interdisciplinary History* 24 (2), 207–31.

McCaa, R. and Gray, A. (1989) 'Isolation or Assimilation? A Log Linear Interpretation of Australian Marriages', *Population Studies*, 43 (1), 155–62.

Marcuse, P. (1993) 'Ethnic Intermarriage and Gender in New York City', *Journal of Interdisciplinary History* 24 (2), 697–720.

Murphy, D. (1993) *The Urban Poor: Land and Housing*. Asian Coalition for Housing Rights, Bangkok.

Naerssen, T. van (1989) 'Continuity and Change in the Urban Poor Movement of Manila, the Philippines', in F. J. Schuurman and T. van Naerssen (eds), *Urban Social Movements in the Third World*. Routledge, London and New York, 199–219.

Nelson, J. M. (1979) *Access to Power: Politics and the Urban Poor in Developing Nations*. Princeton University Press, Princeton, NJ.

Olson, M. (1971) *The Logic of Collective Action*. Harvard University Press, Cambridge, MA.

Poethig, R. P. (1972) 'Life Style of the Urban Poor and People's Organizations', *Solidarity* 7 (1), 37–43.

Sassen, S. (1991) *The Global City: New York, London, Tokyo*. Princeton University Press, Princeton, NJ.

— (1994) 'Identity in the Global City: Economic and Cultural Encasements'. Paper presented at the conference 'The Geography of Identity', University of Michigan, 4–5 February.

Saunders, P. (1985) 'Space, the City and Urban Sociology', in D. Gregory and J. Urry (eds), Social *Relations and Spatial Structures*. Macmillan, Basingstoke and London, 67–89.

— (1986) *Social Theory and the Urban Question*. Hutchinson, London, Melbourne, Sydney, Auckland and Johannesburg (1st edn, 1981).

Schuurman, F. J. (1989) 'Urban Social Movements: Between Regressive Utopia and

Socialist Panacea', in F. J. Schuurman, and T. van Naerssen (eds), *Urban Social Movements in the Third World*. Routledge, London and New York, 9–26.
Smith, M. P. (1980) *The City and Social Theory*. Basil Blackwell, Oxford.
Swyngedouw, E. (1989) 'The Heart of the Place: the Resurrection of Locality in an Age of Hyperspace', *Geografiska Annaler* 71B, 391–403.
Taylor, B. K. (1975) 'The Absence of a Sociological and Structural Problem Focus in Community Studies', *Archives Européennes de Sociologie* 16 (2), 296–309.
Urry, J. (1985) 'Social Relations, Space and Time', D. Gregory and J. Urry (eds), *Social Relations and Spatial Structures*. Macmillan, Basingstoke, 20–48.
Wirth, L. (1938) 'Urbanism as a Way of Life', *American Journal of Sociology* 44 (1), 1–24.

PART III

Rediscovering Islam through the prism of the global

8

Re-imagining the global: relocation and local identities in Cairo

Farha Ghannam

> Short of a certain threshold of likelihood, only magical solutions remain. Magical hope is the outlook on the future characteristic of those who have no real future before them. (Bourdieu 1979: 69)

'Praise the Prophet. Once upon a time, there was an old woman who used to live in an apartment that was as small as that tiny table [pointing to the small table in their living room]. Each time the old woman swept the floor, she found either one pound or 50 piasters [an Egyptian pound is worth around 34 cents] that she kept hidden in a place in her window. The old woman was saving to buy a larger apartment. But one day, a thief stole all the money that she saved. She was very sad. An *afriit* [demon or ghost] appeared and asked the old woman what she would like to have. She asked for a larger apartment. The *afriit* asked her, "Would you like the apartment to have a balcony?" and she answered yes. He asked her, "Would you like a television set, a fan and a bottle of water?" [describing some of the things that were in front of us in the living room]. The old woman said yes. Then he asked her, "And would you like some pictures of Samira Said and Latifa?" [two popular female Moroccan and Tunisian singers whose posters were decorating the wall of the living room]. The woman again answered yes. The *afriit* brought all these things for the old woman. She was very happy and cried out of joy. In the same day, however, she smelled the *birshaam*[1] that was hidden behind the television set which caused her heart to collapse [*gham ala albaha*] and the old woman died' (a story told to me by the five-year-old Amal in Cairo, 1994).

Amal's narrative was contextualized by her family's attempts to find a larger housing unit to move into from the one-bedroom apartment that she, her four sisters and their parents have been occupying since 1980, when the family was displaced from their home in the centre of the city and relocated in al-Zawiya al-Hamra in northern Cairo. Amal's images of the desired home are constructed, as is the case with many other children, from global images transmitted to them through television programmes, school textbooks and visits to different parts of the city. Her dreams, as well as those of her sisters, of the future apartment are informed by the movies and soap operas that they like to watch: a big apartment with a balcony, a spacious kitchen, modern furniture and organized spatial arrangements inside and outside the unit. These images contradict the objective realities of Amal's life and create desires that cannot be satisfied even through some magical means. Like the dreams of many other low-income people, Amal's discourse 'proceeds in a jagged line, the leaps into daydream being followed by relapses into a present that withers all fantasies' (Bourdieu 1979: 69). Death and destruction is the ultimate answer.

Amal, her family and the rest of their neighbours are not fax-users, e-mail receivers, jumbo jet travellers or satellite-owners. They are part of Cairo's working class whose experience of 'the global' is structured by their economic resources and position in social space. In addition to the many consumer goods, especially television sets, that are desired by people and are becoming signs of distinction, Amal's family and many other families experienced the force of the global in their displacement from their 'locality' in the centre of the city. Their houses were demolished to be replaced by buildings and facilities that cater to upper-class Egyptians, international tourists and the transnational community. In this chapter, I focus on relocation, utilized as part of the state efforts to 'modernize' Cairo and its people, to show how global discourses and forces are articulated in contradictory ways at the national and local levels. In the first section, I present a brief review of the history of the relocation of roughly 5000 working-class families from 1979 to 1981 and the state public discourse utilized to justify the project. This discourse strategically appealed to the global in the state's attempts to implement its different economic policies and to construct a modern national identity. In the second part, I draw on my recent ethnographic research in Cairo, or *Umm al-Dunya* (the mother of the world) as Egyptians like to refer to it, to map some of the identities that are attached to and formed by Amal's group to show how the displacement of the local by global processes and national policies brought new changes that paved the way to redefine local communal feelings in ways that help people live in the modern world. I argue that religious identity, as a hegemonic identity in the formation, was consolidated by the changes brought by the global as experienced by the people and as filtered in national policies.

Modernity and the struggle over urban space

> With her vast capabilities, the United States is bound in duty, even naturally expected, to assist all those striving for a better future alike for themselves and for the whole world. (Sadat 1978: 328)

In *Search for Identity* (1978), Anwar el-Sadat presents a strong critique of Nasser's policies that kept the country isolated from its neighbours and the rest of the world and destroyed Egypt's economy. To remedy the country's chronic economic and financial problems, Sadat reversed Nasser's policies by suspending relationships with the Soviet Union and reorienting Egypt towards the West. He turned to the United States in particular for aid in resolving Egypt's conflict with Israel as well as the economic and technological development of the country. After his victory in the 1973 war (at least it was a victory for him), Sadat crystallized his new visions and ideas in declaring 'the open-door policy' or *infitah* in 1974. This policy aimed to 'open the universe ... open the door for fresh air and remove all the barriers (*hawajiz*) and walls that we built around us to suffocate ourselves by our own hands' (Sadat 1981: 12). As he explained to a group of young Egyptian men, Sadat's *infitah* was motivated by his belief that each one of them would like to 'get married, own a villa, drive a car, possess a television set and a stove, and eat three meals a day' (Sadat 1981: 12).

Sadat's policy strived to modernize the country through speeding planned economic growth, promoting private investment, attracting foreign and Arab capital, and enhancing social development (Ikram 1980). Private local and international investments were expected to secure the capital needed to construct modern Egypt. Egyptians were encouraged to work in oil-producing countries and invest their remittances in the building of the country. At the same time, laws were enacted to secure the protection needed to encourage foreign investors and to facilitate the operation of private capital. Investments in tourism were especially important because they were expected to 'yield high economic returns and provide substantial foreign exchange and well-paid employment' (Ikram 1980: 309).

This orientation to the global, the outside, or the 'universe' as Sadat describes it, required a 'distinctive bundle of time and space practices and concepts' (Harvey 1990: 204). Many changes were needed to facilitate the operation of capital and meet the new demands that were created. For example, the growing demand for luxury and middle-class housing for the transnational community and Egyptians who work in oil-producing countries inflated the price of land, especially in the centre of the city, and increased the cost of construction materials (Rageh 1984). The promotion of private and foreign investment also increased the demand for offices and work-oriented spaces. High-rises proliferated around Cairo, using Western design principles and Los Angeles and Houston, Sadat's favourite American cities, became the models that were to be duplicated (Ibrahim 1987).

Two tendencies were expressed in the discourses and policies of urban planning that aimed to promote the *infitah* policies and to rebuild modern Cairo. The first tried to integrate into the modern city areas of significance to Egypt's glorious past (for example, the pyramids and Islamic monuments), which Sadat loved to emphasize and which were visited by tourists. The second tendency, which is the subject of this chapter, attempted to reconstruct the 'less desirable' parts, especially popular quarters, that did not represent the 'modern' image of Egypt and were not fit to be gazed at by upper-class Egyptians and foreign visitors.

The state, the global and the creation of the 'modern' city[2]

> Faust has been pretending not only to others but to himself that he could create a new world with clean hands, he is still not ready to accept responsibility for the human suffering and death that clear the way. (Berman 1988: 68)

As part of Sadat's larger plan to restructure the local landscape and build 'modern' Cairo, around 5000 Egyptian families were moved during the period from 1979 to 1981 from Central Cairo (Bulaq) to housing projects built by the state in two different neighbourhoods: 'Ain Shams and al-Zawiya al-Hamra. Bulaq, once the site of the winter houses of the rich, then a major commercial port and later an industrial centre (Rugh 1979), had become unfit for the modern image that Sadat was trying to construct. This area, which over the years had housed thousands of Egyptian low-income families, is adjacent to the Ramsis Hilton, next to the television station, around the corner from the World Trade Center, across the river from Zamalek (an upper-class neighbourhood), overlooks the Nile, and is very close to many of the facilities that are oriented to foreign tourists. The area then occupied by low-income families became very valuable because Sadat's policies, as he proudly announced, increased the price of the land which was needed to facilitate the operation of capital. The old crowded houses were to be replaced by modern buildings, luxury housing, five-star hotels, offices, multi-storey parking lots, movie theatres, conference rooms, and centres of culture (*al-Ahram* 27 December 1979: 3). Officials thus emphasized the urgent need to remove the residents of this old quarter because many international companies were ready to initiate economic and tourist investment in the area. Expected profits from these investments would contribute to national income and assist the state in securing money to build new houses for the displaced groups (*al-Ahram*, 27 December 1979: 9). The residents' efforts to stop their forced relocation did not materialize and their calls upon the government to include them in the reconstruction of their area were denied. Voices that protested the relocation were quickly silenced and objections raised by the displaced population were considered 'selfish'. Officials emphasized that the benefit of the 'entire nation' should prevail over everything else (*al-Ahram*, 9 July 1979).

The 'local' was also displaced to protect the state orientation to the global. The relocation project took place two years after the famous 1977 riots that protested the increase in the prices of basic daily goods, especially bread. Protesters targeted *infitah*-related facilities such as five-star hotels and nightclubs, and chanted slogans against Sadat's policies (Abd El-Razaq 1979). The neighbourhood, with its narrow lanes and crowded streets, made it impossible for the police to chase those who participated in the riots (*Mayo*, 22 June 1981). The relocated group was seen by the state and the state-controlled press as part of 'a conspiracy organized by communists' that aimed to distort the achievements of the *infitah* and their housing became an obstacle to the promotion of Sadat's policies and to police attempts to crush protest against these policies.

The rhetorical strategies employed by the state were largely based in the appeal to the global. This appeal was manifested by the emphasis on modernity[3] and its objectification in material forms, rational planning, the importance of visual aspects and the tourists' gaze in representing Cairo, the separation of the home from the workplace, international investment, science, health, hygiene, green areas and clean environment, consumer goods and the importance of the productive agent in the construction of a modern national identity.[4] The global was strategically used to offer the people a 'Faustian bargain' (cf. Berman 1988) which forced the relocated group to pay a high price for Egypt's opportunity to be 'modernized'. Using force (police) and seduction (by appealing to the global and offering alternative housing), the project removed them from the centre of the city and deprived them of the benefits associated with the modern facilities and the new changes that promised prosperity for everyone. The group lost a major part of its economic and 'symbolic capital', to use Bourdieu's (1984) term, which was their central geographical location. Relocation destroyed most of the group's informal economy, altered their access to many cheap goods and services, and destroyed their social relationships and reordered their personal lives.

As previously mentioned, the group was divided into two parts, each relocated to a different neighbourhood away from the gaze of tourists and upper-class Egyptians. One part, the focus of this study, was moved to public housing (*masaakin*) units constructed for them in al-Zawiya al-Hamra in northern Cairo. The move into these units, which were labelled as 'modern', promised to improve the lives of the people and turn them into 'healthy modern productive citizens who will contribute in the construction of their mother country' (*al-Ahram*, 27 December 1979). The state's project assumed a transparent relationship between space and identity and totally ignored the role of social actors in transforming and resisting its policies and ideologies. Rather than creating a unified modern city, I argue that these policies created a more fragmented urban fabric and paved the ground for other competing collective identities. Religious identity in particular has successfully presented itself as a powerful alternative that can articulate the various antagonistic identities that are constructed in the relocation site.

Global discourses and local identities

Since Sadat started his open-door policy, Cairo has witnessed the introduction of new forms of communication,[5] more emphasis on international tourism, increasing importance of consumer goods, and a growing flow of ideas related to civil society, democracy and political participation. Theoretical developments in anthropology and cultural studies have demonstrated that these global processes are not producing one dominant culture but present a set of discourses and practices that are juxtaposed in complex ways in local contexts (Hall 1991a; 1993; Massey 1994; Lash and Urry 1994). Thus, contrary to the old conceptualization of the world as becoming a 'global village', local differences and identities are not destroyed but are being reinforced in many cases by global forces and processes (Hall 1991b; 1993; Ray 1993; Massey 1994).

With the growing connectedness between different parts of the globe and with the circulation of global discourses and images facilitated by new systems of communication, the Other is becoming more identified with the self in complex ways. The connectedness and tension between the self and the Other is crucial to understanding how identities are constructed and shift over time and how the Other is simultaneously desired and dreaded. One example can be found in how people in Cairo desire the global (in this case identified as the West) because it is organized, clean, rich and 'democratic' and at the same time they distrust it because it is associated with 'moral corruption', drugs and violence. The focus on the connectedness and tension with the Other is therefore a necessary step to theorize the different ways that the global is reshaping local identities and redrawing their boundaries. This focus will enable us to conceptualize local identifications not as static but as always in the process of formation and constructed of multiple discourses and as composed 'in and through ambivalence and desire' (Hall 1991b: 49).

'Globalization', however, should not be reduced to 'Americanization' as some authors tend to do (Hall 1991a; Hannerz and Lofgren 1994). While the 'American conception of the world' (Hall 1991a: 28) may be hegemonic in various contexts, people experience the influence of other 'globals'. People in al-Zawiya al-Hamra not only experience the American culture that is transmitted to them in movies starring Arnold Schwarzenegger but they also experience the global through oil-producing countries where their children and male relatives work as well as through the mixture of people who visit and work in Cairo from different Arab countries. For example, women use oil for their hair that comes from India via their sons who work in Kuwait and collect their wedding trousseau from clothes, sheets and blankets brought from Kuwait; others visit husbands in Saudi Arabia; and many have accumulated electrical appliances from Libya where husbands and sons work. Despite the fact that many of the consumer goods are produced in the West, their meanings are given to them by their users who live in al-Zawiya al-Hamra. For many, consumer goods are investments that can be exchanged for cash when needed. Several families use their refrigerators to cool water during the summer but turn them into closets during the winter to store household appliances. The global is also introducing new forms of identification between the subjects of its processes. People, for example, enjoy watching television, especially some of the global sports events such as the soccer World Cup. Young men and women follow these games very closely; they know the names of the Brazilian, German and Italian players. While watching these games, different identities compete for priority: they shift from supporting African and Arab teams to cheering for third world teams when they play against European teams (Brazil against Germany, for example). People, thus, do not experience the global as a coherent set of discourses and processes that are transmitted from the West to the rest of the world but experience fragments and contradictory pieces that are filtered through other centres and that do not necessarily present a unified 'conception of the world'. Therefore, 'the global', as an analytical concept, should be expanded to include a mixture of images, discourses and goods that are brought to people through various channels such as state-controlled media, commercial video tapes, audio tapes that are distributed by Islamic activists, and consumer goods brought to al-Zawiya al-Hamra by migrants to Arab countries.

It is also important to remember that, as a theoretical concept, 'the local' should not be confused, as Massey (1994) and Lash and Urry (1994) argue, with the concrete, the empirical or the authentic or a spatially bounded entity (Urry 1995). I use 'local' to mean 'acts of positing within particular contexts' (Tsing 1993: 31). People attach multiple meanings to their localities that vary from one context to another. Despite the fact that geographical space is used as a point of reference for several local identities in Cairo, these different contexts share a set of social relationships and identities that include those who are like us (local people) and exclude people who are not like us (outsiders). Thus, when people identify the relocated group as 'those from Bulaq', they are trying to exclude them from another collective identity that includes people who have been living in al-Zawiya and identify primarily with it. The relocated people still refer to themselves as 'people of Bulaq' despite the fact that they have been living in al-Zawiya for fifteen years. Many also still identify with their old villages and towns that they left more than fifty years ago. In short, there is not one 'local' but there are various 'locals' that are juxtaposed in complex ways with multiple 'globals'.

Old places, new identities

> Here in al-Zawiya, you do not find Pizza Hut and Kentucky Fried Chicken. Such places can never get any profit in areas like this. People are poor and the money they will pay for one meal in one of these restaurants will feed the whole family for a week if not more. (A male shop-owner who works in al-Zawiya but lives in another middle-class neighbourhood)

To understand the local identities that are in the process of formation in al-Zawiya al-Hamra, it is important to remember that state practices and discourses were based on what Foucault calls 'dividing practices' (Rabinow 1984: 8). The project started by separating and stigmatizing the targeted population as an expedient rationalization of policies that aim to modernize, normalize and reintegrate them within the larger community. Not only were the housing conditions attacked by state officials, but the people themselves were stigmatized and criticized. A 'scientific' social study conducted to determine the needs of the relocated group revealed, as stated by the Minister of Construction and New Communities, that the area of Bulaq in general and one of its neighbourhoods (al-Torgman) in particular have been shelters for *qiradatia* (street entertainers who perform with a baboon or monkey), female dancers, pedlars and drug dealers (*al-Ahram*, 27 December 1979: 3). The 'locals' were also represented as passive, unhealthy and isolated people who did not contribute to the construction of the mother-country and who had many social ills.[6] After resettlement, these publicized stereotypes fostered a general feeling of antagonism towards the newcomers. In addition to repeating the same words that were circulated in the media, residents of al-Zawiya added other stereotypes to describe this group such as *labat* (trouble-makers) and *shalaq* (insolent). Women, in particular, were singled out (as they were also singled out by the Minister who described them as dancers or *Ghawazi*); they were described as rude and vulgar, and were used in daily conversation as an analogy for bad manners.

These negative constructions of the relocated group are supported and perpetuated by the physical segregation of their housing (*masaakin*) from the rest of the community. Their public housing is clearly defined and separated from other projects and private houses (*ahali*). Public housing is characterized by a unified architectural design (the shape, the size of the buildings, as well as the colours of walls and windows), whereas private housing has more diversified patterns. This unity in design and shape sharply defines and differentiates public housing from private houses and makes it easier to maintain boundaries that separate the relocated from other groups. In short, neither the discourse of the state nor the shape and location of the housing project enhance the dialogical relationship between the relocated group and other groups in al-Zawiya. After fourteen or fifteen years of resettlement, the relocated group continues to be stigmatized and its interaction with the rest of the neighbourhood is restricted.

The identity of Bulaq With their stigmatization in the state discourse and by the residents of al-Zawiya, and with the hostility that faced them, the relocated population rediscovered their common history and identification with the same geographical area. While people used to live in Bulaq and identify strongly with their villages of origin, after relocation Bulaq became an anchor for the group's sense of belonging and took precedence over other identifications. The attachment to the old place is not single or one-dimensional and Bulaq is remembered and related to differently by gender and age groups. These differences are beyond the scope of this chapter but it is sufficient here to say that Bulaq is of great significance for most of the group in reimagining their communal feelings. Currently, their public housing is called after one of Bulaq's neighbourhoods (*masaakin al-Torgman*) and people express their strong attachment to their old place in songs and daily conversations. Despite the fact that relocation reordered relationships within the group and destroyed a major part of their support system, the old neighbourhood still structures parts of the people's current interaction. They still refer to the people who used to live in Bulaq as '*min 'andina*' (from our place) which not only creates a common ground for identification but also indicates certain expectations and mutual obligations between the people in the current area of residence. At the same time, Bulaq is the point of reference for their identification with those who still live in parts of Bulaq[7] and those who moved to 'Ain Shams.

Through relocation, the group lost, among other things, a major part of its 'symbolic capital'. This is mainly manifested in two important aspects related to group members' identification with the old location. First, they used to live next to an upper-class neighbourhood, Zamalek. Young men and women, as emphasized by the people themselves and documented in an famous old movie (*A Bride from Bulaq*), could even claim that they were from Zamalek because only 'a bridge' separated (or connected) the two neighbourhoods. People also lost the pleasure and satisfaction associated with looking at the beautiful buildings and knowing that people of Zamalek – and much to their shame, as described by one informant – used to see Bulaq with its old and shabby houses.

Second, the group used to live in an 'authentic popular' or *baladi* area and perceives its relocation in al-Zawiya as moving down the social ladder. In Bulaq, the 'authentic popular' quarter, people used to live next to each other, separated only by narrow lanes that allowed close interaction and strong relationships. They remember the old place in the way people used to cooperate and 'eat together'. Their rootedness in the same place over a long period of time provided people with a strong support system, open social relationships, and a sense of security and trust. In contrast, al-Zawiya is a relatively new neighbourhood. It was mainly agricultural fields until the 1960s, when the area started to expand rapidly with the state construction of the first public housing project. This project housed families from different parts of Cairo who could not afford to live in more central locations. Immigrants (mostly Muslims) also came to al-Zawiya from different parts of the countryside and many live in private housing. The heterogeneity of its population is used by its residents, especially members of the relocated group, and people around them to indicate that al-Zawiya is not 'an authentic popular quarter'. Its people are 'selfish', 'sneaky' and 'untrustworthy'. It is seen as located between *baladi*[8] and *raqqi* (upper-class areas) which places it, as described by a male informant, in a tedious or annoying (*baaykh*) position. Al-Zawiya, thus, is geographically and socially marginal compared to Bulaq.

A key word in understanding the differences between what is seen as an 'authentic' neighbourhood such as Bulaq and 'less authentic' newer neighbourhoods such as al-Zawiya is *lama*. This word refers to the growing mixture and gathering of people from different backgrounds who live in the same locality. People from various quarters, villages and religions are coming to live in the same neighbourhood, hang out at the same coffee shop, visit the same market, and ride the same bus. These spaces are defined as *lamin* as compared to a more homogeneous or less *lama* places such as the village and the 'authentic popular' quarter based on long established relationships. Being rooted in a certain area, that is, localized in a particular place, allows the development of strong relationships between people. *Lama* is used to classify different localities and points to the difference between a neighbourhood where people know each other by name and face as opposed to more heterogeneous areas where people are strangers and not to be trusted. *Masaakin* is *lama* as opposed to *ahali* housing. Al-Zawiya is *lama* compared to Bulaq and Cairo is *lama* compared to the villages where the inhabitants originally came from.

Relocation and religious identity

> Hegemony is not the disappearance or destruction of difference. It is the construction of a collective will through difference. It is the articulation of differences which do not disappear. (Hall 1991b: 58)

Despite the significance of Bulaq in how people reimagine their communal feelings, this identity does not facilitate the group's interaction with the rest of the people who live in al-Zawiya al-Hamra. Relocation rearranged local identities and added to the old identifications: people are now identified with a village (the place of origin), as locals of Bulaq (where they resided for generations), as occupiers of *masaakin* (which is stigmatized by dwellers in private housing) and as inhabitants of al-Zawiya al-Hamra (not known for its good reputation in Cairo). But above all, they are mainly Muslims. Religion, rather than nationalism, neighbourhood and the village of origin, became a powerful discourse in articulating and socially grounding the various identities of the different groups residing in al-Zawiya al-Hamra.[9] Only the religious identity promises to articulate these identifications without destroying them.[10] Displaced families, *ahali* and *masaakin* inhabitants, people of Bulaq and al-Zawiya, rural immigrants, *Fallahin* (peasants who come from villages in Lower Egypt) and *Sa'idis* (immigrants from Upper Egypt), who are largely pushed from their villages to Cairo in their search for work and a better life, as well as residents who moved from other areas of Cairo can all find commonality in religion that is expressed in practices such as a dress code and the decoration of houses and shops.

Islam brings people together on the basis of a common religion. Despite the fact that Muslims do not know each other on a personal basis, religion creates a 'safe' space (the mosque), a common ground where they are connected to each other, and a sense of trust and rootedness. This is clearly manifested in how the mosque, of all public spaces, is gaining importance in facilitating the interaction of various groups and the formation of a collective identity. To start with, the mosque's growing centrality in daily life is manifested in the many modern services that are provided to the people in it. Through charitable organizations (*jam'iyyat khayriyya*), the mosque provides socially required services such as affordable education, health care and financial support to the poor. It is also the place where discourses circulate that prescribe and/ or forbid daily practices. Above all, it is the most acceptable and safest social space where various groups can meet and interact.

To understand the importance of the mosque, we need to go back to the word *lama*. As previously mentioned, people tend to distrust areas and public spaces that are labelled as *lama* such as the market, the coffee shop and the bus. These spaces are seen as 'dangerous' and people are very careful when visiting or utilizing them. Compared to such spaces, the mosque, which is a historical space that is legitimated through its naturalized relationship with religion, is currently being actively articulated to frame the interaction between members of different groups as well as to empower emerging meanings, identities and relationships. Those who are labelled as trouble-makers and rude (people who come from Bulaq and live in *masaakin*) as well as the untrustworthy and selfish (people of al-Zawiya as described by people of Bulaq) can all meet in the mosque and collectively identify themselves as Muslims.

Thus, the power of the mosque is being currently reinforced through its promise of an equal and unified community out of a heterogeneous urban population. It is accessible to all Muslims and brings them in on equal terms. The unity of prayers and the importance of communal feelings is manifested in the unifying discourse and the similar movements that are performed simultaneously. The Imam leads the prayer and coordinates the movement of all the attendees through his pronounced signals that indicate when one should bend forward on the knees or stand up straight, and so on. Emphasis is placed upon standing in straight lines, very close to other attendees, in a way that leaves no empty spaces through which the devil could enter among the devout and divide their collectivity.[11]

The feelings that are associated with being part of a collectivity were cited by many, especially by women, as one of the main reasons for going to the mosque. As is the case with most of her neighbours, relocation shattered most of the support system that connected the fifty-five-year-old Umm Ahmed with friends and neighbours who were relocated to 'Ain Shams or to different parts of the new housing project in al-Zawiya al-Hamra. Although she used to perform her religious duties on a regular basis in Bulaq, Umm Ahmed's religiosity gained a different meaning in al-Zawiya al-Hamra. In addition to her adoption of the *khimar* (a head garment that covers the hair and the shoulders), which is seen as the 'real Islamic dress', Umm Ahmed began attending local mosques on a daily basis. She explained that she goes to mosques because the presence of other people strengthens her will and provides her with more energy than when praying alone. Currently, Umm Ahmed frequents five local mosques to perform four out of the five daily prayers. For Friday prayer, she usually selects a large mosque, located within the boundaries of the *masaakin* but that is also attended by some worshippers from the *ahali*. She also visits two small mosques that are identified with an Islamic group active in al-Zawiya al-Hamra. She attends these two mosques, which are located in the *ahali* area, to listen to weekly lessons and participate in Qur'ān recital sessions. Another mosque, which is located next to the vegetable market in the *ahali* area, is a convenient site for the midday prayer when Umm Ahmed is shopping for the family's daily food. For the evening prayer, she chooses a smaller mosque on the edge of the housing project that is attended by a mixture of worshippers from *ahali* and *masaakin* areas. She prefers this mosque, as she explains, because she meets 'wise' women who like to talk to her. Over the last five years, Umm Ahmed has formed strong relationships with other women from different parts of the neighbourhood, especially from the *ahali* area, who attend the same mosque. If one of them does not come to the evening prayer, she goes with other women to ask about their absent friend. At the same time, the mosque not only brings people together from the same neighbourhood but also encourages people to move from one part of the city to the other. Young men and women, for example, use the city bus to tour the city in their search for the 'truth'. They cross the boundaries of their localities to go to other neighbourhoods to attend certain mosques where popular sheikhs preach.

The mosque is also becoming more open to women in al-Zawiya al-Hamra. This is perceived by some Islamic activists as essential to counter other spaces that are open to women, such as universities, the workplace, cinemas and nightclubs. Women are identified by men as more vulnerable to the influence of global (defined here as American) discourses and practices. Women's actions, dress and access to public life are seen as threatening the harmony of the Islamic community and as the source of many social ills. Women have internalized these ideas and hold themselves, and not men, responsible for the safety of the morals of the community. As women repeatedly emphasize, men are weak creatures and cannot resist the seduction imposed on them by women who do not adopt Islamic dress. At the same time, women can be very active in the construction of the Islamic community. More voices have emphasized the positive aspects associated with opening the mosque to women who, as mothers, sisters and wives, can be active agents capable of altering their own practices as well as shaping the actions and values of other family members. Thus, to contain the destructive potential of women and promote their constructive power in the formation of the Islamic community, more attempts are made by Islamic activists to incorporate women within the mosque. Currently, women, especially those without jobs and small children, go to the mosque on a regular basis for prayer and to attend weekly lessons, while working women usually attend the Friday prayer. Women are also becoming more active in the mosque through their roles as teachers, students, workers and seekers of social, educational and medical services. In addition, more women help in taking care of the mosque and participate in mosque-related activities such as preparing food and distributing it to the needy.[12]

Globalization and religious identities

It is important not to confuse my previous discussion of religious identity with 'fundamentalism', 'extremism' or 'militant Islam', which have been the centre of attention of several studies (Ibrahim 1982; Kepel 1993). Fundamentalism especially has been the focus of studies that aim to examine the relationship between globalization and religion (see, for example, Turner 1994; Beyer 1994). Such studies limit discussion of the ideology of the leaders of some radical Islamic groups and tend to present these movements as 'responses' or 'reactions' to the global. The role of ordinary people as active agents in negotiating religious and global discourses in their daily life and the formation of their local identities is largely neglected.

Despite the fact that communal feelings based on religion can be politicized and used as the basis to mobilize the working class (as happened in 1981 in clashes between Muslims and Christians in al-Zawiya al-Hamra), at the daily level religious identity brings people together as connected selves rather than separated and isolated others. It articulates the presence of the group at the neighbourhood level, integrates its members into the mosque and secures a space for them in Cairo. People do not want to relive the past, as some fundamentalists seem to desire, but try to live in the present with its complexity and contradictions. They hence struggle against efforts of some extremist groups who try to impose restrictions on how they appropriate certain aspects of modernity. Nuha, for example, is a twenty-three-year-old woman with a high school diploma who works in a factory outside the neighbourhood. She hears things on the radio, in the mosque and from her friends and then lets her heart and mind judge what she will follow. She expresses her religiosity in adopting the *khimar*. At the same time, she opposes many of the restrictions that extremists try to impose on people, such as forbidding men from wearing trousers and prohibiting eating with a spoon because, as some argue, the Prophet did not do these things. She believes that had these things existed when the Prophet was alive, he would have used them. So it is not a sin (*haram*) to eat with a spoon but, if one chooses to eat with the hands, one will get an extra reward.

There are moments when people directly reject the 'American conception of the world' (Hall 1991a: 28) with its homogenizing tendencies and use this conception to explain the conflict between the state and some Islamic groups. A young woman explained the conflict between the government and religious groups as follows:

> The problem is that the government has strong relationships with the United States which hates Islam and Muslims and is trying to spread its ideas and practices all over the world, especially wearing short clothes, the domination of science, and the destruction of religion. My cousin, who is a Sunni,[13] explained to me that Americans have many methods to achieve their purposes, especially through schools. They try to prove that science is better than religion by using the comparative method. They bring, for example, a candle and a light bulb and ask which is better. The first represents religion and the second represents science. Of course, one will choose the second. They also compare two pictures, one of a man wearing a *gallabiyya* [a long loose gown that the Prophet used to wear] with a beard and a rotten look, while the second picture is of a handsome man who is shaved and looks very clean and tidy. Of course, anyone will choose the second. The whole idea is for science to replace religion and dominate the universe. Islam is compatible with science because one can find all answers in it if examined closely. Science should serve religion.

The opposition to the 'global West', however, is not sufficient to explain the growing importance of the mosque and religious identity in al-Zawiya al-Hamra. There are complex local and national forces juxtaposed with the global to produce religious identity. State oppression, the daily frustrations in dealing with state bureaucracy, alienation, the fragmentation of the urban fabric, and the ability of Islamic groups to utilize various discursive strategies that mobilize people are as important as the economic frustration, the unfulfilled expectations and desires, and the need to have a voice in the global in understanding why religious identity is becoming more hegemonic.[14]

As manifested in the services that are being attached to the mosque in al-Zawiya al-Hamra, certain global discourses and consumer goods are negotiated and appropriated. For example, to avoid state censorship of discourses circulated in the mosque, Islamic activists use cassette tapes to distribute the religious discourse to a large segment of the urban population. Especially for illiterate men and women, tapes provide a powerful means of communication that brings popular preachers (that is, those who are believed to tell the 'truth') from the mosque into the home, the workplace, the taxi and the street. These can be replayed until their meanings become clear to the listener. Women can also pass them on to friends and relatives. On several occasions, women gathered to listen to such tapes and expressed strong emotional reactions to the descriptions of death, the horrible torture of the grave and the soothing visions of heaven.

Various Islamic groups, however, relate differently to the global in general and the West in particular. While there were some Islamic activists who attack the influence of the West on the dress code and practices of Muslims, a major part of the lessons that I attended in the mosque as well as tapes I heard in al-Zawiya al-Hamra did not attack the West but emphasized the horrible nature of torture that unbelievers would go through in the grave and in hell, and, in contrast, the rewards that are awaiting the believers in heaven. Women who do not adopt Islamic dress are singled out and detailed descriptions are presented of how they will be hung from their hair and breasts while huge snakes bite their bodies as they are grilled in hell. Women shivered, cried and prayed hard asking God to protect them from the horrible torture that is awaiting unbelievers. These graphic descriptions contextualize the critique of people's 'un-Islamic' practices and the 'medicine', as one sheikh said, that is provided to heal the ills of the current situation and to win the eternal heaven. The prescribed medicine is to go back to God, ask for his forgiveness, and live according to his commands.

Although the emphasis on the dress code can be seen as a rejection of the influence of the West, I would argue that gender distinctions are the centre of the restrictions applied to women's dress code. Another interesting example could be found in how people negotiate their definition of Islam and modernity. Their rejection of many of the ideas that are circulated by some religious extremists is clearly manifested by the struggle over some consumer goods such as colour televisions, VCRs and tape-recorders which are rapidly becoming signs of distinction. Many families participate in saving associations (*gam'iyyat*) to secure money to buy these goods which are also seen as investments that can be easily exchanged for needed cash. Just as Amal, most people dream of consumer goods and better living conditions that television brings to their homes without objective means to satisfy them. Many families try to solve Ramadan puzzles (these are usually presented daily by popular Egyptian performers) and collect the covers of tea-bags and chocolate bars to mail to the manufacturer in the hope that they may win a 'dish', a familiar English word that is used to refer to the satellite dishes that are spreading in upper-class neighbourhoods, a VCR, a washing machine or a gas stove. Among all the consumer goods that people use, Islamic groups centre their struggle against the television set. This struggle can be interpreted as 'rejection of modernity', but such an analysis fails to see how other aspects of modernity are being selectively incorporated in the struggle of these groups. They use the fax machine, the tape-recorder, the computer and many other modern facilities to achieve their aims. To understand the struggle over the television set, one should look how this medium is being used in people's daily lives.

Television is one of the most popular goods that people incorporate as one of the basic elements of their daily lives. Except for very few people with extreme religious beliefs, there is no housing unit in al-Zawiya al-Hamra without a television set. Each family, regardless of its income, owns a television set that is the centre of attention of all the family members. The television set is a powerful medium that conveys to them many experiences and values that can be described as global and brings the Other closer than ever to the self. The television set and the mosque are competing with each other to connect Muslims in different parts of the world. People of al-Zawiya al-Hamra are connected with other Muslims whom they have never met and who are not assumed to be identical duplicates of the self but are identified as the Other that is closely connected with the self. It is the force that binds people of this neighbourhood with Muslims who fight in Bosnia, Afghanistan and Chechnya. Young men, who are frustrated with the state's restriction on their participation in fighting with the Bosnian Muslims, circulate stories about God's help and support of the Bosnians. People talk about invisible soldiers (angels) and unidentified white planes that bomb the Serbs. Islam, thus, is becoming a force in localizing the global and globalizing the local. The distinction between Muslims who live in al-Zawiya al-Hamra and those who live in the rest of the world (such as the Bosnians) is blurred. On the other hand, television is blamed by Islamic groups for corrupting the people, silencing them, and distracting their attention from God as well as from what happens in their country and the rest of the world. With the total state control of this powerful medium, various Islamic groups do not have any option but to denounce its role in society and try to forbid it.

People are capable of articulating different discourses within their religious identity without seeing contradictions in being oriented to the global and attempting to enjoy what it offers, and being rooted in their religious and local identities. A twenty-year-old factory worker, who was born in Bulaq and was relocated with his family in 1980, dreams of having enough money to buy a villa in Switzerland for skiing during the winter, another villa in India where he will hire singers and dancers to perform for him as he has seen on video tapes, and of a palace in Saudi Arabia to facilitate his performing of pilgrimage every year. As Hall (1991a; 1993) emphasizes, with identity there are no guarantees. The openness and fluidity of identities and the multiple discourses that are competing to shape them make it hard to guarantee whether an identity is going to be inclusive or exclusive.[15]

Conclusion

> Paradoxically in our world, marginality has become a powerful space. It is a space of weak power but it is a space of power, nonetheless. (Hall 1991a: 34)

I have tried to show in this chapter how the articulation of global discourses and processes is producing contradictory identities at the national and local levels. By destroying old neighbourhood relationships, stigmatizing and physically segregating the relocated population, the project that aimed to construct modern subjects has paradoxically produced antagonistic local identities that empowered the basis of a collective identity which is based on religion. I have also aimed to show the important role of active social agents in mediating the different global practices and selectively articulating certain global discourses in the formation of their local identities. Social agents face the global in collectivities rather than as individuals and the struggle between the local and the global is not simply taking place in 'human minds' (Goonatilake 1995: 232). In general, although 'new regimes of accumulation' (Hall 1991a: 30) are appealing to the individual, alienation, racism and uprootedness are being faced collectively. In fact, being part of a collectivity is necessary to feel at home in the modern world with its rapid global changes. Thus, the local is not passive and local cultural identities are not waiting to be wiped out by globalization as some authors suggest (see, for example, Goonatilake 1995).

Amal's dreams should continue to remind us that people experience the global in structured ways. It should also draw our attention to the fact that many of the writings on globalization are conducted by people who feel at home in the global and tend to celebrate the growing efficiency of transportation, electronic communication and the growing connectedness of the globe (see, for example, Friedland and Boden 1994). The freedom of travel, however, while experienced by the privileged, is denied for millions of people who find borders of the global (especially, the USA and Europe) closed to them. The relationship between the local and the global cannot be brushed aside by assuming that they are 'articulated as one' (Friedland and Boden 1994: 43). Such statements reduce the complexity of the interaction between the global and the local and ignore the asymmetrical relationship that is still central to this interaction. The analysis presented in this chapter points to the need for more attention and sensitivity to the structured nature of globalization processes. When people experience the global as a violent attack on their cultural identities and self-images, it is not strange that they do not embrace global discourses and its representatives (such as international tourists). In short, more attention should be devoted to those who live on the margin of the marginal: those who are displaced in their own 'culture' and the millions who cannot find solutions to the growing number of desires that are brought by the global except through magical means, death and destruction or religion that at least promises them a better life and the glories of eternal existence in Paradise.

Notes

I would like to express my appreciation to the Middle East Awards Program in Population and Development, the Wenner-Gren Foundation for Anthropological Research, Inc. and the International Office at the University of Texas at Austin for funding my field work in Cairo. I am also thankful to Benjamin Feinberg, Karen Buckley, Seteney Shami and the editors of this book for their comments on a draft of this chapter.

1. The *birshaam* is a type of drug that is believed to be produced and circulated by the USA and Israel; it is a pill that is taken orally and not sniffed as Amal implies.
2. This phrase should not be taken to mean that the globalization and modernization of Cairo started with Sadat's policies (for a detailed description of Cairo's history, see Abu-Lughod 1971). Modernity, however, became a national project for Sadat and his policies were based on a strong orientation to the rest of the 'universe'. The experiences of many Western countries from the United States and Canada to France and West Germany continue to inform the construction of Cairo.
3. Words such as *hadith* (modern or new), *'asri* (contemporary or modern) and *madani* (civilized or refined) were widely used in the state public discourse.
4. Fifteen years after relocation, no hotels or luxury buildings have been constructed in this area. Many argue that the plan to rebuild the city centre died with

Sadat who was killed a few months after the relocation of the residents of a small part of Bulaq. The piece of land that was evacuated is currently used as a parking lot.

5. For example, one can now watch CNN in Cairo if supplied with cable services, and satellite dishes are added to the roofs of upper-class residential units.

6. See Mitchell (1988) for an analysis of such constructions under the British colonization of Egypt.

7. As previously mentioned, with the death of Sadat, the removal of the rest of Bulaq stopped.

8. *Baladi* is a complex concept that signifies a sense of authenticity and originality. It has been discussed in several studies. See, for example, Early (1993) and Messiri (1978).

9. Although people strongly identify themselves as Egyptians, the state definition of 'modern' Egyptians is exclusive. Different groups are not seen as contributing positively to the construction of their country and the state believes that its task is to cure them of their social ills and pathologies in order to turn them into 'good Egyptian citizens' (Ghannam 1993).

10. Let us not forget that Sadat tried to present himself as *al-Ra'is al-Mu'min* or 'The Believing President'.

11. In the women's section, which I had access to, the Friday prayer was coordinated by a woman who made sure that we were standing correctly and made room to squeeze in newcomers.

12. Despite the incorporation of women, the mosque is still a highly gendered space. It manifest and shapes the ways in which gender is constructed. Inside the mosque, women are spatially separated from men, their access to the mosque is conditioned by the absence of their menstrual period, and within its confines they are required to wear long and loose dress and to cover the hair and chest.

13. Al-Sunniyyin (singular Sunni) is used in daily life to refer to Islamic activists who are considered strict followers of the Prophet's traditions or Sunna.

14. It is important to remember that, although these processes take place at the neighbourhood level, they are part of the transformations that Cairo and Egypt in general have been experiencing in the last two decades.

15. The relationship between Muslims and Christians, for example, in al-Zawiya al-Hamra is very complicated and beyond the scope of this chapter. Religion also plays a central role among Christians who live in al-Zawiya. The church serves a similar role to that of the mosque in bringing Christians together. There is also a strong tension between the two religious groups that resulted in clashes between them in 1981.

References

Abd El-Razaq, H. (1979) *Egypt During the 18th and 19th of January: A Political Documentary Study* (in Arabic). Dar al-Kalima, Beirut.

Abu-Lughod, J. (1971) *Cairo: 1001 Years of the City of Victorious*. Princeton University Press, Princeton, NJ.

Berman, M. (1988) *All That is Solid Melts into Air: The Experience of Modernity*. Penguin Books, New York.

Beyer, P. (1994) *Religion and Globalization*. Sage, London.

Bourdieu, P. (1979) *Algeria 1960*. Cambridge University Press, Cambridge.

— (1989) *Distinction: A Social Critique of the Judgement of Taste*, trans. R. Nice. Routledge, London.

Early, E. A. (1993) *Baladi Women of Cairo: Playing with an Egg and a Stone*. Lynne Rienner, Boulder, CO and London.
Friedland, R. and Boden, D. (eds) (1994) *NowHere: Space, Time and Modernity*. University of California Press, Berkeley.
Ghannam, F. (1993) 'Urban Planning and the "Imagined Community": Relocation and the Creation of Modern Subjects'. Paper presented at the workshop on 'Social Problems in Urban Planning of Modern Middle Eastern and North African Cities', The American University of Beirut, 21–24 September.
Goonatilake, S. (1995) 'The Self Wandering between Cultural Localization and Globalization', in J. Nederveen Pieterse and B. Parekh (eds), *The Decolonization of Imagination: Culture, Knowledge and Power*. Zed Books, London.
Hall, S. (1991a) 'The Local and the Global: Globalization and Ethnicity', in A. D. King (ed.), *Culture, Globalization and the World-System*. SUNY, Binghampton.
— (1991b) 'Old and New Identities, Old and New Ethnicities', in A. D. King (ed.), *Culture, Globalization and the World-System*. SUNY, Binghampton.
— 1993 'Culture, Community, Nation', *Cultural Studies* 7 (3), 349–63.
Hannerz, U. and Lofgren, O. (1994) 'The Nation in the Global Village', *Cultural Studies* 8 (2), 198–207.
Harvey, D. (1990) *The Condition of Postmodernity*. Basil Blackwell, Cambridge.
Ibrahim, S. E. (1982) 'Islamic Militancy as a Social Movement: The Case of Two Groups in Egypt', in A. E. Hillal Dessouki (ed.), *Islamic Resurgence in the Arab World*. Praeger Special Studies, Praeger, New York.
— (1987) 'Cairo: A Sociological Profile', in S. Nasr and T. Hanf (eds), *Urban Crisis and Social Movements*. The Europo-Arab Social Research Group, Beirut.
Ikram, K. (1980) *Egypt: Economic Management in a Period of Transition*. Johns Hopkins University Press, Baltimore and London.
Kepel, G. (1993) *Muslim Extremism in Egypt: The Prophet and Pharaoh*. University of California Press, Berkeley.
Lash, S. and Urry, J. (1994) *Economics of Signs and Space*. Sage, London.
Massey, D. (1994) *Space, Place, and Gender*. University of Minnesota Press, Minneapolis.
Messiri, S. el, (1978) *Ibn al-Balad: A Concept of Egyptian Identity*. E. J. Brill, Leiden.
Mitchell, T. (1988) *Colonising Egypt*. The American University in Cairo, Cairo.
Rabinow, P. (1984) *The Foucault Reader*. Pantheon, New York.
Rageh, A. Z. (1984) 'The Changing Pattern of Housing in Cairo', in *The Expanding Metropolis: Coping with the Urban Growth of Cairo*. The Agha Khan Award for Architecture.
Ray, L. J. (1993) *Rethinking Critical Theory: Emancipation in the Age of Global Social Movements*. Sage, London.
Rugh, A. (1979) *Coping with Poverty in a Cairo Community*. Cairo Papers on Social Science. The American University in Cairo, Cairo.
Sadat, A. el- (1978) *In Search of Identity*. Collins, London.
— (1981) *The Basic Relationships of the Human Being: His Relationships with God, Himself, Others, the Universe, and Objects* (in Arabic). General Agency for Information, Cairo.
Tsing, A. L. (1993) *In the Realm of the Diamond Queen: Marginality in an Out-of-the-way Place*. Princeton University Press, Princeton, NJ.
Turner, B. S. (1994) *Orientalism, Postmodernism and Globalism*. Routledge, London and New York.
Urry, J. (1995) *Consuming Places*. Routledge, London and New York.

9

Formation of a middle-class ethos and its quotidian: revitalizing Islam in urban Turkey

Ayşe Saktanber

Religious revivalism in general, and Islamic revivalism in particular, are often construed as a major example of fragmentation and localization, the inferred opposites of the term globalization. Since Islamic ideologies and movements have universalistic claims, it is difficult to see why the challenge of Islamic activists to the secular ethics of modernity and Western modes of life is assessed as a sign of localism, without examining the basic premises of the term globalization itself.

The term globalization denotes a phenomenal situation of increasing concomitance and synchronization in human affairs in terms of access for *all* to the flow of both specialized and general information, sources of image production, or similar market opportunities. It thus provides a kind of 'master metaphor' in Silber's sense of the term, by 'actually playing a central role in the shaping and controlling of sociological theory and research' (Silber 1995: 324). The peculiarity of the term globalization as a metaphor resides in its ability to offer both a spatial and an orientational image, unlike many of the others which Silber refers to as spatial metaphors used in contemporary sociological theory (Silber 1995: 327).[1] The overall social process labelled globalization, driven by what Castells and Henderson (1987) term 'techno-economic' developments, claims to influence, by its very nature, all forms of human existence without bearing any sort of exclusionary assertion. This can be contrasted with the concept of universalization, for instance, which brings in its wake socio-economic and political problems such as universalism vs particularism. Globalization is seen as immune to these kinds of dichotomic problems inasmuch as it is primarily conceived as the product of the development of high technology industries in general, and of the information technologies in particular. Because of the ability of these developments, especially those in electronic communications, both to penetrate spatially and to influence different social processes and life areas, the possibility of linking the local to larger structures and processes (that is, the global), is seen as greater than ever before, often creating the false impression that this linkage is effortless. The historically cultivated mental background to this process is developed through a sense of one humanity, what Elias (1991) defines as the ultimate source of 'we-identity of I's'. Instead of perceiving the world as divided by the East/West or North/South axes, ranked into the first and third world societies, we have now the hope, through the term globalization, that we can abandon the common tendency to perceive the 'non-us' as the repository of our imagined opposites.

Yet the concept of globalization also implies its counterparts, in that the local stands for the 'Other' of the global. In this context, Islamic revivalism is presumed to be non-eclectic, particularistic, time-bound and memory-loaded, the opposites of which are seen as necessary conditions for the realization of a 'global culture'.[2] The challenge posed by Islamic activists to the secular ethics of modernity and Western modes of life is conceived as opposition to the linkages that the process of globalization offers, and is assessed as a sign of localism despite the universalistic assertions in Islamic ideologies and movements.

My own point of departure in the present chapter is the premise that any meaningful discussion of Islamic revivalism must be couched within a national-yet-globalizing context. Following Sivan (1992) I will posit that the revitalization of Islam in Turkey, as in many other parts of the Middle East and North Africa, should be interpreted as a response of civil society to the failures of the state. It is fair to say that this challenge to prevailing state practices could not have come into being without parallel changes in the understanding of human rights and civil society. The gradual disappearance of the once rigid boundaries between the private and public spheres, which took their most consolidated forms within the framework of the sovereign nation-state and its ways of organizing society, has changed the way in which people define their participation in these two spheres. These developments are bound with the emergence of new 'techno-economic' processes, which have not only entailed the restructuring of industrial production but have also, according to the nature of this restructuring in different societies, led to the emergence of new types of social belonging and identities. The restructuring and readjustment of social class characteristics, for instance, is one important aspect of this change in types of social belonging and identity. But the orientational imagery upon which people's aspirations to social mobility are based has not lost its vertical characteristics with the advent of globalization. The significance of globalization as a social process resides in increasing the possibility of infiltrating different *opportunity spaces* (Mardin 1980) hitherto monopolized by state elites and their practices. In this sense, Islamic revitalization is part of the ongoing globalizing processes which are primarily shaped within the context of the nation-state.

Below, I shall attempt to elucidate the ways in which Islamic revivalism in Turkey has found ways of expressing itself within the social structures of the nation-state, becoming increasingly visible in the national arena primarily as an urban phenomenon. Drawing upon information and insight gained from field experience in a Muslim urban complex in Ankara, I will discuss how the inhabitants have managed to adjust their 'life politics' (Giddens 1991: 215)[3] and social conditions of existence to 'live Islam' as 'conscious Muslims', in the capital city of the secular Republic of Turkey. In so doing, I hope to illuminate how this politically conscious effort to render Islam a living social practice is not merely based upon an image of isolated community, but upon a project of civilization, one that is quite different from that of secularists.

The new visibility of Islam as an urban phenomenon in Turkey

The new visibility of Islam as an urban phenomenon in Turkey since the 1980s represents the unfolding of two intertwined processes. On the one hand, it is part of a politically determined social effort towards the actualization of a middle-class ethos for an Islamic social order. On the other, it is a reflection of the new meanings attributed to the social sphere, so that what used to be defined as private has enlarged its boundaries to cover new areas of sociabilities, and hence has changed its content.

I believe that these processes can be read as an extension of two points of argument upon which this chapter is grounded. My first point derives from the practical implications of Emanual Sivan's (1992) interpretation. If we assume that (1) the revitalization of Islam in Turkey, as in other parts of the Middle East and North Africa, must be conceived as a response of civil society to the state's failures, aimed at 'recapturing the initiative and redrawing the boundaries between the two';[4] and also that (2) this mostly takes the form of a reaction to state practices exercised mainly by a state elite through which the '"presence" of the state has been assured in all walks of life'; then we can argue that in terms of its practical implications this means that an Islamic movement has to create its own intelligentsia capable of replacing the existing one. I would maintain that this also includes the need to create other social agents autonomous enough to be able to compete with the state both in the political and economic spheres as well as in the cultural, in order to build an Islamic social order.

In the Turkish context, the state elites who are, and were, assigned to safeguard the ideals of national civic culture have become the most important target group, and their professional abilities appear something to be attained by the Islamic circles. The civic culture of the present, however, is an extension of a lengthy institution-building process, through which the state has created what might be termed 'national civil religion', with its 'panoply of heroes, symbols, sacred places (monuments, historical sites), sacred times (holidays, memorial days), and founding myths' (Sivan 1992: 99). Therefore, to be able to detach themselves from the 'cultural hegemony of the state' in most areas of social behaviour, hence actualizing a moral transformation, Islamic circles in Turkey also need to create their own middle classes. As social agents, the middle classes can play a leading role in the production, dissemination and consolidation of new models of sociabilities. Indeed, it is only after the successful creation of a middle-class ethos and its quotidian that it becomes possible to conceive Islamic circles in Turkey as a social force capable of setting an alternative to the existing social order.

My second point of argument follows from the premise that the overall motive behind the revitalization of Islam centres upon one major question, that is, the question of moral transformation. If this is so, then it is necessary to ask why the gender identity of women functions as a signpost of moral transformation. Here, I will limit myself to highlighting only one aspect of this process, the vested role of women in organizing the inner spaces of social life, namely, the private sphere. This is the sphere wherein the very constitution of the republican social order once sought to confine religion, thereby making it a private concern. As Şerif Mardin (1989) argues, the revitalization of Islam we witness today has started to make itself visible through practices pertaining to the same sphere. This is not only because, as is often argued, Islam is a religion which tends to organize all aspects of social life including the private everyday life; it is also because, as Mardin once again points out, in the contemporary world the boundaries of the private have been expanded and gained new richness and variety, and thus 'religion has received a new uplift from that privatizing wave' (Mardin 1989: 229). So, as he argues, 'private religious instruction, Islamic fashion in clothes, manufacturing and music, Islamic learned journals, all of them aspects of "private" life, have made Islam pervasive in a modern sense in Turkish society, and have worked against religion becoming a private belief' (Mardin 1989: 229).

To the extent that it is the organization of the 'domestic' space, raising children as 'true' Muslims, and putting effort into expanding the meaning of the 'private' which render Islam a living social practice, women who are the main actors in this process have become crucial agents in the daily articulation and reproduction of Islamic ideologies. Thus women, who were once perceived as an adjunct to the more important issues of polity and social order, have now become the central focus of Islamic revitalization.

Following this line of thinking, it becomes apparent that the process termed 'revitalizing Islam' by the 'outsiders' corresponds, in the experience of so-called Islamist people, to a politically informed effort to render Islam a living practice. Any attempt to comprehend the parameters of lived Islam must therefore come to grips with the production of new models of Islamic sociability, both as a political strategy in the broader sense of the term, and also as the tactical extensions of everyday life strategies, which enable Muslim people to adjust to ongoing changes in a national-yet-globalizing context.

An urban complex of their own: a place to live Islam as 'conscious Muslims'

How do people organize their daily lives according to so-called Islamic precepts which advocate the superiority of an Islamic social order over all others? This was the basic question I had in mind when I began my field research at the beginning of the 1990s, at a time when the call to an Islamic way of life could finally be heard in the very heartland of the urban elite in Turkey.

The urban complex where I conducted my research is located in a densely populated out-district in the north-west of Ankara, the capital city of Turkey, some distance from the city centre. The area contains many of the socio-economic and cultural facilities typically associated with metropolitan life, but in a rather peripheral way. Urban planners in Turkey refer to this kind of development as 'apart-kondu', the analogy being drawn to 'gecekondu', unauthorized squatter houses, but indicating high-rise apartment blocks originally built without official licensing. Through retroactive planning and licensing, however, the area has become one of Ankara's highest-density residential districts, the inhabitants of which are mainly composed of lower- and lower-middle-class people.

The complex itself is actually a small part of this district in terms of population, but it is also one of the well-established and neatly constructed sites. It is composed of five high-rise apartment blocks with seventy flats in each block; one mosque; one small building formerly built for Qur'ān courses; ten dormitory-style flats for university and high school students (one for males and one for females in each block and usually designed to accommodate ten students in each), a large meeting room used for social occasions such as wedding ceremonies, seminars and so on in the basement of one block; one tea-house for men just near the mosque; one nursery school (occupying a flat, with an enrolment of nearly thirty children); one playground for small children; several open areas for the young; one supermarket (which became a multi-storeyed department store two years after I started this research and moved to just outside the complex); and finally some open places used for parking.

The inhabitants of the complex are identified by their neighbours as 'closed', 'religionist' or 'Islamist' people, and are recognizable through their appearance, which is in accordance with the orthodox Muslim codes of contemporary Turkish urban people: women with large headscarves covering their necks, shoulders and chests, and long loose overcoats in pale colours; men with moustaches and/or beards typical of religious Turkish men, and usually formal, simple suits with or without neckties. The residents of this urban complex are not the only people known for their religious reputation in this district. On the contrary, it is quite common to come across people who can be easily typed as religiously conservative among various other sorts of middle- and lower-middle-class people in the district. Nevertheless, since it is known that the inhabitants of this urban complex have rallied around a living space deliberately organized to live in accordance with Islamic codes, they are distinguished from other residents and provided with a virtual identity as members of an Islamic community. Thus, they are not simply identified as Muslims, but are conceived of as 'religionist' and/or 'Islamist', if not actually labelled as religious fanatics, reactionists or obscurantists. The same holds true for the inhabitants of the complex themselves who want to distinguish their own religious identity from that of other 'false', (that is, secular) Muslims by calling themselves, by and large, 'conscious Muslims'.

The inception of the complex dates back to the late 1960s when a group of people came together to establish a construction cooperative to create a living space which would allow them 'to live Islam' as 'conscious Muslims'. The group included the founding fathers of *Milli Görüş* (National Vision) which is a shorthand description of the politico-societal project of Professor Dr Necmettin Erbakan's Welfare Party;[5] some of the leading figures of the Zahid Kotku branch of the Nakşibendi order;

and also some followers of these two movements. Organized around this cooperative, the inhabitants extended their life space into various social organizations ranging from different *wakfs* to youth and women's associations. After coping with many economic and psycho-sociological difficulties, they finally managed to finish the whole complex in 1985. This place should not be thought of, however, as the domain of a closed community under the politico-religious leadership of one branch of Islam. On the contrary, it constitutes a living space in which highly conservative Sunni Muslim families with various political affiliations but similar world-views lead their lives. If I were to attempt to group them together into a single ideological category, they could perhaps best be described in terms of an ideological discourse whose major elements stem from an Islamic fundamentalist meta-narrative wherein the main authority for an Islamic move resides in the written scripture rather than in traditional practices (except for those social practices that took place in *Asr-ı Saadet*, the age of the Prophet Muhammad). These sources, however, can be open to *ictihad* (reinterpretation) in order to rebuild Islam as a 'distinct and integrated' system. The idea of progress is thus contained within this narrative, but in such a way that it dissociates itself from Western-oriented modernization inasmuch as an anti-imperialist voice of third-worldism carries the narrative.

During my ethno-sociological research in the complex, I conducted in-depth interviews with nearly 10 per cent of the families, organized several focus group interviews with men, women and the young separately, participated in several social and religious activities (such as *kandil* celebrations[6] at the largest mosque in Ankara), *tefsir* studies (studies on Qur'ānic commentaries), attended theatrical performances, wedding ceremonies, seminars, reception days of women and the like. Off and on for twenty-eight months, I mainly tried to capture the discursivity, the rhythm and the strategy-generating principles of a given quotidian, all of which set the dialogical boundaries of the making of an Islamic way of life. The imagining of an Islamic community, the gendering of the order of life, the construction of Muslim gender identities, the making of an Islamic way of life, becoming the 'Other', the development of strategies of containment and resistance and the future all appeared as the main topics under which the 'data' obtained could be arranged in an intelligible way. In all these occasions my very first conclusion was that the creation and realization of any sort of Islamic way of life would not be possible without the efforts of women.

What I have learned from this experience is that we cannot proceed with the analysis of Islamic revivalism without considering the dimension of faith. For in terms of such conventional sociological indicators as family type, level of education, income or professional status, the families I studied could easily be placed in the middle or lower-middle stratum of society. Most earned their living as civil servants, self-employed professionals, politicians, journalists and the like. What distinguished this particular group from others similarly placed in the middle ranks of society was 'faith' intermingled with what Bourdieu (1989) calls taste. Hence, without a discussion of how faith functions through the social practices which actually distinguish the group I studied, it is difficult to convey how and in what sense they form the potential middle classes of a yet to be established Islamic order.

Harnessing Islamic faith for an 'activist Utopianism' in a national-yet-globalized context

The common feature of recent analyses of Islamic revivalism is the assumption that Islam has a common stock of cultural knowledge in which the vocabulary of social dissatisfaction can be discerned. In other words, Islam has been thought of as something which functions as a common idiom for the deprived to express their social discontent. Although such an instrumentality, to a certain extent, may depict Islamic revivalism both in Turkey and in other parts of the Muslim world, it falls short of explaining why only some among those who experience similar conditions find Islam so meaningful to resort to as a source when expressing their discontent. To provide an answer to this question it would be helpful to remember the way in which James Piscatori (1986) defines revivalism. For Piscatori, if Anthony Wallace's (1956) explanation of '"revitalization movement" in terms of the severe stress felt by individuals who are dissatisfied with the prevailing social order and identity' (Piscatori 1986: 36) is true, then it also becomes true, to a large extent, to say that 'revival is a sum of individual unhappiness'. However, I agree with James Piscatori that 'to an even larger extent, revival is the sum of individual contentment' (Piscatori 1986: 36). This is because my own field work experiences are similar to the ones he had among many Egyptian, Indonesian and Malaysian Islamists. While asking them why they had become more devout than they had previously been, their answers neither relied on the social, economic or political dislocations that they had experienced, nor did they frame an answer in terms of emotional and psychological distress, regardless of whether they were highly educated professionals or just lay sympathizers.

As Piscatori also argues, 'there is no doubt that social, economic and political factors', as well as international developments, play important roles in the formation of Islamic revivalism and also in people's personal attachments to the movement. Likewise, there is no doubt that 'some Muslims use Islam to achieve their own narrow ambitions' (Piscatori 1986: 37). But the point I am trying to make here is that as a social phenomenon 'faith' deserves as much analytical attention as other sociological factors which make up the analysis of Islamic revivalism.

At this point, as do many who wish to describe the sociology of religion, I shall look at how Durkheim conceptualized the place of 'faith' in modern societies. In his article 'De la Définition des phénomènes religieux' (published in *L'Année sociologique* in 1899; see, Cladis 1992), contrary to assertions he had made in *Division of Labour*, he claimed that religion permeates modern societies. Although its beliefs and practices have changed, at least in Europe, its basic form has not: 'Collective beliefs and practices are still prevalent. The political, economic, and even scientific realms are infused with the religious. Individual rights, notions of economic fair play, and the spirit of free inquiry, for example, are fraught with the sacred' (Cladis 1992: 79).

For Cladis, this reversal of Durkheim does not spring from a radically new understanding of religion *per se* but from a new understanding of modern society. Durkheim's novel approach becomes evident, for instance, in 1899 when he noted: 'between science and religious faith there are intermediate beliefs; these are common beliefs of all kinds which are relevant to objects that are secular in appearance, such as the flag, one's country, some form of political organization, some hero, or some historical events etc.' According to Durkheim, then, many secular beliefs are 'indistinguishable from religious beliefs proper'. It was so because 'modern France, like traditional societies, has a common (even if "secular") faith: The mother country, the French Revolution, Joan of Arc etc. are for us sacred things which we do not willingly permit one to contest the moral superiority of democracy, the reality of progress, and the ideal of equality' (Cladis 1992: 79).

Therefore, as Cladis points out, for Durkheim, 'a common faith was no longer a unique attribute of traditional societies. Modern societies too were in need of, and were developing their own common faiths. Therefore, the relevant distinction between the two types of society now rested on the different contents of their faiths' (Cladis 1992: 79).

Of course, for Durkheim, the question of what constitutes the sources from which these faiths gain their legitimacy was not a valid question; the answer had already been given in his scheme of thought to the extent that in every case these sources should be construed as society, and moreover, as the *conscience collective* through which society permeates individuals. However, this question is particularly relevant for us since our problem is to show the peculiarity of the challenges that new Islamic revivalist movements pose to the secular ethics of modernity. What we need to understand is what gives these demands a religious character in general, and makes them Islamic in particular. It is not enough to observe that the secular ethics of modern societies are also based on the social distinctions drawn between the sacred and the profane, and that in their very structures of morality, there already exist places or junctions which allow religious ideologies to hook themselves up to dominant discourses of morality and thus to enter into the realm of the ordinary. Rather, what we must also see is the extent to which through the same channels they become rivals of the secular ethics of modernity in a national-yet-globalized context.

According to some observers, notably Wilfred Cantwell Smith, the peculiarity of the Islamic faith lies in its different attitude to the notion of belief. In his study *On Understanding Islam*, he argues that you can believe in the correctness of something according to the knowledge or information you have about it, or change your mind depending on the information you get. However, in Islam, 'faith is something that people do more than it is something that people have … it pertains to something that people are, or become' (W. C. Smith 1981: 122), So, the *mümin* (person of faith) is one who accepts, who says 'yes to God … recognizes the situation [God's command] as it is and commits himself to acting accordingly' (W. C. Smith 1981: 124, 126). That is why in Islam, in order to become a Muslim, you do not believe first but you witness. A Muslim is one who witnesses (*şehadet*) and not simply believes that 'there is no God but God, and Muhammad is the messenger of God'. Similarly, John Esposito also argues that, 'for Christianity the appropriate question is "What do Christians believe?" In contrast, for Islam (as for Judaism) the correct question is "What do Muslims do?"' (Esposito 1991: 69). Thus, 'faith places the Muslim on the straight path, acts demonstrate commitment, and faithfulness. In Islam the purpose of life is not simply to affirm but to actualize; not simply to profess belief in God but to realize God's will – to spread the message and law of Islam. Faith without works is empty' (Esposito 1991: 69–70).

I think this understanding of Islamic faith also reveals what so-called Islamist people claim when they say that they want 'to live Islam as conscious Muslims'. In my view they were somehow 'conscious' of the above structural characteristic of Islamic faith; or in other words theirs was an effort to harness Islam for what Al-Azmeh defines as 'activist utopianism', that is, becoming of eschatology and past example – Medinan regime and the prophetic example, which is also the recovery of Adamic order – a Utopia where legalism and moralism give way to political contestation (see, Al-Azmeh 1993: 95–8, for example). How

Islamic activists fill the content of this specific structure of faith and how they interpret it depends on the social and historical context in which they live; nevertheless, we can develop an appreciation of how this understanding of faith functions by examining several social practices which actually constitute distinctive features of the people who call themselves 'conscious Muslims' in my own study.

Making Islamic faith the distinguishing feature of a classification system to create an Islamic way of life

At this point I would suggest that what distinguishes the inhabitants of the urban complex I studied from others similarly situated in the middle or lower-middle stratum, and defines them as the potential middle classes of a yet to be established Islamic order, is 'faith'. Here, Islamic faith works in conjunction with what Bourdieu (1989: 175) calls taste, to inform the choices people make to differentiate their life-style from those similarly situated in social stratification categories. Thus, whether culturally given or newly implemented, or even deliberately avoided, the matrix of social activities in which the inhabitants of this urban complex participate defines the boundaries of an Islamic way of life and confirms Islamic solidarity. This sense of solidarity is also perpetuated by a specific emotional bonding, namely trust, which underpins the personal attachment of its members to this particular living space and allows them to cultivate a sense of security in carrying out daily life in accordance with Islamic precepts.

In a social context where religious affiliation is equated with backwardness, it becomes important for the inhabitants of the complex to show that they are not obscurantist, ignorant and stupid people who cannot comprehend the requirements of the contemporary world. On the contrary, they believe that Islam is not only a religion but also a way of life capable of meeting the needs of all times. The ultimate model for them is the *Asr-ı Saadet*, and they believe it is always possible to create such a life order by following the patterns set by the Prophet's behaviour as enshrined in the *Sünnet*, the norms of religious practice. By taking the behaviour pattern of the Prophet and his companions (especially the senior companions) as models, it is still possible to a certain extent to live Islam today in a secular order, that is, to carry out daily life according to the precepts of Islam. The use of *Hadis* (short narratives purporting to give information about what the Prophet said, did and approved) helps to put Islam into practice, above all in family life.

The creation and realization of any sort of Islamic way of life would not be possible without the efforts of women. In the discourse attributing different roles to men and women in the Islamic structuring of the social world, women are primarily depicted as mothers dedicated to raising and educating new generations of faithful Muslims ready to struggle for the progress of the Islamic community. This is indeed very similar to the responsibility vested in women both at the time of the Ottoman Reforms (since the *Tanzimat*) and under the Republic. But while Westernizing reformers expected women to educate the nation in the name of progress, Muslim women are to educate others to establish God's system on earth and to gain his mercy to live eternally in Heaven.

Moreover, a Muslim woman has to do this without compromising her religiosity. In other words, while living in a secular modern system, she has to reject the precepts of secular Western life since these are seen as incompatible with an Islamic way of life. This is not something which can be fully realized by men since, in order to earn their families' living, they generally have to cope with the requirements of an 'outside' world not organized according to Islamic principles.

In the realization of Islam in daily life, however, the two contesting world-views, Islam and modernity, cannot remain in their pure forms as they can at the ideological discursive level. 'Conscious Muslims' make great efforts to overcome this difficulty. I would suggest that these efforts, which should be considered as a praxis, can be formulated as follows: if modernity functions as an index in which the objective givens of social life are indicated, then Islamic thought serves as a lexicon from which the meanings of these objective givens can be discerned. Thus, the socio-behavioural strategy of 'conscious Muslims' is based on a rather simplistic belief that the more they can learn about that index, the more knowledge they can acquire to alter it. They disregard the fact that the index of modernity is also a product of a variety of ideologies that have flourished from within specific discursive formations and that these ideologies, like all other ideological discourses, are nothing but semantic 'systems of coding reality' (Veron 1971: 68). Thus coded, 'reality' as a lived experience cannot be separated from its ideological definitions, and so no exception can be made for modernity. From this vantage point, the extent to which Islamic ideologies can transform the index of modernity obviously depends on their ability to displace its referential context, norms and idioms.

In the life strategy of the inhabitants of this urban complex which I have outlined above, the aim was not to reject the comforts and opportunities of modern life but to question the moral price a Muslim should pay for their attainment. Otherwise, from home decoration to cooking, from women's indoor dress to ways of receiving guests, the basic framework of their life-style differed little from that of ordinary secular middle- or lower-middle-class families in urban Turkey. Similarly, the voluntary associations they established and the patterns of intellectual activities they engaged in duplicated the urban elite's modern intellectual life, as evidenced by the various charity meetings, seminars and conferences I attended and visited.[7]

They make no concessions, however, to women going out without a headscarf and loose-fitting overcoat or showing themselves to strange men (especially without a headscarf); to the use of interest; the drinking of alcohol; to dancing and gambling as well as other behaviour forbidden by their code. Most important, they strongly reject cultural rituals and celebrations borrowed from the Western Christian world, such as the celebration of New Year's Day, Mothers' Day, and Fathers' Day. This is worth noting because it provides further insight into the maxims of daily life in the urban complex. In so far as these 'rituals' are the signifying practices of a given culture, they define not only the rhythm and periodicity of a cultural life organized according to specific meaning systems, but also regulate culturally identified personal relations through certain types of mannerisms.

In constructing an Islamic way of life, the dangers of creating a cultural gap which could entice the young towards modern Western life-styles are well recognized and carefully avoided, especially by the women. As they are also apprehensive about being labelled as backward, narrow-minded or obscurantist, they try to revise socio-cultural patterns which register modernity in a way which would not violate basic Islamic rules.

They watch television, but selectively. They go to the cinema, but watch only 'religious' films. They may go to the seaside for holidays, but are careful to choose secluded places. They allow brides to wear white, modern, wedding-dresses but insist that their heads be covered. Important rituals such as weddings, circumcisions and women's henna evenings are rarely accompanied by dancing. Although they do celebrate anniversaries and their children's birthdays, they are careful to make them occasions for expressing thanks to God rather than just providing entertainment. Their aim is to protect the young as well as the whole family from being lured into the seductions of modern urban life. Thus, places are set up for young people to get together, segregated by sex of course. These meetings are organized to enable teenagers to improve their fund of religious learning while enjoying the company of their peers and good food. Young women meet to recite holy verses, to write and perform small parodies of Western, non-Islamic life-styles, and to sing hymns. Since men are frequently away from home, they do not have the opportunity to tutor their sons. This duty falls upon older brothers, who socialize boys into the ways of Islam by organizing small group discussions and quizzes on religious subjects as well as on history, literature and science. Mothers prepare the food and provide the encouragement and approval needed to create a warm and loving atmosphere in which such education can be imparted.

Apart from individual prayers and conventional worshipping practices, such as getting together for Friday prayers and *tefsir* studies, women develop various patterns of learning and actualizing Islam and Islamic ideologies. They read passages from the Qur'ān, or other religious books teaching tradition, during their home visits and/or reception days while having tea, discuss many practical questions regarding daily life and organize small groups to discuss specific issues such as masonic guilds, feminism and women's rights in Islam. They frequently organize seminars and panels to discuss the role of women in Islam or current political issues which affect their social position. These occasions make up the very inventive and dedicated activities whereby Islamic women create an intellectually active social milieu intended to facilitate the consolidation of an alternative Islamic life-style and to strengthen their faith in Islam.

Conclusion

As can be seen from these examples, the overall effort that the inhabitants of this urban complex put into leading their lives according to Islamic ideals not only renders Islam a living social practice, but also creates its ethics of quotidian. This is also designed to help Muslims to prepare themselves for the other world. For, above all, it is through this discourse of ethics that their 'ways of operating', 'walking, reading, producing, speaking etc.' are defined, in the sense M. de Certeau (1984: 30) proposes. These ethics constantly remind them that they should dedicate themselves to the creation of an Islamic world in which to realize the will of God in this mortal life, in order to deserve eternal life in Heaven. Thus justified, a social practice termed 'revitalizing Islam' by the 'outsiders' is just perceived as 'living Islam' by them. This can be summed up in one frequently repeated expression: 'What we all do is strive for the mercy of God.' And God responds to this striving by declaring in his book that he will reward them in Heaven. It is this specific dialogical relation, I would argue, which cultivates a sense of reciprocity and urges them to actualize Islamic ideals in deed and thought with confidence. And it is this omnipresence of an 'Islamic God' which distinguishes their ways of attachment to social life from others of similar social status and class.

Yet, for the same Islamic circles, the strategies which provide direction in actualizing the model for an Islamic way of life presumed to have flourished in the *Asr-ı Saadet* are not merely based on an image of isolated community. On the contrary, the peculiarity of imagining an Islamic community also comes from the meaning of community in Islam, which is not a small-scale refuge but the *ümmet*, the single universal Islamic community embracing all the lands in which Muslim rule is established and where Islamic law prevails (see, for example, Lewis 1991: 32). It is possible to think of *ümmet* as a representational image, but what we need to understand, as de Certeau (1984) asks, is how the representation of an image is *used* by the people who are not the original *makers* of it. This brings us to the concept of 'ways of operating', tactical extensions of the strategies of everyday life which I have tried to outline throughout this chapter. It is only through the actualization of these strategies of containment and resistance, that the adjustment of this group of Muslim people to the ongoing structures of national-yet-globalizing Turkish society becomes possible. What makes their praxis local is not simply their way of life but the ways in which they construct their project of civilization. This is an understanding of civilization that is quite different from that of the secularists who see modern civilization as the common property of humanity, since, for the former, in spite of its universal assertions, civilization is something which has to be defined in Islamic terms and originally belonged to Muslims. This is why, perhaps, the music of Cat Stevens did not mean anything to Islamic youth in Turkey until he converted to Islam and became Yusuf Islam. This might also be why some young Muslim women formed NGOs for the first time to participate in the Fourth World Women's Conference in 1995 in China, not to defend gender equality as such, but to support the Islamic ideals of equity between men and women.

Notes

1. I should note that Silber herself does not take up the concept of globalization, as one of the examples which became very influential as an illustration of the 'theoretical usage of spatial metaphors' in exploring not only spatial but also relational dimensions of social processes.
2. I borrow this definition of 'global culture' from Smith's discussion on the possibility of the emergence of such a culture (see A. D. Smith, 1991: 177–80).
3. Giddens uses the concept of 'life politics' to refer to the kinds of political decisions inherent in the ethical question, 'How should we live?', which gives rise to the creation of morally justifiable forms of life that promote self-actualization. See Giddens (1991: 215).
4. Sivan argues: 'In the Middle East and North Africa, the 1950s and 1960s witnesses the high water-mark of the mass mobilizing state, all-pervasive bureaucracy, mass production factory system, and official culture' (Sivan 1992: 96). It was in this context that the presence of the state was assured in all walks of life, assuming the

role for itself of setting a model for the construction of social life. The boundaries between the state and society, then, shifted in favour of the state, but this same economic, social and cultural dynamism also entailed the integration of the masses in the political and economic processes, which not only prepared the conditions for the expansion of civil society but, particularly due to the 'state's failure in certain domains to modify the core values of its people in relation to the ultimate meaning of life' (Sivan 1992: 100), caused the state to lose its cultural hegemony over society.

5. The Welfare Party (founded in 1983) is the continuation of the National Salvation Party (NSP) which was established in 1972 and banned after the 1980 military takeover together with all other political parties. The NSP was the continuation of the National Order Party (1970–71) and was also closed by the Constitutional Court for it violated the Law on Parties which forbade using religion for political purposes. Professor Dr Necmettin Erbakan has appeared as the leader of all these religious political parties. For the formation of this political movement, see, for example, Toprak (1980) and for the Welfare Party, see Çakır (1994). For a recent analysis of how Islam has been politicized in Turkey as it has been developed in the line of NOP-NSP-WP and its overall place in Turkish politics, see Ayata 1996: 40–56.

6. *Kandil* celebrations are four Muslim feasts, celebrating the Prophet Muhammad's conception, the secret night he first received God's revelation, his night ascent, and the 'Night of Power'.

7. For an extended discussion of the ways in which the inhabitants of this urban complex build an Islamic way of life which shapes the identities of Muslim women, see Saktanber (1994).

References

Al-Azmeh, A. (1993) *Islams and Modernities*. Verso, London and New York.

Ayata, S. (1996) 'Patronage, Party and State: The Politization of Islam in Turkey', *Middle East Journal* 50 (1), Winter, 40–56.

Bourdieu, P. (1989) *Distinction: A Social Critique of the Judgement of Taste*, trans. R. Nice. Routledge, London.

Çakır, R. (1994) *Ne Şeriat Ne Demokrasi: Refah Partisini Anlamak*. Metis Yayınları, Istanbul.

Castells, M. and Henderson, J. (1987) 'Techno-economic Restructuring, Socio-political Process and Spatial Transformation, a Global Perspective', in J. Henderson and M. Castells (eds), *Global Structuring and Territorial Development*. Sage, London.

Cladis, M. S. (1992) 'Durkheim's Individual in Society: A Sacred Marriage?', *Journal of the History of Ideas* 53 (1), January and March, 71–90.

de Certeau, M. (1984) *The Practice of Everyday Life*, trans. S. F. Rendall. University of California Press, Berkeley.

Elias, N. (1991) *The Society of Individuals*. Basil Blackwell, Oxford and Cambridge, MA.

Esposito, J. L. (1991) *Islam: The Straight Path*. Oxford University Press, New York and Oxford.

Giddens, A. (1991) *Modernity and Self Identity: Self and Society in the Late Modern Age*. Stanford University Press, Stanford, CA.

Lewis, B. (1991) *The Political Language of Islam*. University of Chicago Press, Chicago and London.

Mardin, Ş. (1980) 'Turkey: The Transformation of an Economic Code', in E. Özbudun and A. Ulusan (eds), *The Political Economy of Income Distribution in Turkey*. Holmes and Meier, New York.

— (1989) *Religion and Social Change in Modern Turkey: The Case of Bediüzzaman Said Nursi*. SUNY Press, Albany.

Piscatori, J. P. (1986) *Islam in a World of Nation States*. Cambridge University Press, Cambridge.

Saktanber, A. (1994) 'Becoming the "Other" as a Muslim in Turkey: Turkish Women vs Islamist Women', *New Perspectives on Turkey* 11, Autumn, 99–134.

Silber, I. F. (1995) 'Space, Fields, Boundaries: The Rise of Spatial Metaphors in Contemporary Sociological Theory', *Social Research* 62 (2), Summer, 323–55.

Sivan, E. (1992) 'The Islamic Resurgence: Civil Society Strikes Back', in L. Kaplan (ed.), *Fundamentalism in Comparative Perspective*. University of Massachusetts Press, Amherst, MA.

Smith, A. D. (1991) 'Toward a Global Culture?', in M. Featherstone (ed.), *Global Culture: Nationalism, Globalization and Modernity*. Sage, London.

Smith, W. C. (1981) *On Understanding Islam*. Mouton, The Hague.

Toprak, B. (1980) *Islam and Political Development in Turkey*. E. J. Brill, Leiden.

Veron, E. (1971) 'Ideology and the Social Sciences', *Semiotica* 3 (2), Mouton.

Wallace, A. F. C. (1956) 'Revitalization Movements', *American Anthropoligist* 58 (2), April, 264–81.

10

Between religion and ethnicity: a Kurdish-Alevi tribe in globalizing Istanbul

Günter Seufert

Discussing tribalism in the context of a global city at first sight appears to be a contradiction in terms. The globalization of Istanbul, the city with which I am concerned in this article, is a very recent phenomenon; indeed, whether it merits the term global city is questionable. Furthermore, the tribe I shall focus upon lacks many of the features conventionally associated with tribalism, such as a nomadic way of existence, constant struggles with neighbouring tribes and revolts against central authority (Bruinessen 1992). Even with these reservations in mind, however, the notions of 'tribalism' and 'globalism' seem incongruous when used within the same analytical framework. This is because globalization is often primarily associated with such universal trends as commodification of everyday life, mass consumerism and the blurring of distinctions between high and low culture which erode local contexts of meaning and communal ties (Turner 1994: 112). Simultaneously, however, globalism entails propinquity of diverse cultures and experience with cultural pluralism, as well as growing awareness of such international discourses as that of human rights through media and information networks with diaspora populations. By providing members of local communities with a new prism of cultural reflexivity, globalization can enable them to act on the international stage. Indeed, the experiences of the tribal group I will discuss in the following pages embodies this 'twofold process of the particularization of the universal and the universalization of the particular' which Robertson (1992: 178) describes as the essence of globalization.

I begin by describing the chain migration of the Koçkiri tribe to Istanbul[1] starting in the 1960s, and its subsequent integration into the economy of the city. In its broad outlines, this is a story which parallels the experiences of various other immigrant groups arriving in Istanbul in the 1960s and 1970s (Gümrükçü 1986). Next I turn to the Alevi religious affiliation of the Koçkiri and discuss how this predominantly religious identity, which served to legitimate the traditional caste-like tribal order, is currently being transformed into a chiefly ethno-political identity among the younger generation, namely that of Kurdish leftist. In the concluding part, I argue that this shift of identity is related to the rediscovery of one's own culture through the grid of modern values and global discourses.

The process of migration and acquiring a foothold in Istanbul

Before its migration to Istanbul, the Koçkiri tribe was settled in about twenty-eight villages towards the east of the central Anatolian city of Sivas, in a region whose boundaries were marked by the town of Suşehir in the north, Kemah in the east, Divriği in the south and Hafik in the west. This chapter focuses on the Saran clan, whose homeland includes four villages. The Saran used to be cattle-breeders and bee-keepers, and they also worked in open-cast salt- and coal-mining. Until the turn of this century, tribesmen were able to establish new villages whenever the population of a village became overcrowded. Although real poverty was already evident in the 1940s, when overpopulation was exacerbated by the war economy, the first clan members started to migrate in the mid-1960s. In the 1970s, whole families began to move in increasing numbers, reaching a peak between 1975 and 1977. Today, only four small settlements remain of the original twenty-eight villages in the tribal region.

It was generally the young, single men, often not older than twenty, who first ventured to Istanbul. In the mid-1960s Istanbul was a city of less than two million, barely a fraction of its current population estimated at around twelve million. But it was already surrounded by a peripheral ring of squatter housing, built by rural immigrants who arrived in ever increasing numbers from different regions of Anatolia. For the Saran clansmen, who initially had to seek accommodation in dilapidated rooming houses in the city centre, the move to one of these newly emerging squatter districts constituted the first step up the social ladder. In this first phase, building plots had to be bought on the informal land market. But later on, as the urban clan-community grew in numbers and became powerful enough to occupy new land and defend it against competing immigrant groups, newcomers no longer had to pay for building sites. Houses were generally constructed by fellow tribesmen, who would often continue to work at weekends, roofing the first couple of rooms overnight.

No more than one or two skilled craftsmen were directly employed, often at very low wages. It was only in the early 1980s, when the migration of clan members from Anatolia ended, that construction workers began to be paid regularly.

Since the early 1980s, the broader settlement patterns have also undergone a shift. Initially clan families were concentrated in the emerging squatter districts of the 1960s, such as Okmeydanı, Fikirtepe or Ümraniye, and lived side by side with their village neighbours. As clan members began to move from these first 'bases' to other parts of the city, such as Tarabya, Çengelköy or Dudullu, living next to work associates, business partners or people of similiar political orientation became much more common. Today, the number of clan households within the boundaries of any single municipal sub-district can range from anywhere between fifteen and fifty households. Each such household includes the father's family together with the families of his sons, who may live in separate buildings in the neighbourhood but maintain close relationships. The number of clan-people linked together in this way over all Istanbul encompasses approximately 5000 people.

Just as settling in Istanbul was achieved as a community, entering into urban economic activity also required the tribesmen's common efforts. The clan's young migration pioneers often started their Istanbul working life as caretakers of private apartment houses, especially in the quarters of Şişli, Kurtuluş and Levent. Living in the cheap basement flats of those apartment houses, caretakers generally do not face accommodation problems. Part of the duties of a caretaker is the carrying of food and fuel, coal or firewood or of household appliances. These activities led to the establishment of a clan-controlled network of carriers, which later spread out over a range of districts such as Pangaltı, Topkapı and Dolapdere. The concentrated power of the united clan members, however, was necessary to compete with already existing carrier-systems in those districts and to establish their own networks, which provided the opportunity to leave the caretaker jobs and to settle in new emerging squatter districts.

In the 1960s, mutual help again, this time in the form of private credit, circulating money and partnership, enabled tribesmen one by one to buy lorries and work as motorized carriers. Today nearly all males of the first migrant generation are working as drivers, most of them self-employed and owning only one lorry. In the words of one of them: 'The load just moved from our backs to the lorry, but we remain carriers.' The decision to stop being porters was strongly supported by the emergence of a group of competitors, Kurds from south-eastern Anatolia, who in some districts drove the clan members out of this field of activity.

It is only members of the younger working generation of the 1980s who had to fight individually to earn their living. They have become lawyers, doctors, painters and technicians, but many of their customers are members of the tribe. There is one large disadvantage in dealing with faithful customers like these: they often do not realize that the work done has to be paid for!

Because of their low level of education, a network of clan members in the civil services has not yet been established and, due to poverty, influential positions in political parties have not been occupied. Solidarity among clan members today can be seen in the way they care for sick people and provide free accommodation for visiting tribe-members from the homeland or from foreign countries, especially Germany.

It is obvious that for the first two generations of migrants success in settlement and vocational life was impossible unless they acted as a unit. But today market relations gnaw at all traditional hierarchies and impose modernization. The new patterns of settlement and the independent careers of the younger generation are distinct signs of the disbandment of predominantly closed and communal relations and for the establishment of primarily open and associational relationships among the migrants.

The tribe's culture: community consciousness and religion

Almost all of the population in the homeland of the Koçkiri tribe is Alevi by religion, but in linguistic terms is divided between Turks and Kurds. Turkish-speaking Sunni Muslims are only a small minority. The Koçkiri tribe, including the Saran clan, has Kurdish as its mother-tongue; indeed, even the name of the tribe is Kurdish, meaning 'those who have migrated'. But one of the thirteen clans that constitute the tribe is Turkish-speaking and correspondingly named *Tirkan* or *Kirveler*.[2]

The synthesis of tribal and religious belonging that had been moulded in the consciousness of the tribesmen can be exemplified by their marriage practice. It is not the tribe that is the unit which practises endogamy, but the religious group, the Alevi, and indeed one is Alevi only by birth (Väth 1993: 213). While marrying a Turk instead of a Kurd causes no negative reaction from the tribe-members, marrying a Sunni Muslim instead of an Alevi is considered a serious offence. Those who desert the faith and become Sunni Muslims, however, are described as *yol düşkünü* (Turkish: those who got lost on the way [to God]). Such a person cannot remain part of the clan; it is difficult for him to maintain contact even with his close relatives. In the same way the institution of life-long fraternity exemplifies that it has not been lingistic but religious criteria that draw insurmountable social borders for tribe-members. Before marrying, every Koçkiri male has to choose another Alevi male as a kind of brother-in-religion, and it is not unusual for a Kurdish-speaking Alevi to choose a Turkish-speaking one. All over Turkey most of the Alevi speak Turkish as their mother-tongue, and even if many of them speak Kurdish[3] (*Kurmanci*) or *Zazaca* (*Zazaki*), the ritual language for all of them is Turkish.

The tribesmen say that, due to the insurrection of March and April 1921, during the Turkish War of Independence, the use of the tribe's name 'Koçkiri' in public risked criminal persecution and still does so even today. The rebellion, initiated by the Koçkiri and carried out in cooperation with other Alevi tribes from the region of Dersim,[4] aimed at the establishment of an autonomous province. A memorandum was delivered to the government in Ankara which declared a state of emergency in the area until the insurrection was suppressed. Although separatism was not pursued after that, official history accepts the rebellion as the first initiative of a separatist Kurdishness (Coşkun 1996).

In religious terms the Koçkiri belong to the Alevi, Turkey's Shia Muslims, who have little to do with the better-known Iranian ones.[5] Nevertheless it was the close contact between the heterodox Muslim milieu in the Anatolia of the fifteenth century and the order of the Iranian Safavids which finally produced a specific Anatolian Alevism. But before the Safavids established themselves as a dynasty, proclaiming the Twelver Shia as the state religion – that is, before a formalized religious doctrine affected the Anatolian Alevi – the Ottoman Empire severed these ties. For this reason Turkey's Alevi, like the Iranian Shia, venerate the fourth caliph Ali ibn Abî Tâlib and the family of the Prophet Muhammad, but do not participate in the Shii version of the Islamic law (Kehl-Bodrogi 1988). The most important event in the Shii calendar is the remembrance of the battle of Kerbala where, in the year 680, Imam Hussain, the son of Ali and the grandson of the Prophet, was murdered together with his family by troops of the Sunni caliph Muawiyya. This also figures as the most salient event in the religious year of the Alevi. While that date is fittingly remembered in Shii Iran with mourning and even with flagellation, it is remembered by Turkey's Alevi in a cheerful atmosphere since it ends a twelve-day fast. Most important, however, is that the feast reminds the Alevi of the basic differences that separate them from the Sunni Muslims. Attitudes towards Kerbala reflect the 'irreconcilable difference' between these two groups.

The heretical belief and the mostly Turkmen tribe-based social structure of the Alevi reinforced each other and made them, particularly since the fifteenth century, suspect in the eyes of the imperial centre. The oppressive stance of the Ottoman Empire, which deemed the Alevi the 'fifth column' of Iran, and in the sixteenth and seventeeenth centuries declared them blasphemers and heretics (Şener and İlknur 1994: 3–4), slaughtering thousands of them (Laçiner 1985: 238), made them strong supporters of the Kemalist Republic, in which they expected to be treated on an equal footing.

In this respect, a world-view, already prepared by religion, seems to have been strengthened by the contemporary history of the tribe. In the meaningful context of both religious and tribal history, the Alevi Koçkiri tend to see themselves as existing in a more or less 'natural' tension with the political centre, be it the Ottoman Empire or the newly founded Republic. The interpretation of this tension, however, used to be expressed in religious terms, and it is the broader imagined community of the Alevi, to which tribe and clan are felt to belong.

Communal social structures and religious knowledge

In contrast to the likewise Shii-influenced but more urban Bektaşi movement, in which any novice can receive the religious training needed to become the master of the lodge, the Alevi accepted as religious authorities an hereditary class of *dede*s. Although in the beginning these *dede*s were appointed by the head of the Bektaşi, they managed through arranged marriages to distinguish themselves as a social class of their own.

The Koçkiri tribesmen used to accept the members of special families of another Kurdish-speaking tribe, which has its homeland in the province of Tunceli, as religious authorities. They were deemed *seyyid*s (that is, descendants of the Prophet Muhammad) and used to visit the Koçkiri in autumn when the harvest was brought in and the religious leaders were able to demand their part of it. The mobile *seyyid*s established a network of information and support between the various Alevi tribes. This system connects kin-based social organizations with similarly kin-based religious leadership. The religious world-view legitimized inherited leadership, distinct castes and a hierarchic social order with unchangeable status, and both the world-view and the social relations of the tribe are to be classified as pre-modern.

This same quality is indicated by the structure of its religious knowledge. Under the circumstances of state-supported Sunni *ulema* in Ottoman times (see Mardin 1989), the teaching of the rural, settled, Alevi was not able to produce an elaborate religious discourse. The religious culture of the Alevi is not grounded in theology and Islamic law, but in narratives, poems and songs which praise the deeds of the fourth caliph Ali and the members of Muhammad's family. These narratives and poems provide various patterns of ideal behaviour for the holder of a specific status. Personal examples from Islamic and Alevi history offer models for the proper behaviour of children, women, warriors and leaders, containing as they do a series of basic ethical patterns.

The community's 'definite other': the Sunni Muslims

Every cultural entity exists only because there is a boundary between it and those who are both outside it, and represent its opposite in terms of values and morality. In this respect, for the stability of every social unit a 'definite other' is needed. For the Alevi it is the Sunni Muslims who function as that 'definite other'. This can be clearly seen in the following answer to a question about what one would have to do to become Alevi: 'Somebody who wants to become Alevi must not be like Sunni men, not cruel, not oppressive or rude. An Alevi must be above this kind of behaviour.' What is true for any other identity is also true for that of the Alevi (and Sunni Muslims): 'Identity is always ... a structured representation which only achieves its positive through the narrow eye of the negative. It has to go through the eye of the needle of the other before it can construct itself. It produces a very Manichean set of opposites' (Hall 1993: 21).

Even today Turkey's official Sunni *ulema* do not recognize Alevism as an Islamic confession. Non-governmental religious authorities sometimes even accuse the Alevi of being incestuous unbelievers.[6] Meanwhile, Alevi spokesmen cast blame on the Turkish government for trying to assimilate them[7] by building mosques in Alevi villages and staffing them with Sunni imams.[8]

This may explain why there was no overt religious practice in the first decade of the Koçkiris' migration to Istanbul. Alevis often resorted to an old element of Shiism, the religious disguise, concealing their Alevi identity. They even sent their children to Sunni-organized Qur'ānic courses. As shanty-town studies show, there is, even today, little contact between Alevi Kurdish groups and Sunni Turkish groups (Wedel 1994: 5; Güneş-Ayata 1990/91), and in some regions of western Turkey violent conflicts between these two groups have recently flared up.[9]

It is the antagonism between these religious–cultural groups which has obviously influenced the political attitude of the Alevi. Ergo, to be a member of the clan, and therefore Alevi and Kurdish, for the tribesmen meant being politically leftist, just because the Sunnis were regarded as rightist. Like the Anatolian Alevi cattle-breeders and farmers two generations ago, the Istanbul Alevi lower middle class until recently voted social democrat because the social democrats were not regarded as religious in a Sunni Islamic way (Yılmaz 1994). Turkey's social democrats have always been aware of the importance of Alevi votes and have not been afraid to exploit the religious–cultural cleavages that run through Turkish society.

To summarize: in the first stage of migration the common efforts of the tribesmen determined the quotidian experience and reinforced the traditional social ties of the clan. The community felt itself isolated in a strange and sometimes even hostile environment and an open confession of religious commitment risked trouble. Religious meetings were rare and at the level of 'understanding' and 'meaning' one may say that there was no development in the clan members' 'understanding' of their own religious culture; that is, they understood their culture in nearly the same way as they had done in their homelands. Instead of being concerned with their own tradition, the Alevi youth joined with the left in political struggles prior to 1980 and, sometimes even physically, attacked Alevi holy men, the *dede*s, for being rural conservatives. Political activism by Alevis pushed their religion into the background. They tended to see themselves as part of the national and international working class. In the European diaspora the situation was no different.

Urban religious life: folklore and tribal-consciousness

The focus of the Alevi religion is the *cem*, a ceremony in which the participants, headed by the *seyyid*s, not only pray and worship, but also solve conflicts that have occurred in the community. Another important religious event is the Birthday of Ali, commemorated as the Feast of the Dervish-Lodge, actually a spring feast of sorts. Religious belief and tribal consciousness used to fuse in the commemoration of the tribe's deceased elders. People then met at the cemetery, listened to verses of the Qur'ān and to traditional tunes played on an Anatolian violin. After that, beginning with those who had died most recently, the names of all the deceased were recited and a common meal was served. In Istanbul today, it is primarily on the occasion of weddings, funerals and the commemoration of the dead[10] that clan members come together. During events whose meanings are traditional and are expressed in religious terms, the clan and the tribe as real entities are resurrected and renewed.

It was not until just after 1980 that culture and religion gained new importance among the Alevi in Istanbul. The military takeover at that time ended the fighting between left and right. During the same period, clan migration came to an end and economic integration into the city was achieved. With the solving of the migrants' most compelling problems, community ties relaxed and the individual members of the clan increasingly had to face the urban environment alone. It was at this stage that religious tradition was to be resurrected. The youth of the tribe and clan in particular began to show a much greater willingness to participate in religious ceremonies, especially *cems*. The *cems* are led by some *seyyid* families who, like the Koçkiri, have migrated to the big cities and continue to visit the Koçkiri circles there. In Anatolia, the *cem* was celebrated either in the open countryside or in the house of the *dede*. In the big cities, however, frequent celebrations of the *cem* required a new institution, a *cem*-house, and the struggle for its foundation became an important issue. Once established, the *cem*-house was also to serve for funeral services which until then had taken place at the mosque, a situation that worried the older tribesmen who never went to a Sunni mosque. Prior to 1993 only two or three *cem*-houses had been established in Istanbul, but the number increased in the run-up to the last local election in March 1994 and has reached about twenty today.

Another concrete expression of the Alevi religious resurgence is the establishment of wedding salons where tribal marriages can be celebrated.[11] These new institutions should provide the conditions necessary for a vibrant Alevi culture in the big city, and lute and folk-dance groups have already been placed at the top of the agenda. In the summer of 1993 the young members of the clan obtained tents and spent the holidays in their tribal 'homeland'. For several years now they have also been organizing a kind of pilgrimage to the small central Anatolian town of Hacı Bektaş, named after the founder of the Bektaşism (see above), the elaborated version of Alevism. A *dede*, accepted as the unofficial head of the Anatolian Alevi, resides near the original lodge, which has now been turned into a museum.

This religious tourism indicates the shift from a rather illiterate version of religious belief to a more literate one. This process of re-creating an intellectually sound religious and cultural identity is not restricted to the youth of the Koçkiri. In fact, there is a growing interest in the culture of the Alevi as a whole, which can be seen in the increased numbers of books on Alevi history and belief, in magazines and in the recording of Alevi-type folk-music. The Alevi, in former times a parochial, spatial and linguistically divided denomination, known for screening itself off from the outside world, have published, within the space of only a few years, about one hundred books in order to research, teach and popularize their culture. Today they publish more than ten monthly journals and run four private radio stations with the aim of reconstructing their own culture and spreading it by modern mass media.

The 'understanding' of traditional religious culture in modern patterns

How are we to explain this new interest in a religious culture, a culture which is inseparably interwoven with traditional forms of sociality, given the fact that, under the pressure of modernity, every traditional culture is challenged? It is challenged because, as a pattern for communal morality, it defines its members in a way which is irreconcilable with market conditions. Market conditions are built upon contracts and therefore are gnawing at all estates and all kinds of hierarchies. In modern cultural patterns the citizen 'is no longer defined in terms of property-holding, gender, racial characteristics, or any such particularistic dimension [which are the bases of traditional social systems, GS] but rather emerges as the abstract bearer of general rights of social participation and membership' (Turner 1994: 82). In addition, the integration of individuals into a free labour market, along with the loosening of communal ties, the experience of cultural pluralism caused by the propinquity of competing cultures, and the spread of information technology, result in a weakening of pure national culture and render traditional contexts of meaning implausible.

But the cultural revival of Alevism is also an outcome of the Alevis' increased confrontation with modernity, a process which is largely a result of their domestic migration, even if the delimitation of the communities from the urban environment has caused a delay. But now the individual members of the clan, especially the youth, are forced to lead their own lives, largely independent of the community. This predicament was described by Bellah: in modern times, life is 'not a one possibility thing but an infinite possibility' (Turner 1994: 195). Here Bellah reiterates a statement already made by Weber for whom life in modern times became a chosen project which required great staying power for conscious realization (Weber 1973: 272).

This self-awareness, however, is to be realized in two different social spheres: in the *world outside the community* and in the *community itself*. Towards his own community, especially for the purpose of gaining personal freedom in and from it, the modern individual is liable to emphasize the already mentioned 'rights of social participation and membership' and to sue for the abstract principles in which they are represented, principles such as 'equality', 'tolerance', 'democracy', 'justice' and 'progress'. Given the cultural cleavages in Turkish society, however, the world outside the community requires a different symbolic system. In order to differentiate himself from the outside world and to define himself within this world, the individual has to restore the cultural heritage of his community, that is to present himself in the way he is already described, (as Alevi).

In every case it is the quotidian 'knowledge' of the individual that serves as symbolic material for the process of gaining personal awareness. For Alevi migrants this 'knowledge' is both embedded and expressed in their religious culture. The specific use made of traditional symbolic material in modern and urban circumstances, however, reshapes it to new requirements. At the level of the individual, the world *inside* and the world *outside* the community are to be integrated and, therefore, the values of modern society function as a grid for interpreting the traditional culture, that is, the meaning of the religion will be interpreted anew according to modern values and orientations.

What happens among the Koçkiri Alevi, therefore, is not the resurrection of traditional culture, even among the so-called defenders of Turkish laicism, but the collective endeavour to make sure of the cultural heritage, realized by increasingly autonomous individuals for their own purposes in modern times.

This argument may be evaluated at two levels in the ongoing Alevi resurgence, first at the level of its religious discourse, and second at the level of its social actors. Starting with the discourse, we observe that the religious knowledge collected by the youth through practice (the performance of *cem*s) and theory (the study of Alevi literature) does not lead them to traditional piety and traditional forms of togetherness. The Koçkiri youngsters in this way reject religious forms which do not fit in with the new personal freedom they have gained from their own community: as traditional religious authorities, the *seyyid*s were considered absolutely necessary for the performance of *cem*s, but today they have become superfluous in the eyes of the youth. Likewise, the religious teacher, the *hoca*, is considered unnecessary for the circumcision of boys, and young parents are also unwilling to send their children to Qur'ānic courses, even if they are organized by the Alevi. Consistently, the strict subordination in religious and sometimes even in social questions that used to shape the relationship between the ordinary Alevi and the members of the *seyyid* families, is no longer the case. Increasing the religious practice and knowledge of the ordinary Alevi, in fact, causes the devaluation of the sacred knowledge of *seyyid*s and *hoca*s, producing an egalitarian effect. We find here, and I use the term without any pejorative connotation, a 'religious life without strong piety', an indigenous secularization.

At the level of social actors, we find nearly all of the Alevi's activities in the urban environment shouldered neither by the village community, nor by tribe or clan, but by new social organizations. Indeed, the revival of religious life has not entailed a revival of the traditional social structures – that is, the pure tribe relations – which in former times were able to gain their meaning and legitimation from religious concepts. Now, beneath the traditional institutions such as tribe, clan or village community, modern institutions exist, institutions with written statutes. The younger generation founded 'village clubs', associations of mutual support which often have as their social basis people originating from the same village, but which are organized in an entirely different manner. Thus the new togetherness, realized on religious occasions, and the new interest in religious knowledge are paralleled by the establishment of a new form of sociality, not based on given but on voluntary membership, and not with inherited but with achieved status.

While tribe, clan or village community, as relatively closed units, produce a barrier between the individual and the environment, associational forms of social organization serve as a bridge to the outside world. While the traditional community is an end in itself, the clubs are for individual members. The club allows the integration of non-tribesmen, be they business associates, political comrades or merely neighbours, into an organization which is, in principle, an open one. Not only is the Koçkiri tribe undergoing a transformation of its social system from traditional and communal to modern and associational forms of social relations, but so too are the urban Alevi as a whole. Today there are about 120 Alevi associations in Istanbul alone, and, nationwide, a 'Council of the Representatives of the Alevi' has been formed, even including associations from Europe. This shift in the social reality of the Alevi is moulding the 'understanding' of their religion: most of the Alevi spokesmen and most of its intellectuals today interpret Alevism as a system of tolerance, equality, justice, progress and democracy. Consequently they argue for the cancelling of the borders that divide the hereditary religious leaders from the simple Alevi and also vote for the acceptance of converts in the communities (Vorhoff 1995: 162ff). It is the principle of the individual's vocational decision that now prevails in a community formerly built entirely on given estates. One consequence of this transformation is that the urban Koçkiri do not stay in contact with any other eastern or south-eastern Anatolian tribes whose members have also migrated to Istanbul. To be a 'tribe member' is not a valid social classification in the urban environment and produces no useful patterns of behaviour.

As far as 'religion' is understood as the specific symbolic legitimation of traditional social relations, we observe a process of rapid secularization in the midst of the resurgence of Alevism because the specific interpretation of Alevism that justified traditional structures is rendered implausible. At the same time, however, we might not overlook the sanctification of the 'ultimate concern' that is now emerging: the 'embodied self' of the individual. In countries like Turkey, this 'ultimate concern' of the late twentieth century (Kofler 1975: 121), in contrast to Europe and the West, is symbolized to a great extent not in secular but in religious terms. In these countries even in modern times, religion is not an invisible (Luckmann 1991) but a very visible force. Istanbul, which was under the political and cultural hegemony of the lay bureaucratic and economic elite at the time of the Koçkiri arrivals in the 1960s, has been ruled since March 1994 by a mayor of the Islamistic Welfare Party. And the Alevi urban communities, which were neither influential nor even well known in the 1960s, find themselves today courted by the ruling party which, for the first time since the founding of the Republic, promises government support for their religious institutions.

Personal self-awareness in global times

In the big cities the Alevi are confronted with modernity in which, according to Berger and Luckmann, a market of worlds prevails, rendering the life worlds of distinct communities relative (Berger and Luckmann 1967: 192). No doubt, the mentioned self-reflexivity of individuals is not a new issue, but one that has been frequently described and analysed in classical sociology. What is new in global times, however, is that enhanced self-awareness today occurs not merely in fully industrialized societies or in the upper classes of developing societies, but even in their lower strata: 'The confessional, the diary, the mirror and spiritual practices were techniques specifically directed at the elite. By contrast the project of the embodied self in the late twentieth century is a mass movement which is bringing a new conception of self to the whole of society' (Turner 1994: 195).

The integration of individuals into the free labour market and the disbandment of communal ties coincide today with the experience of cultural pluralism, caused by the propinquity of competing cultures and the enlarged extent of information technology, ushering in a weakness of formerly state-preserved national culture. The economic dimension of globalization, especially the emergence of a world economic system with the freeing of financial and labour markets, caused distorted modernization and urbanization outside the industrial centres, producing global islands in local life-worlds. Cultural globalization enters the stage in the form of the influence on local life-worlds of global life-styles based on consumerism, gratification, leisure and hedonism; in short, on individualistic values, ushering in a cultural atmosphere of modernity without the real modern conditions of quotidian life, that is, fully industrialized circumstances: 'Cultural globalization therefore, forces upon modern societies, and upon intellectuals in particular, a new reflexivity about the authenticity of cultures, their social status and the nature of cultural hierarchy' (Turner 1994: 194).

This analysis is valid in Turkey not only for the Alevi but also for their 'definite others', the Sunni Muslim groups, and it explains to a fair degree the current Islamization trend in the country. The shift from illiterate to literate religion and the critical perspective towards tradition is on the agenda of Sunnism too. Likewise we find also among the Sunnis, the establishment of associational forms of religious–political organization (for example, the party) and the interpretation of the traditional symbolic material (religious texts and practices) through the grid of modern values and orientations. In terms of rediscovering the indigenous culture within modern frameworks, and in criticizing the elders for not having an appropriate understanding of it, the youth of both groups show a lot of parallels. In both camps the struggle is led by the young, who are convinced that they are involved in a decisive moment of history. Like the revival of Alevism, the revival of Sunni Muslim religious culture is not conceivable without the domestic migration that brought into social propinquity communities which were formerly clearly demarcated one from the other.

In this respect, migration and globalization confront Turkey with its history: the society of the Ottoman Empire was not conceived as an all-encompassing whole; rather it was made up of separate communities. Even if in some cases ethnic and religious criteria coincided, it was religious terms which defined individuals' affiliations to various communities and the place of the individual inside the community itself (İnalcık and Quatert 1994; Karpat 1973; Eryılmaz 1992). Thus the rank of the individual, in relation to others and in relation to the state, was fixed according to his membership of one of the great religious communities (*millet*s), which were religiously (that is, culturally) and judicially autonomous. The world-view of these communities and their religion related their members to the cosmos and provided them with a cosmology; that is, a consciousness of their place in creation. The decay of the empire and the founding of the Republic led to great shifts in the structure of the population and transformed it from multi-religious (mostly Muslim and Christian) to multi-ethnic (almost completely Muslim). Its community-centred characteristics, however, remained (Schiffauer 1993; Andrews 1989).

Today, members of the different groups in quotidian life are confronted directly with each other, and opposing life-styles are claiming ground. Cultural diversity and propinquity, which in global times are seen generally as the motor of enhanced reflection of the respective cultures, appear multiplied: 'This cultural diversity cannot be simply ignored and my argument, therefore, is that globalization requires a new cultural reflexivity, which in turn gives a special role to the intellectual as passing a judgement on the nature of national cultures' (Turner 1994: 184).

Beneath the parallels between the Alevi and the Sunni Muslims' evaluation, reassessment and judgement of their own cultures, there remains a great difference. This difference, in my eyes, is closely related to the problem of the individual's 'reconciliation of his commitment to the local community on one hand and, on the other, his achieved commitment to (often only imaginary) groups on the global level' (Turner 1994: 112). I argue that, for the members of local groups, together with the emergence of global media networks and global discourses (like the human rights doctrine), every *Weltanschauung* is credible only under the precondition that it is – at least in the eyes of its adherents – embedded in a global one.

In this issue, however, an important difference occurs between the Alevi and the Sunni Muslims' religious resurrection. In the matter of the reconciliation of local and global commitments, both groups walk in opposing directions. The Sunni Islamic side tenaciously works out a new 'understanding' of its religion according to secular parameters, creating 'Islamic economies', 'Islamic welfare systems' and 'Islamic political institutions'. At the same time, political Islam is becoming a social movement which 'attempts to secure political hegemony within the global political structure' (Turner 1994: 78). Indeed, Sunni political Islam in Turkey is boosted by each success achieved by Islamic movements in any part of the world, and Islamic doctrine to a great extent gains its credibility from its global presence.

The situation for the Alevi, however, is quite different. On the global scale, Alevism is a very singular and isolated occurrence, and that detracts from its persuasiveness to a great extent, especially for the younger generation. Apart from that, its relatively unelaborated doctrine does not open up possibilities for the construction of a framework that could meet all the theoretical and philosophical requirements of a politicized youth, a youth which has to work out for itself an 'international' and, with that, a 'valid' identity. That is the reason why the Alevi youth is liable not to understand the secular world in religious terms (as do the Sunni Muslims) but use religious doctrine for the sanctification of secular ideologies.

In the past, its religious culture related a community and its members to the cosmos by fixing its place in creation. Today the same culture is required to mark the community's – and within that community, the individual's – place in the globe. And it is only the latter mode – that is, the rank of that culture in the global world – that proves the value of the various cultures, the different 'systems of meaning', in global times.

That is one of the reasons why today the literate youth of the Koçkiri projects not his Alevism but his Kurdishness. In a world in which nationalism is the only working religion (Lukacs 1993), the young Alevi of the Koçkiri feel the need not to turn their backs on their religion but to accept their linguistically defined ethnicity as the ultimate base of their identity. As one of them said: 'It is nationalism which brings us home, which causes us to find ourselves.'

For the young tribesmen of the Koçkiri, Alevism today is no longer a religion but a 'life-style', and the significance of this perception should not be underestimated. Indeed, at least among the youth, the process of rediscovering their own religion in modern concepts has begun to veer into the opposite; secular concepts prevail and become actual.

Now that Kurdishness, instead of a tribal identity or Alevism, is chosen as the ultimate reference, the 'ignorant' elders have to be taught by the youth. In their own words: 'Unlike me, my father speaks fluent Kurdish but he sees himself first as an Alevi and only second as a Kurd. He names the Sunni Kurds[12] *guro*, which in Kurdish means illiterate and a boor. The Alevi Turks, however, he calls *tirki bireh* and its meaning is Turks who found the way. What a contradiction!'

While, for their fathers, the religious Alevi and the secular social democrat identity made up two halves of a whole, for the young men, nationalist Kurdishness and 'rebellious' Alevism are the same thing. The teaching of Alevism is romanticized as a 'tradition of rebellion and fight against assimilation'[13] and, according to this, it is asserted that the majority of Alevi have Kurdish as their mother-tongue. In the same way, linguistic and religious dimensions need to be harmonized, and Iranian Zoroastrianism is now accepted as the source of Alevism, and has been promoted to the rank of 'the old Kurdish religion'.[14] Likewise, the Iranian/Kurdish spring feast *newroz* is said to be the origin of the Alevi spring feast at which they used to celebrate the birth of the fourth caliph Ali. But this is no surprise because:

> What is the point of identity if it isn't one thing? That is why we keep hoping that identities will come our way because the rest of the world is so confusing: everything else is turning, but identities ought to be some stable points of reference which were like that in the past, are now and ever shall be, still points in a turning world. (Hall 1993: 22)

While the Kurdish-speaking Alevi youth in this way construe that 'one thing' which identity has to be, by interpreting Alevism as a Kurdish issue, a remarkable percentage of the Turkish-speaking Alevi tend to see in Alevism the embodiment of pure Turkishness. These circles accept the official Turkish Thesis on History, that regards pre-historical Anatolian civilizations, such as the Sumerians, as ethnically Turkish and treat similarities between the cultural practices of those civilizations and the cultural practices of the Alevi as proof of their Turkish ethnicity (Demirci 1993: 9). Similarities in Alevi rites and rites of Central Asian Turkish people serve as further evidence for that claim (Şener and İlknur 1994: 2). In the 1950s and 1960s this view was part of the ideology of the extreme right-wing Nationalist Movement Party which, after a period of serious self-Islamization in the 1970s and 1980s, has in the last few years been cautiously returning to such positions, and is trying to organize the Turkish-speaking Alevi (Bora and Can 1990: 243). But today it is not only the Turkish-speaking Alevi who vote for a Turkish identity. Increasing tension over the Kurdish issue reminds the older Koçkiri generation in particular of the Turkish proverb 'Politics is a shirt made of fire',[15] and they consequently tend to view themselves as Turkish. In this direction, those poems and legends which show the East Iranian region of Khôrasân as the homeland of great Alevi teachers, and which in former times were considered to be evidence of the religious credibility of their disciples, are today increasingly understood as proof of the ethnically Turkish origin of the Alevi.

Conclusion

With the opening up of the closed parochial communities and the migration of their members to the big cities, the orally mediated and simple folk-beliefs of the Alevi are confronted by an outside world which cannot be integrated into their traditional religious parameters. The Alevi's narrow social basis of tribe and village communities, and their isolated conditions of life, resulted in a mystic world-view which failed to objectify itself in a widespread written tradition. Its restriction to a small and weak region in the world affords little credibility today in an era in which the consciousness of a steadily growing number of people is shaped by global media networks. In contrast to the Sunni Islamic movements, which use religious terms to define secular modern issues, the Alevi youth are forced to interpret their religious culture in terms of secular ideologies, such as socialism and/or nationalism.

For its members in the global city, the tribe plays an important role in their cultural and political identity. This role emerges at two different levels. First, the tribe provides the individual with a meaningful history. As a member of the Koçkiri, you have, this 'history' tells you, always been in opposition to Sunni Muslim Turkism. You were always peripheral and you have always been suppressed and outlawed. The entities in which this contrast occurs may have changed from the 'Alevi Tribe vs Sunni Muslim Empire' confrontation to the 'Kurdish Socialist vs Turkish-ruled Capitalist State' confrontation, but the frontier is still seen as the same.

The second level at which tribe membership influences identities is its provision of relatively closed social units, in which the transformation of the indigenous, local culture is worked out according to global patterns. The tribe members face the new and differently structured 'meaningful systems' (which emerge as global and therefore valid ones) as a community. The production of identities – that is, ideally and typically, the transformation of an Alevi tribe member into a Kurdish leftist – happens in a community from which one can remove oneself only at the cost of being ostracized. Interestingly enough, the descendants of religious authorities sometimes become the strongest political activists. For Alevi and Sunni Muslims, for Turks and Kurds, and for all the different cultural camps in Turkish society, however, it may be argued that it is, to a large extent, the community of origin which plays a decisive role in placing its members in a specific segment of the political spectrum.

Urban environment and the impact of a free labour market lead to a sudden decay of traditional social structures and force the individual to build up 'its own' personal identity. It is the tension between atomizing social relations and the individual's self-understanding in religious concepts which leads to the discovery of modern and individualistic values in traditional creeds. That modern identities are construed with religious symbolical material is a clear hint at global and postmodern times. It could be suggested that the postmodern critics of universalistic approaches and solutions that emerge together with globalism (Turner 1994: 9) encourage religious intellectuals to present religious patterns of life-conduct as serious alternatives to secular ones.

There is, however, as the example of the clans' migration into global conditions has shown, no need to raise hopes that the mixing of local and global culture will usher in 'a new melting pot of multiculturalism' (Turner 1994: 186). Rather, we may experience the systematization and rationalization of the doctrines of local cultures, which then function as modern political ideologies.[16]

Notes

1. The data were collected by participant observation, narrative interviews and group discussions with members of the concerned clans during various meetings in the years 1993 and 1994 in Istanbul.

2. *Tirkan*, (Kurdish (Kurmancı): Turks, *Kirveler*, Turkish: godfathers, the word is used for the man who holds the boy during the circumcision. The denotation refers to a quasi-kinship established out of fulfilled social and religious duties.

3. It is asserted that about one in three Kurds in Turkey is Alevi (Şener and İlknur 1994: 9).

4. Almost the same as the region that today makes up the province of Tunceli; the name of the province was changed by the Turkish government.

5. For the theology of the Alevi, see Mélikoff (1992); 20–25 per cent of the Republic's population are assumed to be Alevi (Steinbach 1993: 23). For Twelver Shia, see Ende 1984.

6. *Cumhuriyet*, 13 May 1993, p. 3; for the judge of the *ulema* see Topaloğlu (1993: 11–12) and Yiğenoğlu (1993: 1).

7. For a witness, see Şener (1993: 20).

8. So did Selahattin Özel, president of the Alevi Federation of Hacı-Bektaş Associations, and the Alevi researcher Lütfü Kaleli, both cited in Karakoyun and Araş (1994: 24 and 25).

9. See the cover story of *Nokta*, 6 March 1994.

10. On the seventeenth, fourteenth and fifty-second after the day of decease.

11. Apart from religious feasts, marriages are the most important events in a Turkish village. They are celebrated by all the villagers who, during the celebrations, legitimize the new affiliations which are established by the marriage (Seufert 1983). To inscribe the new affiliations in the memories of as many people as possible, the new city-dwellers need very large wedding salons.

12. Who make up the respectable majority of the Kurds in Turkey.

13. Nearly the same words are used by the *dede* Musa Ateş (1992).

14. See, for this thesis in the new Alevi literature, for example, Bender (1991). The 'Kurdish influence' on the Alevi culture is also underlined by Bulut (1991).

15. '*Siyaset, ateşten gömlek*.'

16. For the character of modern ideologies, see Bendix (1964).

References

Andrews, P. A. (ed.) (1989) *Ethnic Groups in the Republic of Turkey*. Reichert Verlag, Wiesbaden.

Ateş, M. (1992) 'Allah Türkçe bilmiyor mu?', *Nokta*, 20 May.

Bender, C. (1991) *Kürt tarihi ve uygarlığı*. Mesopotamya Yayınları, Istanbul.

Bendix, R. (1964) 'The Age of Ideology', in D. Apter (ed.), *Ideology and Discontent*. Free Press of Glencoe, New York.

Berger, P. and Luckmann, T. (1967) *The Social Construction of Reality*. Allen Lane, London.

Bora, T. and Can, K. (1991) *Devlet, ocak, dergâh*. İletişim Yayınları, Istanbul.

Bruinessen, M. van (1992) *Agha, Shaikh und State: The Social and Political Structures of Kurdistan*. Zed Books, London.

Bulut, F. (1991) *Belgelerle Dersim Raporları*. Tümzamanlar Yayınları, Istanbul.

Coşkun, Z. (1996) *Öteki Sivas*. İletişim Yayınları, Istanbul.
Demirci, K. (1993) 'Ayna tutum yüzüme, Ali göründü gözüme', *İzlenim*, May.
Ende, W. (1984) 'Der schiitische Islam', in W. Ende and U. Steinbach (eds), *Der Islam in der Gegenwart*. Beck Verlag, Munich.
Eryılmaz, B. (1992) *Osmanlı devletinde Millet Sistemi*. Agaç Yayınları, Istanbul.
Gümrükçü, H. (1986) *Beschäftigung und Migration in der Türkei*. Beiträge zur Arbeitsmarkt- und Berufsforschung 104, Hamburg.
Güneş-Ayata, A. (1990/91) 'Gecekondularda kimlik sorunu', *Toplum ve Bilim* 51–2, 89–101.
Hall, S. (1993) 'The Local and the Global', in A. D. King (ed.), *Culture, Globalization and the World-System* (2nd edn). Macmillan, London.
İnalcık, H.and Quatert, D. (eds) (1994) *An Economic and Social History of the Ottoman Empire*. Cambridge University Press, Cambridge.
Karakoyun S. and Araş, V. (1994) 'Aleviler yeniden yapılanıyorlar', *Yön*, 31 July.
Karpat, K. H. (1973) 'An Inquiry into the Social Foundations of Nationalism in the Ottoman State', in P. Brass (ed.), *Ethnic Groups and the State*. Ottowa, 1985.
Kehl-Bodrogi, K. (1988) *Die Kızılbaş Aleviten*. Schwarz Verlag, Berlin.
Kofler, L. (1975) *Soziologie des Ideologischen*. Kohlhammer Verlag, Stuttgart.
Laçiner, Ö. (1985) 'Der Konflikt zwischen Sunniten und Alewiten in der Türkei in Blaschke', in J. and M. van Bruinessen (eds), *Religion und Politik in der Türkei*. Express Edition, Berlin.
Luckmann, T. (1991) *Die unsichtbare Religion*. Suhrkamp, Frankfurt am Main.
Lukacs, J. (1993) 'The 20th Century and the End of Modern Times', *Harpers*, January.
Mardin, Ş. (1989) *Religion and Social Change in Modern Turkey*. University of New York Press, Albany, NY.
Mélikoff, I. (1992) *Sur les traces du soufisme Turc*. Eren Yayınları, Istanbul.
Robertson, R. (1992) *Globalization, Social Theory and Global Culture*. Sage, London.
Schiffauer, W. (ed.) (1993) *Familie und Alltagskultur*. Kulturantropoligische Notizen, Frankfurt am Main.
Şener, C. and İlknur, M. (1994) 'Şeriat ve Alevilik'. Series in *Cumhuriyet* beginning 16 August.
Seufert, G. (1983) 'Kinderehen in der Türkei', *Materialien zum Problembereich ausländische Arbeitnehmer* 39.
Steinbach, U. (1993) *Türkei*. Informationen zur politischen Bildung, BfpB, Bonn.
Topaloğlu, B. (1993) '"Sünni-Alevi" diyaloğuna taraftarım', *İzlenim*, May.
Turner, B. S. (1994) *Orientalism, Postmodernism and Globalism*. Routledge, London and New York.
Väth, G. (1993) 'Zur Diskussion um das Alevitum', *Zeitschrift für Türkeistudien* 2.
Vorhoff, K. (1995) *Zwischen Glaube, Nation und neuer Gemeinschaft*. Schwarz Verlag, Berlin.
Weber, M. (1973) 'Der Sinn der "Wertfreiheit" der Sozialwissenschaften', in J. Winkelmann (ed.), *Max Weber, Soziologie, Universalgeschichtliche Analysen, Politik*, 5. Kroner, Stuttgart.
Wedel, H. (1994) 'Neue Kräfte in der Kommunalpolitik: Problemlösungsstrategien von *Gecekondu*-Frauen'. Unpublished paper of a lecture given at the Institute of the Deutsche Morgenländische Gesellschaft, Istanbul, 30 March.
Yiğenoğlu, Ç. (1993) 'Ölü ozanlar kenti Sivas'. Series in *Cumhuriyet* beginning 8 July.
Yılmaz, Ş. H. (1994) 'Alevilerde yerel seçim sendormu', *Nokta*, 16 January.

11

Travelling Islam: mosques without minarets

Jan Nederveen Pieterse

Historical and cultural differences within Islam are so considerable that the category 'Islam', with its unitary ring and its homogenizing aura, may need to be put in quotes. Like Christianity, Islam is a term that works at a distance; at close range, finer distinctions are necessary. There is a common core to the diverse expressions of Islam but what is in the core, its size and halo vary considerably. The collective self-awarenesses that identify and proclaim the existence of Islam are not unproblematical. Further, to what extent is it justified to call migrants from Muslim countries 'Muslims'? They may be categorized in that way by administrative and clerical authorities in their countries of origin and residence, thus serving the interests of discursive and administrative neatness, but to what extent is Islam central to their lives? There may be cultural and religious Muslims, nominal and observant Muslims. For some, Islam may be part of what they have moved away from. Besides the mosque communities there is the circuit of coffee-houses and, in addition, there are those who frequent neither. The meaning of Islam, then, is not to be taken for granted; statistics are to be bracketed, their significance is not obvious.

The relationship between the global and the local is one of recurrent tension in Islam. Islam has a universalist vocation but no single organizational structure. Islam is a form of globalism that is organized mainly in local structures. Islam is a holistic religion, an ideology of alignment between religion and politics, society and state, but it survives and is revitalized amidst the process of differentiation which is a feature of complex societies.

For centuries Islam has spread worldwide carrying a universalist vocation, as part of the historical momentum of globalization. Intercontinental

Muslim trade and knowledge networks have long been part of the infrastructure of what is now called world capitalism (Abu-Lughod 1989) and which is presented as if it were an invading force alien to the world of Islam, rather than one whose momentum the Islamic world has helped to shape. What is the place of Islam in contemporary globalization? According to Hassan al-Turabi, the leading ideologue of the Muslim Brotherhood of Sudan: 'If pan-Islam is partly an outcome of the increasing internationalisation of human life, it would also give an impetus to that momentum' (Turabi 1993: 18). The Muslim diaspora, like other diasporas, may be viewed as part of an emerging global civil society: yet how does this accord with the integrist claims of Islam? Will Islam in the West be 'secularized' as it is exposed to the same influences that have led to the gradual depopulation of Christian churches (in Europe, more than in the Americas), the creeping impact of urbanization, education, the media, as part of the process of acculturation? Will the Muslim diaspora merge with the host cultures and generate new, hybrid forms? In Asia and Africa Islam has generated new forms and articulations: what is the course of Islam in the West?

Migration is induced by global differentiation and at the same time an attempt to cushion and negotiate its impact. The question considered here is migration/refiguration, or how does Islam *change* in the process of migration? One of the fallacies in thinking about cultural difference is the reification of difference, viewing it in solid and static terms. Both migrants and host cultures tend to be represented with a peculiar emphasis on their allegedly uniform and unchanging cultural characteristics – except for the young of the second and third generations. This is odd if only because migration is a travel experience and in most cultures travel is one of the central metaphors of change. Or, may migration also be viewed as a process of cultural conservation and reconstruction?

The first part of this chapter deals with travelling Islam generally, and the second part deals with Islam travelling in the West and with some of the patterns of intercultural cohabitation: mosques without minarets. 'Travelling Islam' deals with internal migration, the changing political economy of overseas migration, and compares the impact of internal and overseas migration. 'Islam in the West' considers the patterns of intercultural cohabitation shaped by the historical treatment of cultural differences in societies, as reflected in legislation and ideological orientations: it is within these contexts that immigrant culture is reconstructed. Thus there are distinct differences between multi-culturalism in Britain and pillarization in the Netherlands, but both have in common that they define immigrant groups in terms of 'ethnicity' rather than 'religion'. Finally, the boundaries that mark cultural identities and their degree of fluidity are discussed. The rise and decline of boundaries is one way of looking at the encoding and recoding of identity constructions: do enclave cultures persist or are hybrid identities emerging?

Travelling Islam

Migration/urbanization Internal migration and urbanization entails leaving village life behind and entering a complex, differentiated social world. In the urban centres one's social world and religious community no longer coincide, as in village Islam. Religion becomes privatized (Schiffauer 1988). It becomes optional and no more than a segment of life. Part-time Muslims may become Islamists precisely because of this, to compensate for the effect of segmentation. But not all migrants adhere or turn to Islam nor would it carry the same meaning for those who do. The overall relationship between religion and society changes. If society is primarily defined as secular, as in Turkey, religious communities may become counterforces to secular society and the relationship becomes one not of complementarity but of opposition, and Islam can become a vehicle of protest (Schiffauer 1988: 152).

Migration from the countryside is encouraged in the first place by the opening up of rural economies as a consequence of the advance of capitalist relations. When this occurs in conjunction with the retreat of the state from its welfare functions, as now increasingly happens in many countries, Islam in some form may step into the space left by the state. Likewise, Islam steps into the ideological void left by the waning appeal of nationalism and socialism. Where communal relations have been shattered, political Islam reinstates a moral economy that claims to reunite the community of believers. Offering ideals of social justice, a politics of redistribution that is egalitarian and provides a place for the poor, it presents a moral economy in the vernacular of tradition. In the process tradition is being reconstructed. Circumstances have also changed and, under the banner of sameness, Islam has changed. Islam is being politicized in a manner unlike both the official 'Islam of the powerful' and the popular Islam of the village.

If the twin processes of integration into world capitalism and the retreat of the state are crucial conditions for the reorientation of political Islam and the emergence of Islamism, in a broad kind of sense the same may hold for religious revival movements such as Hindutva in India, and ethnic and separatist movements in other societies: vernaculars of discontent, negotiating the present by reclaiming and reworking the past. In reinvoking and reconstructing moral economies these movements attempt to serve as a buffer against and vantage point amidst the advance of capitalism. They are a socio-cultural expression of the process of informalization induced by the tide of market globalization, part of the cultural politics of informalization, and part of the global politics of post-Cold War emancipation. The question is, can they be more effective than nationalism and socialism which, each in different ways, have sought either to channel or to counter the impact of capitalism? At any rate, power accrues to a wide variety of religious and ethnic entrepreneurs who give their own ideological and political inflection to this process.

What changes does Islam undergo when travelling? Initially it may become more central and prominent in some people's lives than it used to be in the countryside. Delocalized from the village Islam may show increasing orthodoxy. A tendency towards growing 'scripturalism' has been in evidence throughout Islam since the nineteenth century, as manifested in an increasing emphasis on Qurʾānic teaching, Islamic education and mosque-building (Geertz 1968; Gellner 1992). The scripturalist tendency comes at the expense of the folk Islam of saint worship, healing, sufism and local brotherhoods and guilds. The imam rather than the saint, marabout or sage becomes the central figure. The tendency of clericalization is reinforced in the migration process. When Islam leaves its original landscape, what travels are not the marabout shrines nor the rural folk practices and brotherhoods, but the Qurʾān and Qurʾānic teachings: the Qurʾān is portable Islam. The return to scriptures, while presented as an orientation to unchanging revelation and a holding fast to tradition, is itself a mode of modernization and a major indicator of change, because it makes cultural reproduction independent of local circumstances. It turns on literacy which, according to Bourdieu, is the benchmark of modernity. High Islam is modern Islam, modern precisely because of its scriptural orthodoxy. Because of this translocal orthodoxy, high Islam can travel. In the plural, of course, as Sunni and Shia orthodoxies. How these modern orthodoxies work out depends on the journey and the destination of travel.

Besides providing shelter from the storm of economic uprooting, the mosque serves as the university of the poor: offering orientation, basic education, a sense of historical depth. The imams are the intellectuals of the migrant working class. 'The holy text or traditions give certainty in a world of moral void; they are a sure protection against the dehumanizing impact of cynicism' (Parekh 1993: 141). In addition, mosques are platforms of power, arenas of contestation, aligned with the state, with non-state circuits of power or with emerging forces.

In Turkey, Şerif Mardin distinguishes various streams of Islam: the official Islam of the state, the localistic Islam of the *tarikas*, and the craft

Islam of the bazaar; but notes that the multi-dimensionality of Islam has been ignored in Turkish research. 'That Islam has been conceptualized as a unitary rather than segmental is probably due to the prevalence of a latent, "Turkish folk-model" of Islam most prevalent among the *Sunni* of exemplary piety' (Mardin 1977: 280). Which illustrates Gramsci's observation: 'Every religion is in reality a multiplicity of distinct and contradictory religions' (Pred and Watts 1992: 45).

These different streams have not been static over time nor have they remained neatly separated. One angle is to interpret the changes that have been taking place in Islam as the expression of tension between different kinds of Islam, as the cultural capital shared and claimed by a variety of social forces, in between the polarities of cosmopolitan Islam and village Islam. Cosmopolitan Islam, extending through caravan and maritime trade, through diasporas and settlements, through knowledge networks and through military expansion, has given shape to the historical dynamics of globalization, of which world capitalism is one manifestation. Village Islam has been part of the tribal underpinnings of this global expansion. The two have both overlapped (when tribal leaders came into political and economic power, when power followed communitarian imaginaries) and clashed (when village Islam urbanized and contested the power of the official Islam of the powerful).

What forms this takes differ from place to place as each locality brings together a different ensemble of influences. The vortex of rural–urban cohabitation shapes the local play of class and culture, of economic and political forces and ways of experiencing and viewing them through maps of meaning. Local histories of rural–urban relations, patterns of state–society relations and the local mix of regional and global influences make for different alignments in Egypt, Algeria, Turkey, Sudan and northern Nigeria. Recognizing the specific local ensemble of global influences makes for what Doreen Massey calls 'a global sense of place': 'a sense of place which is extra-verted, which includes a consciousness of its links with the wider world, which integrates in a positive way the global and the local' (Massey 1993: 66).

There is no firm or stable demarcation between the global and the local because, like different kinds of dough in a marble cake, they mingle and interpenetrate. The global and the local are not merely geographical categories but also ways of seeing, optical devices, discursive frames. A stable demarcation or contradiction between them may seem to exist only from a particular point of view, a fixed point in space and time. With a slight turn of the kaleidoscope, however, the relations may change altogether: the local appears in its global aspect, the global as an assemblage of travelling local features.

Islam itself is a form of globalism, a global civilizational ethos and, as pan-Islam, an aspiring world order (Beeley 1992). More than in other religions of the book, in Islam religion has been secularized in that spiritual order and temporal power are merged, making religion equivalent to political formation. In some respects this is a particularly modern feature and one reason why Islam, including contemporary political Islam, should not be viewed as an anti-modernity, as is common in contemporary polemics, but rather as an alternative modernity (for example, Al-Azmeh 1993). The terminology of 'fundamentalism' and the associated dichotomy between tradition and modernity are profoundly inadequate and misleading, as I have argued elsewhere (Nederveen Pieterse 1994). It is rather the modernity of political Islam which needs to be assessed. Nevertheless, conventional wisdom has it that Islam is at odds with the modern state and nationalism and thus, it has been argued, unable to accommodate modern international relations (George 1993: 4). Yet, if it is true that we are entering a postnationalist phase, what would this mean for the possible futures of Islam?

Islam in the shadow of the World Trade Center In colonial times the cities in the colonies were the most internationalized; now another kind of internationalization is occurring in the postimperial metropolitan centres. The skylines of global cities have been changing under the influence of the restructuring of corporate activity over the past decades. In the in-between places of the metropolitan centres, beneath the shadow of the glossy façades of megacapital, with a view of the changing skylines from below, an immigrant workforce instals itself. Saskia Sassen observes the presence of a migrant or immigrant workforce in the United States especially 'in major cities, which also have the largest concentration of corporate power'.

> We see here an interesting correspondence between great concentrations of corporate power and concentrations of an amalgamated 'other' ... The fact that most of the people working in the corporate city during the day are low-paid secretaries, mostly women – many of them immigrant or African-American women – is not included in the representation of the corporate economy or corporate culture. And the fact that at night a whole other, mostly immigrant workforce installs itself in these spaces ... and inscribes the space with a whole different culture (manual labor, often music, lunch breaks at midnight) is an invisible event. (Sassen 1993: 101)

Internal migration in Muslim countries was largely induced by world capitalism travelling overseas, whereas overseas migration means travelling *into* the sphere of world capitalism, seeking shelter in the shadow of the World Trade Centers. 'By destroying traditional means of livelihood, and by proletarianizing a greater part of the population in some regions, foreign investment encourages the movement of people very often in the direction where capital is coming from' (Pellerin 1994: 5). On the one hand, the internationalization of economies promotes the outflow of labour and, on the other, the casualization of the labour market in global cities makes for an expansion in the supply of low-wage jobs generated by major growth sectors. This twofold process both produces new migrations and facilitates their absorption (Sassen 1991: 316–19).

Islam and capitalism may both be described as 'world processes' (Pred and Watts 1992: 45) and as such they intersect in the matrix of migration. In Islam, 'the institutions of *hajj* (annual pilgrimage to Mecca) and *hijra* (the religious obligation of Muslims to migrate and simultaneously break ties, distance oneself from evil, and form new bonds of religious brotherhood) have over the centuries institutionalized migration' (Antoun 1994: 160; Eickelmann and Piscatori 1990). Thus, according to the imam of the London Central Mosque, migration may be described 'as a traditional Islamic way of life' (Darsh 1980: 75). He quotes a hadith saying that 'migration would not stop until repentance stopped and repentance would not stop until the sun rose in the West. The Hijrah will continue until the Last Day.' He continues: 'If we consider the different patterns of early Muslim migration, we shall discover a number of common factors between them and the present-day migrations. Some resulted from persecution, some from trading connections and others from desire for financial betterment' (Darsh 1980: 76). Migration in the quest for knowledge abroad is also a motif that has been recognized since medieval Islam.

Still, this reinterpretation papers over the actual controversy of the migration issue in Islam. It ignores an important distinction in the pattern of migration: 'In some sense these communities [Muslim communities that have settled in the West] by emigrating *into* rather than *away from* the non-Muslim world, have challenged the basic Muslim concept of Muslim solidarity exemplified by Muhammad's own *hijra* from Mecca to Medina' (Christie 1991: 459). From an extreme orthodox Islamic or Islamist point of view, travelling to the West, like imitating the West, may be a form of 'westoxification' and a betrayal of Islam. For instance, in the words of an orthodox Muslim leader in Turkey, Shaykh Zahid Kotku: 'To voyage to foreign countries simply to earn more money is irresponsible' (Mardin 1993: 222).

There are different ways, then, of preserving orthodoxy in a changing world. The imam's reading of migration both accommodates and obcures the episode of world capitalism; in a narrative of continuity, history is side-lined. The key issue is that while generally travel is a metaphor for transformation, in Islam, under the image of the *hajj* and the *hijra*, travel serves as a metaphor for reconstitution: both of these are journeys undertaken to preserve the faith. (There are similar notions of migration and diaspora as regrouping in Judaism, where it is combined with endogamy.) This is an intrinsic tension within Islam and part of the paradox of travelling Islam: is travelling out acknowledged in Islam or only travelling in?

In the matrix of migration, local and global processes interpenetrate. The global standing and aspirations of Islam are locally meaningful: they inspire a sense of identity and self-worth among the Muslim diaspora; they maintain the transnational infrastructure of Islamic culture, from the *hajj* to subventions and donations from various quarters of Muslim power. At the same time, global Islam is fragmented along denominational, political and ethnic lines and the awareness of global unity and momentum is simultaneously an awareness of fragmentation, division and conflict. The Muslim diaspora is the counter-image of the *hajj* in Mecca, an outflow as compared to an in-gathering. In the Muslim diaspora the paradox of Islam becomes manifest: a global project organized in local structures. In terms of organizational structure, Islam resembles Protestantism (strong localism, weak overarching structures), not Roman Catholicism.

As a form of globalism, Islam both colludes and competes with world capitalism. As mentioned before, the intercontinental trade networks of the Muslim world are part of the infrastructure of world capitalism. Along the oil trail multi-faceted networks of cooperation with global capitalism have been generated. While investments from oil-rich Muslim countries, through the recycling of petro-dollars since the 1970s, underpin the expansion of world capitalism, there has also been an investment in contesting the cultural and political manifestations of global capitalism in Muslim countries. Capitalism is being nourished on the investment end and being rejected, on the ground, on the consumer end ('Western decadence'). This overlaps with a wider contradiction which can be summed up as: 'Western technology, Islamic values'. The same funds, even the same centres, have been actively involved both in the economics of the consolidation of world capitalism and in the politics of defiance, in a complex configuration of collusion and contestation. Forces within the world of Islam have been on the defensive, participating in world capitalism so as better to defy it, while being riven, like the heartlands of capitalism themselves (see, D. Bell 1979), with inner contradictions. The bombing of the World Trade Center in New York presumably by a militant Islamist group from Egypt, which may have been sponsored by orthodox forces in Saudi Arabia, illustrates the dramatic scope and intensity of contradictions within Islam.

The ramifications of post-*infitah* economies in Muslim countries are contested by orthodox and militant groups who are – or until recently were – financially and ideologically supported from the very centres which participate in, enhance and benefit from the process of capitalist expansion. This inconsistency is part of the weakness of the *pax Islamica*, which in turn reflects the inability of its moral economy either to encompass or fundamentally to challenge world capitalism. Another indication of this is the marginal character of 'Islamic economics' (Kuran 1993).

Part of this are the dialectics of the Cold War. For decades Islam was viewed as a valuable ally in the struggle against communism and sponsored to the point that Islam itself became a form of political defiance in the hands of new social forces. Washington (the Mujahideen), Riyadh (the Muslim Brotherhood), Tel Aviv (Hamas) and Cairo all took part in this and found themselves together at the Khyber Pass, in support of the Mujahideen in Afghanistan. These Cold War alignments criss-crossed the Islamist foreign policies of Iran and Libya. Presently the armed militants in Algeria and Egypt are known as the 'Afghanis' because it is the Afghanistan connection that has been the source of arms, training, international organization and militarization of Islamists. Thus, the logic of Cold War security has become the basis of post-Cold War instability. It is the old story of the mercenaries at the borders of the empire armed and trained by the metropolis, trying to take over.

Part of the flipside of the contradictory politics of post-Cold War Islam is that the negative media reporting generated by the defiance and contestation on the part of the new forces rubs off on the Muslim diaspora. It contributes to a 'problem' image of Muslim minorities in the West who are thereby kept on the periphery of the social imaginary (cf. Hargreaves and Perotti 1993).

Mosques without minarets in the Netherlands What is the difference between internal migration and overseas migration, as the deterritorialization of Islam mark 2? The long-term tendency towards growing orthodoxy and clericalization may be reinforced in either mode of migration. In other respects the experience of migration is shaped and differentiated by many factors, such as the status of migrants – rural or urban, illiterate or educated; the gender of migrants and their position in the family; the character of migration – as traders or workers, for gain, knowledge or refuge; the direction of travel – East or West. To Asia and sub-Saharan Africa, Muslims came as traders and *ulamā* at times when Islam was in the ascendant. Their settlements often formed separate quarters within towns where they sometimes enjoyed a distinct legal status as trading minorities. The recent migrations of Muslims to the West, however, involve workers and take place at a time when, on the whole, global Islam has been on the defensive.

Does it make sense to generalize about migration experiences? What shapes the migration experience and the formation of local Muslim cultures in global spaces are the patterns of intercultural cohabitation which differ from country to country and the mix of transnational and cross-cultural influences which Muslims encounter. This is best looked at in specific terms. We will consider the case of Muslims in the Netherlands and then turn to Britain for a contrasting case.

The general point of this part of the chapter is to engage the paradox of travelling Islam, the complexity of the Islamic diaspora: on the one hand, the *umma* is being affirmed and realized in the diaspora, and, on the other, Islam while travelling is fractured along multiple lines – through cultural differentiation or 'ethnicization', political differentiation among and within nationalities, and generational differentiation.

In the West, mosques and minarets may be controversial markers of cultural presence. If the presence of migrants in the corporate city centres is marginal, little noticed or invisible – such as the cleaners who come in as the white-collar workers leave – in the neighbourhoods the immigrant presence may be highly visible. Reflecting on the reactions to the construction of a minaret in Dalston in the north-east London borough of Hackney, Gilsenan observes:

> Imagine – and it is very difficult for those who have not experienced the world of the colonized – the effect that outside forces, over a relatively short period of time, can have on the transformation of the *whole* of the relations that make up urban space, including its sacred geography and unquestioned givens of the way things are in cities. Imagine, not only one building being constructed on an alien model, but an entire system of urban life in its economic, political, and symbolic-cultural forms being imposed upon already existing towns and cities that have been organized on quite different bases. (Gilsenan 1982: 195)

'Mosques without minarets' evokes a fractured image of Islam on the move. Among Muslims a preferred image would be 'from prayer rugs to minarets' (Landman 1992), an image that reflects the gradual process of institutionalization of travelling Islam (Waardenburg 1988). In the course of thirty years, from the first labour migrations in the 1960s to the present, Muslim workers in Europe, many of them illiterates from the countryside, have brought over their families, set up enterprises, sent their children to school and have worked themselves up to establish a cultural presence. 'From prayer rugs to minarets' is a narrative of achievement and social mobility: from humble origins to proud attainment.

Mosques without minarets evokes the image of a subculture on the margins. In the Netherlands, a number of newly built mosques do in fact feature minarets, although the large majority does not – being converted school buildings, old churches or synagogues, old factories, or homes converted for use as prayer halls. What minarets there are do not tower above other buildings, do not claim prominent public sites, as is most often the case in Muslim countries, especially for newly built mosques. The minarets are lower than the high-rise offices of capital, lower than the World Trade Centers, lower even than the apartment high-rises among which they are nestled, proud and yet modest, substantial and yet, to outsiders, hardly noticeable. What is the cultural silhouette of a two-storey mosque with a slightly higher minaret, located next to a twenty-storey apartment high-rise?

In some ways the place of the new mosques matches that of the old churches, as part of wider shifts in the sacred geographies, the maps of meaning and profiles of power in the West. The status and function of Christian churches have changed over time: long gone are the days of *ecclesia triumphans* when churches were the dominant structures in the land- and townscapes. Gone are the days when the church in height and location competed only with the palace or town hall. Now banks and corporate real estate, towering on the model of the World Trade Center, dominate the cityscapes spatially and architecturally. Inner-city churches are being vacated, converted to galleries, shops, offices or apartments, and new churches are built on the outskirts, in architectures that are usually more abstract, modest, introverted.

In the Netherlands, the main groups of Muslims are Turks, Moroccans and Surinamese. These reflect different migration histories: colonial migration for the Surinamese and labour migration. Colonial migration is multi-class and involves greater familiarity with and a greater degree of integration in the metropolitan culture, in terms of language, education and jobs. The Surinamese are more integrated in Dutch society and on the whole rank higher in the cultural status hierarchy than Turks and Moroccans. Over time the composition of migration flows has changed. Family reunification brought greater numbers of women. Recent chain migration is bringing new marriage partners from the home countries. The shift to the migration of refugees and dissidents reflects economic and political instability in the countries of origin as well as the closing off of labour migration in Western Europe. Asylum seekers often break ties with their country of origin and thus stand in a different relationship to the community centres in which the culture of origin is reconstructed. Immigrants are further differentiated, of course, according to their regional origin, time of migration, the generation they belong to, political and religious affiliations, level of education, and employment.

The numbers of Muslim immigrants in the Netherlands are modest compared to Britain (with a much more differentiated South Asian component), France (with a greater North African and Middle Eastern presence) and Germany (with a large Turkish presence). The largest groups are the Turks (estimated at 200,000), Moroccans (numbering approximately 150,000), and Surinamese Muslims (22,000). They are mainly concentrated in the four largest cities (Amsterdam, Rotterdam, The Hague, Utrecht) where in 1991 they constituted, on average, 13.4 per cent of the total population, with the highest concentration in Amsterdam (15.5 per cent). In Amsterdam in 1991 the total number of inhabitants was 702,731, out of whom 108,861 were of foreign origin, including Turkish citizens (24,128), Moroccan citizens (33,902), Surinamese citizens (6,004). If we include Dutch citizens of Surinamese and Antillean ethnic origin, the percentage of inhabitants of alien origin is 24.3 of the total city population (Amersfoort 1992: 444). In other words, a quarter of the inhabitants of Amsterdam is of foreign origin, of which roughly a third are Turks and Moroccans.

It follows that Islam is broken down into cultural units: Turkish, Moroccan, Surinamese, Pakistani, Moluccan, and so on. Considering that the nationhood of 'others' tends to be classified as 'ethnicity', this means that many Muslims are categorized in terms of 'ethnicity'. This clashes with 'a key principle of Islam that religious identity should prevail over ethnic identity' (Christie 1991: 457). On the one hand, the *umma* is reconfirmed in the diaspora while, on the other, it is broken up in national and cultural differences.

The spatial location of the various mosques differs: Turkish mosques are often centrally located in cities and secondly in neighbourhoods; Moroccan mosques are typically found in low-income city neighbourhoods; Surinamese/South Asian mosques in low-income suburbs or neighbourhoods; while smaller communities congregate in rural towns, such as the Moluccan Muslims with their mosque in Ridderkerk (Slomp 1984).

What is being carried along the routes of labour migration is not a sophisticated form of Qur'ānic teaching. As the imam of the London Central Mosque notes, 'most of the Imams in this country lack the basic training required to lead the prayer in a village mosque, not to mention in a place of worship in a more sophisticated and intellectually superior society' (Darsh 1980: 89), and this applies more generally. For the first generation of migrants who came to Western Europe as 'guestworkers' in times of economic boom and who on the whole occupy a weak socio-economic position, Islam serves as a form of cultural identification and belonging: 'Most of the Muslim groups here feel at home when they get an Imam who is from the same village or area as the one from which they themselves came and who speaks the same language as they do and who is capable of reciting or reading a few chapters of the Holy Qur'ān' (Darsh 1980: 89). In France, the difficulties of the four million Muslims are summed up as follows: 'fragmentation on ethnic lines, absence of proper representation, guidance provided by untrained imams, and financial pressures from Arab countries that bankroll the community' (*Le Monde*, 14 July 1995).

There are many different nodes to the Islamic world network and each locality brings together a different ensemble of diverse currents. A brief overview of mosque communities in the Netherlands and their cultural, national, ethnic and political diversities may illustrate the mix of global and local influences and the way the Muslim diaspora is implicated in the vicissitudes of transnational politics and political economy.

Among Turkish Muslims the main organization is the Netherlands Islamic Foundation (Hollanda Diyanet Vakfi) which comes under the governmental Directorate for Religious Affairs in Ankara. This subsidizes the construction and upkeep of mosques and brings over imams schooled in Turkey. Presently it owns around 150 mosques and rents another ten. The aim of this government involvement is to control the growth of orthodox and extreme Muslim groups in Europe, presumably also because it could affect the political situation in Turkey. The head of the organization in The Hague is seated under a portrait of Kemal Ataturk. For several years the world Muslim organization Rabita (Rabitat al-Alam al-Islami) in Mecca sponsored the Turkish imams sent to the Netherlands, but one of the conditions was that they preach in Arabic; since 1986 Turkey has paid for the imams (Waardenburg 1988).

One of the competing organizations among Turkish Muslims in Western Europe is the Teblig movement led by Cemalettin Kaplan in Cologne, also known as the 'Khomeini of Cologne'. With funding from Iran shrinking, the mosques associated with Kaplan have been decreasing as well (down to three in 1989); the funds for the upkeep of mosques and imams were simply lacking. Another orthodox Turkish association is Milli Görüscu (National Vision) which runs some fifteen mosques throughout the country (Beunders and Huygen 1989).

Of the approximately 250 mosques in the Netherlands in 1989, 100 are Moroccan (Sijtsma 1989: 150). The Moroccan government also exercises influence over Moroccan mosques but without the tight organization of the Turkish government and without providing funding. UMMON (Union of Moroccan Mosques in the Netherlands) and Amicales are influential government arms, but the mosques are run by local foundations. Moroccans in the Netherlands hail mainly from the Rif mountains and from the south, rural populations who are newcomers to orthodoxy and among whom regional divisions play a large part. Some years ago a few Moroccan mosques turned for funding to the Islamic Call Society in Libya, founded by Gadaffi in 1972, a loose organization which seeks to merge Islam with Gadaffi's Green Book ideas of socialism and women's emancipation. In order to quell Moroccan infighting this organization sent Libyan and Filipino imams to the Netherlands.

Surinamese and South Asian Muslims are organized in the World Islamic Mission which controls some forty-two mosques for Surinamese, Pakistanis and Indians, united by Urdu as a common language. Established in 1976 the Mission is affiliated with the Muslim World Congress headquartered in Karachi. Affiliated with the Mission are the large mosques in the Bijlmer (a suburb of dormitory high-rises constructed in the 1970s in the south-east of Amsterdam which houses many immigrants) and in Utrecht, which were originally established with funding from Saudi Arabia and other Arabic states. (The intercultural character of the Bijlmer is evocatively described by Hannerz 1992.) Surinamese Muslims further maintain an Islamic Parliament, headquartered in Arnhem, and the Aqaidul Islam organization in The Hague.

There are many other Muslim organizations active in the Netherlands, such as the Ahmaddya movement, the Süleymanci group and several Sufi orders. Attempts to establish a federation of Muslim organizations, a central Muslim council and umbrella institutions such as Islamic broadcasting have failed repeatedly. Instead there is a coming and going of organizations, councils and federations that are unevenly funded from various quarters including Saudi Arabia, Kuwait and Libya. Establishing Muslim institutions is also a form of transnational fundraising and job creation, a way to establish silver links with oil-rich Muslim countries. According to the imam of the London Central Mosque: 'In one small area with a population of approximately 3,000 people, I counted no less than six Muslim societies' (Darsh 1980: 80). It shows the dispersed and scattered infrastructure of global Islam: one Mecca, many centres.

The relationship between home government control and government financial means affects the scope for autonomy: Turkey exercises greater influence over its Muslim diaspora in the name of Kemal Ataturk, than Morocco does over Moroccan Muslims in the name of King Hassan II. The ups and downs of oil revenues further affect the degree of orthodoxy and the ebb and flow of 'fundamentalism'.

Local encounters, such as between Surinamese and South Asian Muslims in the Netherlands (typically in the port city of Rotterdam), make for new formations, such as the World Islamic Mission. Overseas colonial history informs local cultural mixing: thus the Lalla Rookh organization in Utrecht serves as a meeting place for Surinamese Muslims and Hindus. Islam is preached in the Netherlands in several languages: Turkish, Arabic, Urdu, English and Dutch, three of which are transnational languages. Travelling Islam is intercultural Islam, much more so than in its countries of origin.

Islam in the West

Vortexes of cohabitation The Netherlands is a relatively open country with a higher degree of international interdependence than neighbouring countries: a much higher percentage of Dutch GNP is generated abroad, through trade, services and investments, than in the neighbouring countries. This openness goes back a long time in Dutch history. From the twelfth century onwards the Low Countries developed a special niche in the region in which they competed with their neighbours on the basis of openness as a selling point. By deliberate strategy, merchants and nobles combined in imposing no limitations on trade with foreigners and non-Christians, setting low tolls and permitting the right of return of ships and cargo in time of war. Elsewhere I have termed this the political economy of tolerance (Nederveen Pieterse 1983). This also found expression in cultural orientations, such as the fifteenth-century saying, in defiance of Catholic Spanish–Habsburg domination, 'Better Turkish than Popish'. It found expression in welcoming religious and political dissidents and persecuted minorities from abroad – Sephardic Jews from Portugal and Spain, Huguenots from France, Pilgrims from England – who through their skills, assets and networks contributed enormously to the Dutch economy. For the Dutch 'tolerated' minorities have historically been *traits d'union* to the world economy. All of this is now long forgotten but the principle of toleration remains a value in Dutch culture. A brief comparison between English and Dutch ways of relating to cultural difference may illustrate the role of cultural orientations and their political ramifications.

In England, the head of state is the head of the Church of England and other denominations have a less privileged status. English legislation does not take account of Islam: the blasphemy law does not apply to Islam and ritual slaughter, polygamous marriage and female circumcision are not recognized. Muslims are treated as ethnic minorities under statutes derived from human rights conventions. Religious institutions receive no general support from the state but can be recognized as charities and be granted tax exemptions: in 1985, 329 mosques were thus recognized (Rath et al. 1991: 106–8). (For a wider discussion of multi-culturalism and liberalism in Britain, see Parekh 1994.)

In the Netherlands since the early nineteenth century the principle of equality of religions has been anchored in the constitution. Equal rights in terms of state support for education was granted to Catholics only in 1917. State financing of schools founded by religious organizations established the system of 'pillarization', also known as the 'silver strings' between the state and Christian denominations. In the revised constitution of 1983 the principle of equality also extends to non-religious convictions. Accordingly Muslims are placed in the same position as Jewish, Hindu or Humanist groups. The blasphemy law also applies to Islam and days off for Islamic holidays are also legally recognized. In 1987 the rules applying to the ringing of church bells were extended to calls to prayer from mosques. State support for establishing places of worship is a recommended policy, on the argument that religious self-organization for those who come from societies where religion plays an important part is natural. At the same time, Muslims are legally recognized as 'ethnic minorities' rather than as a religious category. As a consequence those groups who are not recognized as ethnic minorities, such as Palestinians and Pakistanis, do not fall under the terms of state support (Rath et al. 1991: 108–11).

While multi-culturalism in Britain has been patterned on the colonial experience (Ali 1992: 104) as the main way in which cultural difference has been historically recognized, that is as an experience taking place *outside* the nation, pillarization, the Dutch mode of cultural pluralism from the 1910s to the 1970s, refers to the history of religious and political differences *within* the nation, among Catholics, Protestants and the non-church affiliated. Pillarization valorizes cultural difference from the angle of religion; multi-culturalism in Britain 'ethnicizes' cultural difference. At the same time, Dutch policies follow a double track in recognizing ethnic difference or national origin over religious difference.

In the Netherlands one reaction to migrants, once it became clear that they were immigrants, was to reinstate pillarization. Pillarization seemed a logical mode in which to incorporate the newcomers. Thus Christian democrats, not without nostalgia for the old pillars, spoke of 'emancipation within one's own circle', just as sixty years earlier this applied to Catholics and Protestants who each received state subsidies for their schools and institutions. But the differences between denominational and multi-cultural pillarization were overlooked. The confessional pillars shared power at the top, together their elites made up a roof over the pillarized society. But the pillars of the newcomers with their low socio-economic status do not reach that high, theirs are only mini-pillars. This truncated mini-pillarization did involve subsidies for immigrant institutions but did not add up to a position of power brokering. The overall timing was another difference: multi-cultural mini-pillars emerged in an urbanized and secularized society in which religious pillarization was past and denominational differences were becoming a background rumour (Knippenberg and Pater 1988). In the course of the 1980s the pillarization model gave way to a greater emphasis on integration, advocated by social democrats and assimilation, endorsed by free market conservatives. In the 1990s this takes the form of policies emphasizing learning the language, courses in citizenship skills, and immigrant employment schemes with a reporting system for companies.

A further dynamic is the relationship between residential patterns, employment and other indices of social participation. It has been argued that in postindustrial welfare states such as the Netherlands this relationship has become quite weak: 'In postindustrial societies the labour market no longer appears to be the primary field of interaction determining other spheres of societal interaction. Housing, work and education have become (relative) autonomous circuits' (Amersfoort 1992: 439). The welfare state and especially municipal councils in which the Labour Party predominates, as in the big cities where immigrants are concentrated, control the allocation of social housing.

> In the first years of immigration, 1964–1974, unemployment among immigrants was very low. The great social problem connected with immigration was the housing situation, with overcrowded lodging houses and associated ills. The housing situation is presently more or less satisfactory, but it seems impossible to solve the unemployment problem. In the welfare state tradition, the Netherlands people ... look to the Government for a solution to social problems. But the Government has less control over the labour than over the housing market and a solution is not in sight. (Amersfoort 1992: 453)

Unemployment among Moroccan and Turkish immigrants is high and their level of schooling is low. 'The vanguard which has managed to find a paying job either does the same work as the first generation or works for their own ethnic group in jobs in which vertical mobility is virtually lacking' (Aboutaleb and van der Burght 1986: 189). For some time unemployment has been at the top of the agenda, for native as well as allochthonous citizens. For immigrants this has led to the adoption of a compulsory reporting system on hiring practices by companies and to policies of fostering integration by making learning Dutch obligatory for newcomers.

The Amsterdam skyline is lower than that of New York, London or Paris, and high-rises are scattered around rather than located within the inner city. There are concentrations of multinational capital around the World Trade Centre, as part of the south axis of corporate real estate extending towards Schiphol airport. Other areas of corporate concentration are in the south-east and the teleport on the north axis of the city (*Boomtown* 1988). It is in the interstices of the edifices of megacapital that migrant labour finds a place. In sweatshops, particularly in the garment industry, the migrant workforce delivers the goods for just-in-time capitalism. Turkish-owned sweatshops form an important infrastructure of the Amsterdam garment industry.

There may be a different way of looking at migrants and the role they play in economic restructuring: 'Rather than being a marginal mass of workers, or a specific category in the segmented market, they become a "vector" of restructuring' (Pellerin 1994: 14). Specifically, the situation in many industrialized receiving countries allows:

> the coexistence of high levels of unemployment among the indigenous labour force, and economic decline more generally, with significant levels of employment amongst foreign workers, or at least some categories of foreigners. Consequently, rather than regulating economic cycles, migrants seem to participate in the deregulation of the productive process in many industries. (Pellerin 1994: 13)

In the context of the prevailing political economic regime, there may well be a limit to minority employment schemes and to expectations for the gradual integration of immigrants in the primary labour market and society at large. With or without diplomas, the second and third generation may not find enough jobs, because they compete with indigenous white- and blue-collar sectors whose unemployment has been growing, in an environment where cultural capital counts. Are immigrants destined then to remain in enclaves, economically and culturally? Two qualifiers may alter this picture. One is that in intercultural society, *intercultural capital* itself becomes an asset, that is, ethnic entrepreneurship and hybrid entrepreneurship may themselves be generators of growth. The second is the role of cultural cross-over which enhances the ability of immigrants to compete in the labour market.

The rise and decline of boundaries Common understandings of the way Muslims define their boundaries with Dutch society focus on the areas of purity, sexuality and religion (Bartels 1989). Purity relates to food and drink (pork, halal meat, alcohol) and habits of cleanliness. Sexuality relates to the position of women. And with respect to religion,

Muslims might view Dutch culture as anti-Islamic because of its degree of secularization and separation of church and state. Such boundaries give a sense of self-worth. Purity and sexuality provide a sense of moral superiority which may compensate for class inferiority.

Non-Muslims construct similar boundaries of cultural difference with shifts in emphasis and meaning, focused on the suppression of women; notions of 'backwardness' – as in common comparisons, benevolent or otherwise, between immigrants and Dutch people in the past; and religion – as in ideas about Islamic orthodoxy and 'fundamentalism' (Bartels 1989). These boundaries provide Dutch people with a sense of superiority which justifies class differences, and which is helpful in a society otherwise suffused with a rhetoric of egalitarianism. The cliché of Muslim suppression of women diverts attention from the marginal status of Dutch women, in a society where there is a discrepancy between a high level of feminist rhetoric and a low level of actual women's emancipation. Orthodoxy and 'fundamentalism' reflect, on the one hand, popular media images of global Islam from Iran and Algeria to Bradford, and on the other, popular reactions to Muslim life-styles, such as traditional dress and veiled women.

How firm and stable over time are these boundaries? To each there are elements of stretch and in-built boundary-crossing moments. The purity boundary may be the most permeable. The higher the level of education, the more likely Muslims are to ignore dietary restrictions and integrate with Dutch society; here the same pattern prevails as in internal migration. Another effect is manifested in cities with Muslim concentrations: in the marketplace cultural boundaries are increasingly being crossed. Due to recession and unemployment which reduce immigrant purchasing power, ethnic entrepreneurs turn to native or cross-ethnic customers and adjust their products accordingly. Dutch retailers have long been stocking 'ethnic' produce: a fish stall which first imported fish from Spain and Portugal, then from the Caribbean, now stocks Moroccan fish. This is obvious in places such as the Albert Cuyp market, a popular ethnically mixed food market in Amsterdam (Obbema 1994).

The boundary of sexuality and the position of women in some respects clash with Dutch laws and customs as regards the scope of parental authority, obligatory schooling, marriage and life-style. Over the years there have been a series of clashes between municipal or state authorities and Muslim parents on restrictions imposed on women and daughters, reported in the popular press. Without going into details, it is obvious that this is an unstable and conflict-ridden boundary, particularly for youngsters of the second and third generations (Vries 1987; Feddema 1992).

'The first generation of migrants often becomes more religiously active than they were in their homeland' (Lans and Rooijackers 1992: 56). The second generation faces a different situation: 'To follow the parental religious model, to adopt an alternative style of Islamic observance or to give up religious identity at all will become a matter of choice for them' (Lans and Rooijackers 1992: 56). In the process, the meaning of religion itself changes. Religious discourse not only structures experience but is also structured and changed by the different circumstances (Sunier 1992). Thus deterritorialized Islam, when no longer a reflection of village reciprocity, in its new settings acquires an ethical function of upholding norms that society does not but should follow (Schiffauer 1988).

Ooijen (1992) asks a pertinent question: do Islamic organizations promote emancipation or isolation? The degree of choice experienced by the second generation is also a matter of educational level. Among Moroccans, the general educational level is lower than among other Muslims in the Netherlands. As a consequence also their international connections are not as well developed as are those of other nationalities. For Moroccans Islam remains the most important basis for self-help organizations. Hence van Ooijen criticizes attempts to impose government-controlled emancipation patterns, for instance by channelling subsidies to non-religious institutions for migrants.

All the same, Islam is exposed to the same secularizing pressures that have eroded Dutch pillarization: rising education levels, media exposure, urbanization. There are ample manifestations of everyday syncretism: Muslims who respect Ramadan but also buy presents and a Christmas tree so that their children will not feel left out; mosques that would like to use the Qur'ān-classrooms to offer computer courses, also to have something to empower the jobless second generation; hybrid figures such as the 'educated believer' (Lithman 1988).

To Dutch stereotyping of Muslim immigrants there is an in-built time slide: 'backwardness' may be overtaken by social climbing or, at least, by the adoption of symbolic markers of integration in dress and life-style. The test of how these boundaries are constructed, deconstructed and redrawn is in the neighbourhoods. Here residential familiarity makes it possible for distinctions to become fine, rather than crude generalizations, and to identify where they fade or are redefined. 'Our neighbour is a modern Turk', a statement made in an Amsterdam neighbourhood report, refers to the neighbour speaking Dutch (van Soest 1994). Similar distinctions are drawn in neighbourhoods in Haarlem (Jong 1990). In Amsterdam neighbourhoods, Moroccan youths have taken over the spots and streetcorners where previously Surinamese Creole boys gathered. The latter have moved on from the streets to youth centres and thence to coffee shops and other commercial venues, a path that was followed earlier by white working-class youth (Sansone 1992: 177). Accordingly, class tracks and careers may prove to be stronger than patterns based on cultural difference.

In France, the second and third generation of *beurs*, the audience of raï and rap, claim 'le droit à l'ambiguité', which is resisted by ethnonationalists and Islamists (Gross et al. 1992). In the Netherlands cultural crossover is the common trend among second and third generation immigrants from Muslim countries and resistance to cultural mixing is weak (Feddema 1992; Lans and Rooijackers 1992). What comes across in many reports is that what matters in the neighbourhoods is socio-economic prospects – jobs, education, living conditions, moving to a better neighbourhood – and municipal and state policies, rather than cultural difference or 'ethnicity'. That these concerns are shared by immigrants and natives alike shows a common reaction to living in the postindustrial welfare state.

By way of conclusion

This chapter has raised questions about the meaning of travel in Islam: does Islam recognize only travelling in or also travelling out? And it has raised questions about the complexity of the Islamic world mirrored in the Islamic diaspora. Rather than revisiting the rhetorics of unity and homogeneity – upheld by advocates and opponents alike – it has considered some of the fractures and divisions in the world of Islam on the move.

High Islam is modern Islam, which ironically is more orthodox than local Islam. Modern Islam travels well because it does not depend on local circumstances for its cultural reproduction, but what if travel leads outside the ring of Islam? What scope for intercultural mixing does Islam offer? The tension within Islam – a global project organized in local structures – is affirmed in the Muslim diaspora. If Islam is varied enough within the Arab world and in adjacent Iran and Turkey, the new Islams that have developed in the peripheries of this heartland, in Asia, Africa and more recently in Europe and North America, further add to the Muslim *mélange*.

Part of the paradox of the Islamic world is its complex pattern of collusion and contestation with world capitalism. The Islamic presence in the West is both substantial and modest; Europe's second largest religion boasts many mosques but mosques without minarets, in a word, religion without power. To an extent this is made up for by prestige architecture such as the new mosque in New York and the new mosque in Rome: Europe's largest mosque for Europe's second largest religion erected in the spiritual capital of Europe's largest religion.

In the diaspora the *umma* is affirmed and broken up in cultural sub-units, some of which generate novel combinations. The sites of diaspora produce their own opportunity structures. In the Netherlands the combined tendencies of pillarization, ethnicization and integration makes for a different field than in Britain with its predominant discourse of racialized cultural difference, while in France secularism and *laicité* make for yet another arena of difference.

Smaller countries in the West such as the Netherlands may offer greater opportunities for crossover culture than the larger countries: when the numbers of immigrants are smaller, immigrant enclaves are too small to sustain reproduction, either culturally or economically, and cultural chauvinism is weaker. Hence opportunities and incentives for hybridization are greater. This offers yet another form of peripheral Islam. But of course these conditions also exist in different localities within the larger countries.

Acknowledgement

I am indebted to Azza Karam for her comments on an earlier version of this chapter.

References

Aboutaleb, A. and van der Burght, F. (1986) 'De Helden van de Tweede generatie – jonge Turken en Marokkanen in Nederland', in S. Franke et al. (eds), *Maak er een gewoonte van: racismebestrijding in de grote stad*. De Populier, Amsterdam.

Abu-Lughod, J. L. (1989) *Before European Hegemony: the World-System A.D. 1250–1350*. Oxford University Press, New York.

Ahmed, A. S. and Donnan, H. (eds) (1994) *Islam, Globalization and Postmodernity*. Routledge, London.

Al-Azmeh, A. (1993) *Islams and Modernities*. Verso, London.

Ali, Y. (1992) 'Muslim Women and the Politics of Ethnicity and Culture in North England', in G. Saghal and N. Yuval-Davis (eds), *Refusing Holy Orders: Women and Fundamentalism in Britain*. Virago, London.

Amersfoort, H. van (1992) 'Ethnic Residential Patterns in a Welfare State: Lessons from Amsterdam 1970–1990', *New Community* 18 (3), 439–56.

Antoun, R. T. (1994) 'Sojourners Abroad: Migration for Higher Education in a Post-peasant Society', in A. S. Ahmed and H. Donnan (eds), *Islam, Globalization and Postmodernity*.

Bartels, E. (1989) 'Moslimvrouwen en Moslim-identiteit', in R. Haleber (ed.), *Rushdie Effecten*.

Beeley, B. (1992) 'Islam as a Global Political Force', in A. G. McGrew, et al. (eds), *Global Politics*. Polity Press, Oxford.

Bell, D. (1979) *The Cultural Contradictions of Capitalism*. Vintage, New York.

Beunders, H. and Huygen, M. (1989) 'Een zuil zonder fundament', *NRC Handelsblad*, 22 April.

Boomtown Amsterdam: ontwerpen om de Stad (1988) ARCAM/ Meulenhoff, Amsterdam.

Christie, C. J. (1991) 'The Rope of God: Muslim Minorities in the West and Britain', *New Community* 17 (3), 457–66.

Darsh, S. M. 1980 *Muslims in Europe*. Ta-Ha, London.

Eickelmann, D. F. and Piscatori, J. (eds) (1990) *Muslim Travellers: Pilgrimage, Migration, and the Religious Imagination*. University of California Press, Berkeley.

Feddema, R. (1992) *Levensoriëntatie van jonge Turken en Marokkanen in Nederland*. PhD thesis. Utrecht University.

Geertz, C. (1968) *Islam Observed: Religious Development in Morocco and Indonesia*. Chicago University Press, Chicago.

Gellner, E. (1992) *Postmodernism, Reason and Religion*. Routledge, London.

George, D. (1993) 'Pax Islamica: an Alternative New World Order'. Unpublished paper, University of Newcastle.

Gerholm, T. and Lithman, Y. G. (eds) (1988) *The New Islamic Presence in Western Europe*. Mansell, London.

Gilsenan, M. (1982) *Recognizing Islam*. Pantheon, New York.

Gross, J., McMurray, D. and Swedenborg, T. (1992) 'Rai, Rap and Ramadan Nights: Franco-Maghribi Cultural Identities', *Middle East Report* 22 (5), 11–16.

Haleber, R. (ed.) (1989) *Rushdie Effecten: Afwijzing van Moslim-identiteit in Nederland?* SUA, Amsterdam.

Hannerz, U. (1992) *Culture, Cities and the World*. Centrum voor Grootstedelijk Onderzoek, Amsterdam.

Hargreaves, A. G. and Perotti, A. (1993) 'The Representation on French Television of Immigrants and Ethnic Minorities of Third World Origin', *New Community* 19 (2), 251–62.

Jong, A. Tj. de (1990) 'Interetnische verhoudingen in een overbelaste nieuwbouwwijk', Ministerie van WVC, *Onderzoek en Perspectief* 12, Rijswijk.

Knippenberg, H. and de Pater, B. (1988) *De Eenwording van Nederland*. SUN, Nijmegen.

Kuran, T. (1993) 'The Economic Impact of Islamic Fundamentalism', in M. Marty and R. Scott Appleby (eds), *Fundamentalisms and the State*.

Landman, N. (1992) *Van mat tot minaret*. VU, Amsterdam.

Lans, J. M. van der and Rooijackers, M. (1992) 'Types of Religious Belief and Unbelief among Second Generation Turkish Migrants', in W. A. R. Shadid and P. S. van Koningsveld (eds), *Islam in Dutch Society*.

Lithman, Y. G. (1988) 'Social Relations and Cultural Continuities: Muslim Immigrants and their Social Networks', in T. Gerholm and Y. G. Lithman (eds), *The New Islamic Presence*.

Mardin, Ş. (1977) 'Religion in Modern Turkey', *International Social Science Journal* 29 (2), 279–97.

— (1993) 'The Nakshibendi Order of Turkey', in M. Marty and R. Scott Appleby (eds), *Fundamentalisms and the State*.

Marty, M. and Scott Appleby, R. (eds) (1993) *Fundamentalisms and the State*. The Fundamentalism Project, Vol. 3. University of Chicago Press, Chicago.

Massey, D. (1993) 'Power-geometry and a Progressive Sense of Place', in J. Bird et al. (eds), *Mapping the Futures: Local Cultures, Global Change*. Routledge, London.

Nederveen Pieterse, J. (1983) 'Transnational Alliances and the Dutch Revolution: the

Politics of the Transition from Feudalism to Capitalism'. Unpublished paper, Binghamton, NY.
— (1994) '"Fundamentalism" Discourses: Enemy Images', *Women Against Fundamentalism* 1 (5) 2–6.
Obbema, J. (1994) 'Winkelen Met een Tas Vol Heimwee', *NRC Handelsblad*, 10 March.
Ooijen, H. van (1992) 'Religion and Emancipation: a Study of the Development of Moroccan Islamic Organizations in a Dutch Town', in W. A. R. Shadid and P. S. van Koningsveld (eds), *Islam in Dutch Society*.
Parekh, B. (1993) 'Between Holy Text and Moral Void', in A. Gray and J. McGuigan (eds), *Studying Culture*. Edward Arnold, London.
— (1994) 'Equality, Fairness and Limits of Diversity', *Innovation* 7 (3), 289–308.
Pellerin, H. (1994) 'Global Restructuring and the Transnationalisation of Migration Limits and Promises of the Movement of People in the Emerging World Order'. Unpublished paper.
Pred, A. and Watts, M. J. (1992) *Reworking Modernity: Capitalisms and Symbolic Discontent*. Rutgers University Press, New Brunswick, NJ.
Rath, J., Groenendijk, K. and Penninx, K. (1991) 'The Recognition and Institutionalisation of Islam in Belgium, Great Britain and the Netherlands', *New Community* 18 (1), 101–14.
Sansone, L. (1992) *Schitteren in de Schaduw: Overlevingsstrategieën, Subcultuur en Etniciteit van Creoolse Jongeren Uit de Lagere Klasse in Amsterdam 1981–1990*. Spinhuis, Amsterdam.
Sassen, S. (1991) *The Global City: New York, London, Tokyo*. Princeton University Press, Princeton, NJ.
— (1993) 'Rethinking Immigration', *Lusitania* 5, 97–102.
Schiffauer, W. (1988) 'Migration and Religiousness', in T. Gerholm and Y. G. Lithman (eds), *The New Islamic Presence*.
Shadid, W. A. R. and van Koningsveld, P. S. (eds) (1992) *Islam in Dutch Society*. Kok Pharos, Kampen.
Sijtsma, J. (1989) 'De Rushdie Affaire in de Marokkaanse Moskeeën in Nederland', in R. Haleber (ed.), *Rushdie Effecten*.
Slomp, J. (1984) 'Moskeeën in Nederland', *Prana* 38, 47–53.
Sunier, T. (1992) 'Islam and Ethnicity among Turks: the Changing Role of Islam and Muslim organizations', in W. A. R Shadid and P. S. van Koningsveld (eds), *Islam in Dutch Society*.
Turabi, H. al- (1993) 'Islam as a Pan-national Movement and Nation-states: an Islamic Doctrine on Human Association'. Unpublished paper.
Vries, de M. (1987) *Ogen in je Rug: Turkse Meisjes en Jonge Vrouwen in Nederland*. Samsom, Alphen aan de Rijn.
Waardenburg, J. (1988) 'The Institutionalization of Islam in the Netherlands 1961–86', in T. Gerholm and Y. G. Lithman (eds), *The New Islamic Presence*.

Index